NALOPÀKHYÀNAM,

OR,

THE TALE OF NALA.

NALOPÀKHYÀNAM,

OR,

THE TALE OF NALA;

CONTAINING THE SANSKRIT TEXT IN ROMAN CHARACTERS,

FOLLOWED BY

A VOCABULARY

IN WHICH EACH WORD IS PLACED UNDER ITS ROOT, WITH REFERENCES TO DERIVED WORDS IN COGNATE LANGUAGES,

AND

A SKETCH OF SANSKRIT GRAMMAR.

BY THE

REV. THOMAS JARRETT, M.A.

TRINITY COLLEGE,

REGIUS PROFESSOR OF HEBREW, LATE PROFESSOR OF ARABIC, AND FORMERLY FELLOW OF ST CATHARINE'S COLLEGE, CAMBRIDGE.

EDITED FOR THE SYNDICS OF THE UNIVERSITY PRESS.

NEW EDITION REVISED.

Cambridge:
AT THE UNIVERSITY PRESS.
1882

THE following pages are intended for the benefit of those persons who are deterred from the study of Sanskrit in consequence of the complicated characters in which that language is usually printed. The transliteration here employed differs from that hitherto adopted; but will, it is believed, be found more simple in several respects.

The annexed Table will show the sound to be given to each symbol:

a,	as	a	in	America; an obscure sound between *a* in *man* and *u* in *but*.
ȧ	,,	a	,,	father.
ı	,,	i	,,	bit.
i	,,	i	,,	machine.
u	,,	u	,,	put.
u̇	,,	u	,,	truth.
e	,,	e	,,	there.
o	,,	o	,,	no.
ai	,,	i	,,	nigh.
au	,,	ou	,,	thou.
ṛı	,,	ri	,,	writ.
ṛi	,,	ree	,,	reed.
k	,,	k	,,	book.
g	,,	g	,,	log.
n·	,,	n	,,	think.
c	,,	ch	,,	much.
ȷ	,,	j	,,	join.
ṅ	as	n	in	inch.
ṭ	,,	t	,,	trumpet.
ḍ	,,	d	,,	drain.
ṇ	,,	n	,,	no.
t	,,	t	,,	tongue.
d	,,	d	,,	den.
n	,,	n	,,	content.
p	,,	p	,,	pen.
b	,,	b	,,	bind.
m	,,	m	,,	me.
y	,,	y	,,	you.
r	,,	r	,,	rise.
l	,,	l	,,	long.
v	,,	v	,,	vine.
ṡ	,,	ss	,,	session.
ṣ	,,	sh	,,	shine.
s	,,	s	,,	sun.
h	,,	h	,,	hot.

ḥ is a gentle aspiration used only at the end of a syllable.

ṃ is an obscure nasal used as a substitute for m or n in certain cases.

When h follows any consonant, it is to be sounded separately from that consonant, instead of combining with it; as, *gh* in *log-house*, and *th* in *pent-house*.

TRUNCH RECTORY,
Oct. 1, 1874.

CAMBRIDGE
UNIVERSITY PRESS

University Printing House, Cambridge CB2 8BS, United Kingdom

Published in the United States of America by Cambridge University Press, New York

Cambridge University Press is part of the University of Cambridge.

It furthers the University's mission by disseminating knowledge in the pursuit of education, learning and research at the highest international levels of excellence.

www.cambridge.org
Information on this title: www.cambridge.org/9781107621978

First published 1882
First paperback edition 2014

A catalogue record for this publication is available from the British Library

ISBN 978-1-107-62197-8 Paperback

CONTENTS.

CORRIGENDA IN NAḶOPĀKHYĀNAM.

PAGE 1,	first line,	*for* Vṛıhadaṣva	*read* Vṛihadaśva
,,	verse 4*a*,	*for* samyat'-	*read* saṃyat'-
,,	,, 7*b*,	*after* saha	*insert* comma
,, 2,	,, 10*b*,	*after* prápa	*dele* comma
,,	,, 21*a*,	*for* tvad anyam	*read* tvad-anyam
,,	,, 22*a*,	*for* agamans	*read* agamaṃs
,, 3,	,, 23*b*,	*for* sa	*read* sá
,,	,, 24*b*,	*for* khagamans	*read* khagamaṃs
,,	., 24*b*,	at end	*insert* colon
,,	,, 27*b*,	*for* Aśvıno	*read* Aśvınoḥ
,, 4,	,, 2*b*,	*after* babhúva	*dele* full stop
,,	,, 3*b*,	at end, *for* comma	*put* full stop
,,	,, 4*a*,	*after* na	*dele* hyphen
,,	,, 5*a*,	*for* asvastháṃ	*read* a-svastháṃ
,,	,, 6*a*,	*for* nar' eśvare	*read* nar-eśvare
,,	,, 9*a*,	*for* 8 (above line)	*read* 6
,,	,, 10*a*,	*after* sarve	*dele* comma
,,	,, 11*b*,	*for* dṛıṣyaır	*read* dṛıśyaır
,,	,, 11*b*,	*after* dṛıṣyaır	*dele* comma
,, 5,	,, 12*b*,	*for* 'vasans	*read* 'vasaṃs
,,	,, 15*a*,	at end	*dele* comma
,,	,, 16*a*,	*for* avayoḥ	*read* ávayoḥ
,,	,, 17*a*,	*for* vaċaḥ	*read* vacaḥ
,,	,, 17*b*,	*for* tyakta-jivıta, yod-hınaḥ	*read* tyakta-jivıta-yodhınaḥ
,,	,, 18*a*,	at end, *for* semi-colon	*read* comma
,,	,, 19*a*,	*for* ksatrıyáḥ	*read* kṣatrıyáḥ
,,	,, 21*b*,	at end	*insert* full stop
,,	,, 23*a*,	*for* ratna bhútam	*read* ratna-bhútám
,, 7,	,, 4*a*,	*for* apám patıḥ	*read* apám-patıḥ
,,	,, 10*b*,	*for* "pravekṣyas' itı	*read* "pravekṣyas'" itı
,, 8,	,, 12*b*,	over line, *for* 35	*read* 36
,,	,, 12*b*,	*for* vapuṣa	*read* vapuṣá
,,	,, 13*b*,	over line, *for* 16	*read* 19
,,	,, 17*b*,	*for* bhavıṣatı	*read* bhavıṣyatı

PAGE 8,	verse	20*b*,	*for* 'sy'	*read* 'sy
,,	,,	21*a*,	*for* full stop	*read* ?
,,	,,	23*b*,	*for* sobhane	*read* śobhane
,, 9,	,,	4*a*,	*for* mam	*read* mám
,,	,,	6*a*,		*dele* comma
,,	,,	6*b*,	*for* páda raȷasá	*read* páda-raȷasá
,,	,,	7*a*,	*for* vıprayam	*read* vıprıyam
,,	,,	7*b*,	*after* mám	*insert* comma
,, 10,	,,	10*a*,	end	*dele* comma
,,	,,	11*a*,	*for* dharm' átmanam	*read* dharm'-átmánam
,,	,,	12*a*,	*after* lokapálánám	*insert* colon
,,	,,	14*b*,	*after* bhartáram	*insert* colon
,,	,,	16*a*,	*for* devatánám	*read* devatánáṃ
,,	,,	17*a*,	*after* dharmo, *for* comma	*read* colon
,,	,,	17*a*,	end, *for* full stop	*read* comma
,,	,,	17*b*,	*for* sv' árthaṃ	*read* sv'-árthaṃ
,,	,,	17*b*,	*after* karısyámı, *for* comma	*read* colon
,,	,,	20*a*,	*for* twáṃ	*read* tvam
,,	,,	20*b*,	*after* sarve	*insert* comma
,,	,,	20*b*,	*for* swayaṃ	*read* svayaṃ
,,	,,	20*b*,	end	*insert* full stop
,,	,,	21*a*,	over line	*dele* 6
,, 11,	,,	23*a*,	end of line	*insert* comma
,,	,,	28*a*,	*for* varṅyamáneṣu	*read* varṇyamáneṣu
,,	,,	29*a*,	*after* mám	*dele* comma
,,	,,	31*b*,	end of line	*insert* ('')
,, 12,	,,	1*b*,	*for* svayam-vare	*read* svayaṃ-vare
,,	,,	2*b*,	end of line	*insert* full stop
,,	,,	4*b*,	end of line	*insert* full stop
,,	,,	5*b*,	*for* comma	*read* full stop
,,	,,	6*b*,	end of line	*insert* full stop
,,	,,	7*b*,	end of line	*insert* comma
,,	,,	11*b*,	*for* abhyaȷánán	*read* ábhyaȷánán
,, 13,	,,	17*a*,	*for* srutvá	*read* śrutvá
,,	,,	22*a*,	*after* karuṇam	*dele* comma
,,	,,	22*a*,	over line, *for* 62	*read* 60
,,	,,	23*b*,	*for* yath' oktaṃ	*read* yath'-oktaṃ
,,	,,	24*a*,	end, *for* semi-colon	*read* comma
,, 14,	,,	27*a*,	over line, *for* 69	*read* 65
,,	,,	28*b*,	*for* sabdo	*read* śabdo
,,	,,	35*a*,	*for* yaȷne	*read* yaȷṅe
,, 15,	,,	40*b*,	*after* Damayantyá	*dele* comma
,, 16,	,,	12*b*,	*after* Kale, *for* full stop	*read* comma
,, 17,	,,	15*b*,	*for* sahayyaṃ	*read* sáháyyaṃ
,,	,,	4*a*,	*for* Nalaṃ samipam,	*read* Nalaṃ, samipam
,, 18,	,,	8*a*,	*for* ná	*read* na
,,	,,	8*a*,	end of line	*insert* colon

PAGE 18,	verse	8*b*,	*for* Vaidarbhyaḥ	*read* Vaidarbhyâḥ
,,	,,	16*a*,	*for* rucir-âpân·gi	*read* rucir-âpân·giṃ
,,	,,	17*b*,	*for* duḥkh'-ârtâ	*read* duḥkh'-ârttâ
,,	,,	18*a*,	*after* Puṣkarasya	*dele* comma
,,	,,	18*b*,	*after* mâsân	*insert* comma
,, 19,	,,	9*a*,	*for* -paran·mukhân	*read* parân·mukhân
, 20,	,,	11*a*,	*for* Vṛihatsena	*read* Vṛihatsenâ
,,	,,	17*a*,	*before* and *after* manye	*insert* commas
,,	,,	22*b*,	*after* âropya	*insert* comma
,, 21,	,,	1*a*,	*for* Puṇyślokasya	*read* Puṇyaślokasya
,,	,,	3*b*,	*for* sadhu	*read* sâdhu
,, 22,	,,	9*a*,	*after* tasya	*dele* comma
,,	,,	18*b*,	*for* prâṇa-yâtram	*read* prâṇa-yâtrâm
,,	,,	20*b*,	*for* bharto	*read* bhartâ
,, 23,	,,	24*a*,	end of line	*dele* comma
,,	,,	24*b*,	*for* ârto	*read* ârtto
,,	,,	25*a*,		*dele* commas
,,	,,	27*a*,	*for* -trisâ-	*read* -tṛiśa-
,,	,,	28*a*,	and 30*b*, *for* -ârtasya	*read* ârttasya
,,	,,	30*a*,	*after* Damayanti	*dele* comma
,,	,,	30*b*,	end of line	*insert* full stop
,, 24,	,,	34*b*,	*for* ato nimittaṃ	*read* ato-nimittaṃ
,,	,,	1*a*,	*after* mama	*insert* comma
,,	,,	2*a*,	end of line, *for* colon	*read* comma
,,	,,	2*b*,	end of line, *for* full stop	*read* ?
,,	,,	3*b*,	end of line	*insert* full stop
,, 26,	,,	18*b*,	*for* sabh' oddeśe	*read* sabh'-oddeśe
,,	,,	29*a*,	*for* naṣṭ' âtmâ	*read* naṣṭ'-âtmâ
,, 27,	,,	2*b*,	*for* mahâ-raj	*read* mahâ-râj'
,,	,,	4*a*,	*for* nânu	*read* nanu
,, 28,	,,	10*a*,	*for* râj' endra	*read* râj'-endra
,,	,,	10*b*,	end of line	*dele* (?)
,,	,,	16*a*,	*after* duḥkh'-ârtto	*dele* comma
,,	,,	18*b*,	end of line	*dele* full stop
,,	,,	21*a*,	*for* 'byâgatâm	*read* 'bhyâgatâm
,,	,,	22*b*,	end of line	*insert* full stop
,, 29,	,,	23*b*,	*for* kim artham	*read* kim-artham
,,	,,	30*a*,	*for* tvam'	*read* tvam,
,,	,,	30*a*,	*for* abhyâgatâ	*read* âbhyâgatâ
,,	,,	34*b*,	*for* -ârtas	*read* ârttas
,, 30,	,,	1*a*,	*for* nihitya	*read* nihatya
,, 31,	,,	13*b*,	*after* iha	*dele* comma
,,	,,	17*a*,	end of line	*dele* comma
,,	,,	17*b*,	*after* Manu-ja-vyâghra	*insert* comma
,,	,,	18*a*,	*after* arhasi	*insert* comma
,, 32,	,,	26*b*,	end of line, *for* full stop	*read* comma
,,	,,	29*b*,	end of line, *for* ?	*read* comma
,,	,,	30*a*,	end of line, *for* comma	*read* ?

Page 32,	verse 30*b*,	end of line, *for* full stop	*read* comma
,, 33,	,, 32*a*,	*for* asan·kıtâ	*read* aśan·kıtâ
,,	,, 36*b*,	*for* sâgaram gamâm	*read* sâgaraṃ-gamâm
,,	,, 37*b*,	*for* n'aıka-varṇaır	*read* n'-aıka-varṇaır
,,	,, 40*a*,	end of line	*insert* comma
,,	,, 40*b*,	end of line	*insert* comma
,,	,, 44*b*,	*for* câtur-varṇyasya	*read* câturvarṇyasya
,,	,, 45*a*,	*for* râȷa-sûya	*read* râjasûya
,, 34,	,, 45*b*,	end of line, *for* full stop	*read* comma
,,	,, 47*b*,	*for* upasthıthâm	*read* upasthıtâm
,,	,, 50*a*,	end of line	*insert* comma
,,	,, 57*a*,	*for* atmânam	*read* âtmânam
,, 35,	,, 59*a*,	*after* ṛıddhâm	*insert* comma
,,	,, 60*b*,	*for* dıṣam	*read* dıśam
,,	,, 63*a*,	end of line	*insert* comma
,,	,, 64*a*,	end of line, *for* full stop	*read* comma
,,	,, 68*a*,	*for* vınayâ 'vanatâ	*read* vınayâ-'vanatâ
,, 36,	,, 72*b*,		*dele* comma and full stop
,,	,, 76*b*,	*after* Bhimo	*dele* comma
,, 37,	,, 99*a*,	*after* puṇya-ȷalâ	*dele* comma
,, 38,	,, 101*b*,	end of line	*insert* colon
,,	,, 108*a*,	*for* ârtâ	*read* ârttâ
,,	,, 111*a*,		*dele* commas
,, 39,	,, 118*b*,	*for* asi	*read* ası
,,	,, 120*a*,	*for* vâ, tvam	*read* vâ tvam,
,,	,, 125*b*,	end of line	*insert* full stop
,,	,, 126*a*,	*for* nṛı-patıṃ ksıpraṃ,	*read* nṛi-patım, kṣıpram
,, 40,	,, 129*b*,	*for* krıtsne	*read* kṛıtsne
,,	,, 131*a*,	*for* banıȷaḥ	*read* baṇıȷaḥ
,,	,, 2*a*,	end of line	*dele* comma
,,	,, 3*a*,	*for* banıȷaḥ	*read* baṇıȷaḥ
,, 41,	,, 7*a*,	end of line, *for* comma	*read* colon
,,	,, 14*c*,	*after* patıtâ	*dele* comma
,,	,, 16*b*,	end of line	*insert* colon
,,	,, 17*a*,	*after* gṛıṇidhvaṃ	*insert* comma
,, 42,	,, 26*a*,	*for* krıtvâ	*read* kṛıtvâ
,,	,, 26*b*,	*for* comma	*read* full stop
,,	,, 28*b*,	*after* loṣṭabhıḥ *and* trı-ṇaıḥ	*dele* commas
,,	,, 28*b*,	*after* aıva	*insert* comma
,,	,, 29*a*,	*for* krıtyakâm	*read* kṛıtyakâm
,, 43,	,, 32*b*,	*after* vâcâ, *for* comma	*read* colon
,,	,, 38*a*,	*after* yûthena	*insert* colon
,,	,, 38*a*,	end of line	*insert* colon
,,	,, 39*b*,	end of line, *for* comma	*read* colon
,,	,, 40*a*,	end of line, *for* comma	*read* full stop
,,	,, 42*a*,	end of line, *for* comma	*read* colon
,,	,, 44*a*,	*for* pâra-gaıḥ	*read* pâragaıḥ

Page 44,	verse 50*a*,	śaraṇ' ârthini	*read* śaraṇ-ârthini
"	" 50*b*,	*after* paśyâmi	*insert* comma
" 45,	" 70*b*,	*after* kartavyaṃ	*insert* comma
"	" 72*a*,	*after* kariṣyâmi	*insert* colon
" 46,	" 1*b*,	*for* mahântam	*read* mahântaṃ
"	" 5*b*,	*for* sapto	*read* śapto
"	" 7*b*,	*after* śreyas	*insert* colon
"	" 8*b*,	*after* bhaviṣyâmi	*insert* colon
" 47,	" 20*b*,	between ved' and âkṣa,	*dele* hyphen
" 48,	" 23*a*,	*for* soke	*read* śoke
"	" 26*a*,	*for* datvâ	*read* dattvâ
" 49,	" 8*b*,	*for* Vârsneya	*read* Vârṣṇeya
"	" 13*b*,	*after* nâri	*insert* colon
"	" 17*b*,	*after* puṇyena	*insert* comma
"	" 18*b*,	*after* ân·gi	*insert* comma
" 50,	" 2*a*,	*for* datvâ	*read* dattvâ
"	" 6*a*,	*for* râstrâṇi	*read* râṣṭrâṇi
"	" 8*b*,	end of line, *for* full stop	*read* comma
"	" 10*a*,	end of line, *for* full stop	*insert* colon
"	" 10*b*,	*for* śriyam	*read* Śriyam
" 51,	" 12*b*,	end of line, *for* full stop	*read* comma
"	" 13*b*,	end of line	*insert* comma
"	" 18*a*,	*after* second hinâm	*dele* comma
"	" 20*b*,	*after* dehaṃ	*insert* comma
" 53,	" 2*b*,	*after* Punyaślokasya	*dele* comma
"	" 2*b*,	*for* dhimatah	*read* dhimataḥ
"	" 6*b*,	*after* asyâś	*insert* comma
"	" 8*a*,	*after* rûpaṃ	*insert* colon
"	" 8*a*,	end of line	*dele* comma
" 54,	" 19*a*,	*after* bhaviṣyati	*insert* comma
" 55,	" 25*b*,	end of line, *for* full stop	*read* comma
" 56,	" 37*b*,	*for* utsrijya	*read* utsṛjya
"	" 39*a*,	end of line, *for* full stop	*read* comma
"	" 43*b*,	*for* ânri-saṃsyam	*read* ânṛiśaṃsyam
" 57,	" 3*b*,	end of line, *for* comma	*read* full stop
"	" 8*b*,	*after* jita-svargâ	*insert* comma
"	" 9*a*,	end of line	*insert* colon
" 58,	" 12*a*,	*after* vâ 'pi	*insert* comma
"	" 23*b*,	*for* svaṃ-varam	*read* svayaṃ-varam
" 59,	" 6*b*,	*after* api	*insert* colon
" 60,	" 10*b*,	*after* -vyâghra	*insert* comma
"	" 10*b*,	*after* -nagariṃ	*insert* comma
"	" 11*a*,	*for* aśvânâm	*read* aśvânâṃ
"	" 14*a*,	*for* prithu	*read* pṛithu
"	" 15*b*,	*after* kartum	*insert* colon
"	" 18*a*,	end of line	*insert* colon
"	" 18*b*,	*for* mânyase	*read* manyase
" 61,	" 31*a*,	*after* Vâhukasya	*dele* comma

PAGE 62,	verse	37*a*,	*for* san·grahaṇe	*read* san-grahaṇaṃ
,,	,,	5*b*,	*for* àhartum	*read* àhartuṃ
,, 63,	,,	13*b*,	*for* paro-'kṣatá	*read* parokṣatà
,,	,,	18*a*,	*for* kuru	*read* Kuru
,, 64,	,,	26*b*,	beginning of line	*insert* (")
,,	,,	26*b*,	*for* vıśàra-dam	*read* vıśàradam
,,	,,	29*a*,	end of line	*insert* colon
,,	,,	29*b*,	*after* me	*dele* comma
,,	,,	31*a*,	*for* àrtasya	*read* àrttasya
,, 65,	,,	39*a*,	àdrıśyata	*read* àdṛıśyat
,, 66,	,,	6*a*,	end of line, *for* comma	*read* colon
,,	,,	6*b*,	*for* sıkınaḥ	*read* sıkhınaḥ
,,	,,	7*a*,	end of line	*dele* full stop
,,	,,	7*b*,	end of line	*insert* full stop
,,	,,	9*b*,	*after* viraṃ	*insert* comma
,, 67,	,,	12*b*,	*after* ràj-endro	*insert* comma
,,	,,	19*a*,	end of line	*dele* comma
,, 68,	,,	27*b*,	*for* s' itı	*read* 's' " itı
,, 69,	,,	7*a*,	*for* kım artham	*read* kım-artham
,,	,,	8*b*,	bhavıtá śva	*read* "bhavıtá śva"
,, 70,	,,	15*b*,	gùḍhas	*read* gùḍhaś
,,	,,	18*b*,	utsrıȷya	*read* utsṛıȷya
,, 71,	,,	22*a*,	end of line	*dele* comma
,,	,,	24*b*,	end of line, *for* comma	*read* full stop
,,	,,	25*b*,	*after* ȷıta-svargà	*insert* comma
,,	,,	29*a*,	*after* và 'pı	*insert* comma
,,	,,	30*b*,	*after* soḍhum	*insert* comma
,, 72,	,,	1*b*,	*for* va	*read* vaı
,,	,,	11*a*,	*for* prakṣ-àlan'	*read* prakṣàlan'
,, 73,	,,	16*b*,	end of line	*dele* comma
,, 74,	,,	3*a*,	end of line	*insert* colon
,,	,,	3*a*,	*after* ekaḥ	*insert* colon
,, 75,	,,	10*b*,	*for* utsrıȷya	*read* utsṛıȷya
,,	,,	12*b*,	*for* utsrıȷya	*read* utsṛıȷya
,,	,,	20*a*,	*before* and *after* tapasà	*dele* commas
,, 76,	,,	24*b*,	*for* utsrıȷya	*read* utsṛıȷya
,, 77,	,,	39*b*,	*after* kàryà	*insert* colon
,, 78,	,,	3*a*,	end of line	*insert* colon
,,	,,	4*a*,	*for* pratıgrıhya	*read* pratıgṛıhya
,, 79,	,,	6*b*,	end of line	*read* colon
,,	,,	7*b*,	end of line	*read* full stop
,,	,,	16*b*,	*after* ıcchàmı	*insert* comma
,, 80,	,,	18*b*,	*for* hrıdayaṃ	*read* hṛıdayam
,,	,,	8*a*,	*after* dyutaṃ	*insert* comma
,,	,,	8*b*,	*after* àstu	*insert* vaı
,, 81,	,,	9*b*,	*after* upàyena	*insert* comma
,,	,,	14*a*,	*for* upasthàsyàtı	*read* upasthàsyatı
,,	,,	14*a*,	*after* upasthàyàtı	*dele* comma

PAGE 81,	verse	14*a*,	*after* vyaktaṃ	*insert* comma
,,	,,	14*a*,	*for* Sakram	*read* Śakram
,, 82,	,,	32*a*,	*for* paura-ıâna-padâś	*read* paura-ȷânapadâś
,,	,,	33*b*,	*after* prâptâ	*insert* comma
,,	,,	33*b*,	*for* śata-kratum	*read* Śata-kratum
,,	,,	35*a*,	*for* sat-krıtya	*read* sat-kṛıtya

NAL'-OPÀKHYÀNAM.

I.

Vṛihadaṣva uvàca,[3]
àsid[31] ràjà, Nalo nàma, Virasena-suto,[33] bali,
upapanno guṇair[12] iṣṭai,[30] rùpavàn, aśva-kovidaḥ; 1
atiṣṭhad[36] manu-j'-endràṇàm mùrdhni, deva-patir iva,
upary upari sarveṣàm, àditya iva tejasà; 2
brahmaṇyo, veda-vic, chùro, Niṣadheṣu mahi-patiḥ,
akṣa-priyaḥ, satya-vàdi, mahàn, akṣauhiṇi-patiḥ, 3
ipsito[10] vara-nàriṇàm, udàraḥ, samyat'-endriyaḥ,[1]
rakṣità, dhanvinàm śreṣṭaḥ, s'-àkṣàd iva Manuḥ svayam. 4
tath' aiv' àsid[31] Vidarbheṣu Bhimo, bhima-paràkramaḥ,
śùraḥ, sarva-guṇair yuktaḥ,[2] prajà-kàmaḥ, sa c'àprajaḥ. 5
sa prajà-'rthe paraṃ yatnam akarot[16] susamàhitaḥ.[43]
tam abhyagacchad[19] brahma-'rṣir Damano nàma, Bhàrata. 6
taṃ sa Bhimaḥ, prajà-kàmas, toṣayàmàsa[39] dharma-vit,
mahiṣyà saha ràj'-endra, sat-kàreṇa suvarcasam. 7
tasmai prasanno[37] Damanaḥ sa-bhàryàya varaṃ dadau,[40]
kanyà-ratnaṃ, kumàràṅś ca trin, udàràn, mahà-yaśàḥ, 8
Damayantiṃ, Damaṃ, Dàntaṃ, Damanaṃ ca suvarcasam,

upapannán guṇaiḥ sarvair, bhimán, bhima-parákramán.　　9

Damayanti tu rúpeṇa, tejasá, yaśasá, śrıyá,

saubhágyena ca lokeṣu yaśaḥ prápa, sumadhyamá.　　10

atha tám, vayası prápte, dásinám samalaṃ-kṛıtam

śataṃ śataṃ sakhinám ca paryupásac Chacim ıva.　　11

tatra sma rájate Bhaımi, sarv'-ábharaṇa-bhúṣıtá,

sakhi-madhye, 'navady'-áṅ·gi, vıdyut saudámını yathá,　　12

ativa rúpa-sampanná, Śrir ıv', áyata-locaná.

na deveṣu, na yakṣeṣu, tádṛıg rúpavati kvacıt　　13

manuṣeṣv apı c' ányeṣu dṛıṣṭa-púrvá, 'tha vá śrutá,

cıtta-pramáthını bálá devánám apı, sundari.　　14

Nalaś ca nara-śárdúlo, lokeṣv apratımo bhuvı,

Kandarpa ıva rúpeṇa múrtımán abhavat svayam.　　15

tasyáḥ samipe tu Nalam praśaśaṃsuḥ kutúhalát;

Naıṣadhasya samipe tu Damayantim punaḥ punaḥ.　　16

tayor adṛıṣṭa-kámo 'bhút, śṛıṇvatoḥ satataṃ guṇán;

anyo-'nyam pratı, Kaunteya, sa vyavardhata hṛıc-chayaḥ.　　17

aśaknuvan Nalaḥ kámam tadá dhárayıtuṃ hṛıdá,

antaḥ-pura-samipa-sthe vana áste, raho gataḥ.　　18

sa dadarśa tato haṃsán, játa-rúpa-parıṣ-kṛıtán;

vane vıcaratáṃ teṣám ekaṃ jagráha pakṣıṇam.　　19

tato 'ntar-ikṣa-go vácaṃ vyájahára Nalaṃ tadá,

"hantavyo 'smı na te, rájan, karıṣyámı tava prıyam.　　20

Damayanti-sa-káśe tvám kathayıṣyámi, Naıṣadha,

yathá tvad anyam puruṣam na sá maṃsyatı karhıcıt."　　21

evam uktas tato haṃsam utsasarja mahi-patıḥ.

te tu haṃsáḥ samutpatya Vıdarbhán agamans tataḥ.　　22

Vidarbha-nagarîṃ gatvâ[19], Damayantyâs tadâ 'ntike
nipetus[11] te garutmantaḥ, sa dadarśa[42] ca tân gaṇân. 23
sâ tân adbhuta-rûpân[14] vai dṛiṣṭvâ[42], sakhi-gaṇ'-âvṛitâ[4],
hṛiṣṭâ[24], grahitum[20] kha-gamâns tvaramân'[38] opacakrame[17] 24
atha haṃsâ visasṛipuḥ[35] sarvataḥ pramadâ-vane;
ek'-aikaśas tadâ kanyâs tân haṃsân samupâdravan[41]. 25
Damayanti tu yaṃ haṃsaṃ samupâdhâvad[44] antike,
sa, mânuṣîṃ giraṃ kṛitvâ[16], Damayantim ath' âbravit[13], 26
"Damayanti, Nalo nâma Niṣadheṣu mahi-patiḥ,
Aśvino sadṛiśo rûpe, na samâs tasya mânuṣâḥ. 27
tasya vai yadi bhâryâ tvam bhavethâ[14], vara-varṇini,
sa-phalaṃ te bhavej[14] janma, rûpaṃ c' edaṃ, sumadhyame. 28
vayaṃ hi deva-gandharva-mânuṣ'-oraga-râkṣasân
dṛiṣṭavanto[42], na c' âsmâbhir dṛiṣṭa-pûrvas[42] tathâ-vidhaḥ; 29
tvaṃ c' âpi ratnaṃ nâriṇâṃ, nareṣu ca Nalo varaḥ;
viśiṣṭâyâ[29] viśiṣṭena saṃgamo guṇavân bhavet[14]." 30
evam uktâ[3] tu haṃsena Damayanti, viśâm pate,
abravit[13] tatra taṃ haṃsaṃ, "tvam apy evaṃ Nale vada[7]." 31
tath' ety uktvâ[3] 'ṇḍa-jaḥ kanyâṃ Vidarbhasya, viśâm pate,
punar âgamya[19] Niṣadhân, Nale sarvaṃ nyavedayat[8]. 32

iti Nal'-opâkhyâne prathamaḥ sargaḥ.

1. yam.	9. man	17. kram	25. râj	33. su	41. dru
2. yuj	10. âp	18. kath	26. śaṃs	34. sṛij	42. dṛiś
3. vac	11. pat	19. gam	27. śak	35. sṛip	43. dhâ
4. vṛi	12. pad	20. grah	28. śru	36. sthâ	44. dhâv
5. vṛidh	13. brû	21. car	29. śiṣ	37. sad	45. dhṛi
6. viś	14. bhû	22. han	30. iṣ	38. tvar	46. jan
7. vad	15. bhûṣ	23. hṛi	31. as	39. tuṣ	
8. vid	16. kṛi	24. hṛiṣ	32. âs	40. dâ	

II.

Vṛhadaśva uvāca[2],

Damayanti tu, tac chrutvā[29] vaco haṃsasya, Bhārata,
tataḥ prabhṛti na sva-sthā, Nalam prati, babhūva[13] sā. 1
tataś cintā-parā, dinā, vivarṇa-vadanā, kṛśā,
babhūva[13]. Damayanti tu niḥ-śvāsa-paramā tadā, 2
ūrdhva-dṛṣṭir, dhyāna-parā babhūv', onmatta[7]-darśanā,
pāṇḍu-varṇā kṣaṇen' ātha, hṛc-chay'-āviṣṭa[3]-cetanā, 3
na-śayy'-āsana-bhogeṣu ratiṃ vindati[1] karhicit;
na naktaṃ, na divā śete[28], "hā h'" eti rudati[27] punaḥ. 4
tām asvasthāṃ tad-ākārāṃ sakhyas tā jajnur[23] iṅgitaiḥ.
tato Vidarbha-pataye Damayantyāḥ sakhi-janaḥ 5
nyavedayat[5] tām asvasthāṃ Damayantiṃ nar' eśvare.
tac chrutvā[29] nṛ-patir Bhimo Damayanti-sakhi-gaṇāt, 6
cintayāmāsa[21] tat kāryaṃ sumahat svāṃ sutāṃ prati[30].
"kim iyaṃ duhitā me 'dya n' āti-sva-sth' eva lakṣyate[24]?" 7
sa samikṣya[39] mahi-pālaḥ svāṃ sutām prāpta[8]-yauvanām,
apaśyad[38] ātmanā kāryaṃ Damayantyāḥ svayaṃ-varaṃ. 8
sa sannimantrayāmāsa[8] mahi-pālān viśām patiḥ,
"anubhūyatām[13] ayam, virāḥ, svayaṃ-vara," iti, prabho. 9
śrutvā[29] tu pārthivāḥ sarve, Damayantyāḥ svayaṃ-varam,
abhijagmus[20] tato Bhimaṃ rājāno Bhima-śāsanāt, 10
hasty-aśva-ratha-ghoṣeṇa pūrayanto[10] vasuṃ-dharām,
vicitra-māly'-ābharaṇair balair dṛśyaiḥ, sv-alaṃ-kṛtaiḥ. 11
teṣām Bhimo mahā-bāhuḥ pārthivānām mahā-'tmanāṃ

yathâ 'rham akarot[17] pûjâm; te 'vasans[4] tatra pûjitâḥ.[9] 12
etasminn eva kâle tu surâṇâm ṛṣi-sattamau,
aṭamânau[34] mahâ-'tmânâv, Indra-lokam ito gatau,[20] 13
Nâradaḥ, Parvataś c' aiva, mahâ-prâjnau, mahâ-vratau,
deva-râjasya bhavanam viviśâte[8][9] supûjitau. 14
tâv arcayitvâ[25] Maghavâ tataḥ kuśalam avyayam,
papracch'[11] ânâmayam c' âpi tayoḥ sarva-gatam[20] vibhuḥ. 15
Nârada uvâca,
"avayoḥ kuśalam, deva, sarvatra gatam, îśvara,
loke ca, Maghavan, kṛitsne nṛi-pâḥ kuśalino, vibho." 16
Vṛihadaśva uvâca,
Nâradasya vacaḥ śrutvâ papraccha[11] Bala-Vṛitra-hâ,
"dharma-jnâḥ pṛithivi-pâlâs, tyakta-jivita,[35] yodhinaḥ, 17
śastreṇa nidhanam kâle ye gacchanty[20] aparân-mukhâḥ;
ayam loko 'kṣayas teṣâm, yath' aiva mama kâma-dhuk; 18
kva nu te ksatriyâḥ śûrâ? na hi paśyâmi[38] tân aham
âgacchato[20] mahi-pâlân, dayitân[37] atithin mama." 19
evam uktas tu Śakreṇa Naradaḥ pratyabhâṣata,[15]
Nârada uvâca,
"śṛiṇu[29] me, Maghavan, yena na dṛiṣyante[38] mahi-kṣitaḥ. 20
Vidarbha-râjno duhitâ, 'Damayanti' 'ti viśrutâ,[29]
rûpeṇa samatikrântâ[18] pṛithivyâm sarva-yoṣitaḥ 21
tasyâḥ svayam-varaḥ, Śakra, bhavitâ[13] na cirâd iva.
tatra gacchanti[20] râjâno, râja-putrâś ca sarvaśaḥ. 22
tâm ratna bhûtâm[13] lokasya prârthayanto[26] mahi-kṣitaḥ;
kân-kṣanti[16] sma viśeṣena, Bala-Vṛitra-niṣûdana." 23
etasmin[19] kathyamâne tu loka-pâlâś ca s' âgnikâḥ

áȷagmur[20] deva-ráȷasya samipam amar'-ottamáḥ. 24

tatas te śuśruvuḥ[29] sarve Náradasya vaco mahat,

śrutv'[29] aıva c' ábruvan[12] hṛıṣṭáḥ,[22] "gacchámo[20] vayam apy uta." 25

tataḥ sarve mahá-ráȷáḥ sa-gaṇáḥ saha-váhanáḥ

Vıdarbhán abhıȷagmus[20] te yataḥ sarve mahi-kṣıtaḥ. 26

Nalo 'pı ráȷá, Kaunteya, śrutvá ráȷnáṃ samágamam,

abhyagacchad[20] adin'-átmá, Damayantim anuvrataḥ. 27

atha deváh pathı Nalaṃ dadṛıśur[38] bhú-tale sthıtam[32]

s'-ákṣád ıva sthıtam múrtyá Manmatham rúpa-sampadá. 28

taṃ dṛıṣṭvá loka-pálás te bhráȷamánaṃ[14] yathá ravım,

tasthur vıgata-san·kalpá[20] vısmıtá[31] rúpa-sampadá. 29

tato 'ntar-ikṣe vıṣṭabhya[33] vımánánı dıv-aukasaḥ,

abruvan[12] Naıṣadhaṃ, ráȷann, avatirya[36] nabhas-talát, 30

"bho bho Naıṣadha, ráȷ'-endra, Nala, satya-vrato bhaván;

asmákaṃ kuru[17] sáháyyaṃ, dúto bhava,[13] nar'-ottama." 31

ıtı Nal'-opákhyáne dvıtiyaḥ sargaḥ.

1. vınd	9. púȷ	17. kṛı	25. arc	33. sthambh
2. vac	10. púr	18. kram	26. arth	34. aṭ
3. vıś	11. pracch	19. kath	27. rud	35. tyaȷ
4. vas	12. brú	20. gam	28. śi	36. tṛi
5. vıd	13. bhú	21. cıt	29. śru	37. de
6. mantr	14. bhráȷ	22. hṛıṣ	30. su	38. dṛıś
7. mad	15. bháṣ	23. ȷná	31. smı	39. ikṣ
8. áp	16. kán·kṣ	24. lakṣ	32. sthá	

III.

Vṛihadaśva uvâca,

tebhyaḥ[23] pratijnâya Nalaḥ "kariṣya,"[17] iti, Bhârata,

ath' aitân paripapraccha[10] kṛit'-âñjalir upasthitaḥ[35], 1

"ke vai bhavantaḥ? kaś c' âsau yasy' âhaṃ dûta ipsitaḥ[8]?

kiṃ ca tad vo mayâ kâryaṃ[17]? kathayadhvaṃ[20] yathâ-tatham." 2

evam ukte[2] Naiṣadhena, Maghavân abhyabhâṣata[16],

"amarân vai nibodh'[13] âsmân Damayanty-artham âgatân[21]. 3

aham Indro, 'yam Agniś ca, tath' aiv' âyam apâm patiḥ,

śarir'-ânta-karo nṛiṇâṃ Yamo 'yam api, pârthiva. 4

tvaṃ vai samâgatân asmân Damayantyai nivedaya[7],

'loka-pâlâ mah-endr'-âdyâḥ sabhâṃ yânti[40] didṛikṣavaḥ[37], 5

prâptum[8] icchanti[31] devâs tvâṃ Sakro, 'gnir, Varuṇo, Yamaḥ.

teṣâm anyatamaṃ devam patitve varayasva[3] ha.'" 6

evam uktaḥ sa Śakreṇa Nalaḥ prâñjalir abravit[12],

"ek'-ârtha-samupetam[1] mâṃ na preṣayitum[31] arhatha[27]. 7

kathaṃ tu jâta-san-kalpaḥ[22] striyam utsahate[34] pumân

par'-ârtham idṛiśaṃ vaktuṃ[2]? tat kṣamantu[18] mah'-eśvarâḥ." 8

devâ ûcuḥ[2],

"'kariṣya', iti saṃśrutya[80] pûrvam asmâsu, Naiṣadha,

na kariṣyasi kasmât tvam? vraja[4], Naiṣadha, mâ-ciram." 9

Vṛihadaśva uvâca,

evam uktaḥ sa devais tair Naiṣadhaḥ punar abravit,

"su-rakṣitâni[26] veśmâni praveṣṭuṃ[6] katham utsahe[34]?" 10

"pravekṣyas' iti taṃ Śakraḥ punar ev'[16] abhyabhâṣata.

sa jagáma, tath' ety uktvá, Damayantyá niveśanam. 11
dadarśa[37] tatra Vaidarbhiṃ sakhi[3]-gaṇa-samávṛtám
dedipyamánáṃ[35] vapuṣa, śriyá ca vara-varṇinim, 12
ativa su-kumár'-áṅ·giṃ, tanu-madhyáṃ su-locanám,
ákṣipantim[16] iva prabháṃ śaśinaḥ svena tejasá. 13
tasya dṛṣṭv' aiva vavṛdhe[5] kámas táṃ cáru-hásinim,
satyaṃ cikirṣamánas[17] tu dhárayámása[38] hṛc-chayam. 14
tatas tá Naiṣadhaṃ dṛṣṭvá[37] sambhrántáḥ[15] param'-áṅ·ganáḥ
ásanebhyaḥ samutpetus[11] tejasá tasya dharṣitáḥ[39], 15
praśaśaṃsuś[28] ca su-prítá[41] Nalaṃ tá vismay'[1]-ánvitáḥ,
na c 'ainam abhyabháṣanta[16], manobhis tv abhyapújayan[9], 16
“aho rúpam! aho kántir! aho dhairyam mahá-'tmanaḥ!
ko 'yaṃ devo, 'tha vá yakṣo, gandharvo vá bhaviṣati[14]?” 17
na tás tu śaknuvanti[29] sma vyáhartum[24] api kiṅcana,
tejasá dharṣitás[39] tasya lajjávatyo var'-áṅ·ganáḥ. 18
ath' ainaṃ smayamánaṃ[33] tu smita[33]-púrvá 'bhibháṣiṇi
Damayanti Nalaṃ víram abhyabháṣata[16] vismitá[33], 19
“kas tvaṃ, sarv'-ánavady'-áṅ·ga, mama hṛc-chaya-vardhana,
prápto 'sy' amaravad, víra, jnátum[23] icchámi[31] te, 'nagha, 20
katham ágamanaṃ c' eha, kathaṃ c' ási na lakṣitaḥ[25].
su-rakṣitaṃ[26] hi me veśma, rájá c' aiv' ogra-śásanaḥ.” 21
evam uktas tu Vaidarbhyá Nalas tám pratyuváca[2] ha,
“Nalam máṃ viddhi[7], kalyáṇi, deva-dútam ih' ágatam. 22
devás tvám práptum icchanti Śakro, 'gnir, Varuṅo, Yamaḥ.
teṣám anyatamaṃ devam patiṃ varaya[3], sobhane. 23
teṣám eva prabhávena praviṣṭo[6] 'ham alakṣitaḥ[25].
praviśantaṃ[6] na máṃ kaścid apaśyan[37], n' ápy avárayat[3]. 24

etad-artham aham, bhadre, preṣitaḥ[31] sura-sattamaiḥ;
etac chrutvà[30], śubhe, buddhim prakuruṣva[17] yath' ecchasi[31]. 25

iti Nal'-opàkhyàne tṛtiyaḥ sargaḥ.

1. i	8. àp	15. bhram	22. jan	29. śak	36. dip
2. vac.	9. pùj	16. bhàṣ	23. jnà	30. śru	37. dṛiś
3. vṛi	10. pracch	17. kṛi	24. hṛi	31. iṣ	38. dhṛi
4. vraj	11. pat	18. kṣam	25. lakṣ	32. as	39. dhṛiṣ
5. vṛidh	12. brù	19. kṣip	26. rakṣ	33. smi	40. yà
6. viś	13. budh	20. kath	27. arh	34. sah	41. pri
7. vid.	14. bhù	21. gam	28. śaṃs	35. sthà	

IV.

Vrihadaśva uvàća,

sà namas-kṛitya devebhyaḥ prahasya[24] Nalam abravit,
"praṇayasva[9] yathà-śrad-dhaṃ, ràjan, kiṃ karavàṇi[17] te; 1
ahaṃ c' aiva hi yac c' ànyan mam' àsti[31] vasu kiñcana,
tat sarvaṃ tava; viśrabdhaṃ kuru praṇayam, iśvara. 2
haṃsànàṃ vacanaṃ yat tu, tan màṃ dahati[36], pàrthiva.
tvat-kṛite hi mayà, vira, ràjànaḥ sannipàtitàḥ[13]. 3
yadi tvaṃ bhajamànàm[15] mam pratyàkhyàsyasi[19], màna-da,
viṣam, agniṃ, jalaṃ, rajjum àsthàsye[34] tava kàraṇàt." 4
evam uktas tu Vaidarbhyà Nalas tàm pratyuvàca ha,
"tiṣṭhatsu[34] loka-pàleṣu, katham mànuṣam icchasi[30]? 5
yeṣàm ahaṃ loka-kṛitàm, iśvaràṇàm mahà-'tmanàm
na pàda rajasà tulyo, manas te teṣu vartatàm[6]. 6
vipriyaṃ hy àcaran[22] martyo devànàm mṛityum ṛicchati[27].
tràhi[35] màm anavady'-àn·gi, varayasva[4] sur'-ottamàn. 7
virajàṃsi ca vàsàṃsi, divyàś citràḥ srajas tathà,

bhûṣaṇâni ca mukhyâni, devân prâpya[10] tu bhun·kṣva[16] vai. 8
ya imâm pṛithivim kṛitsnâm saṃkṣipya[18] grasate[21] punaḥ,
Hut'-âśam, iśaṃ devânâṃ, kâ taṃ na varayet[4] patim? 9
yasya daṇḍa-bhayât sarve bhûta-grâmâḥ sam-â-gatâḥ,
dharmam ev' ânurudhyanti[28], kâ taṃ na varayet patim? 10
dharm' âtmânam, mahâ-'tmânaṃ, daitya-dânava-mardanam,
mah'-endraṃ sarva-devânâṃ, kâ taṃ na varayet patim? 11
kṛiyatâm[17] aviśan·kena manasâ, yadi manyase[8]
Varuṇaṃ loka-pâlânâṃ su-hṛid-vâkyam idaṃ śṛiṇu[29].” 12
Naiṣadhen' aivam uktâ sâ Damayanti vaco 'bravit,
samâplutâbhyâm[11] netrâbhyâṃ śoka-jen' âtha vâriṇâ, 13
“devebhyo 'haṃ namas-kṛitya sarvebhyaḥ, pṛithivi-pate,
vṛiṇe[4] tvâm eva bhartâraṃ satyam etad bravimi te.” 14
tâm uvâca tato râjâ vepamânâṃ[2] kṛit'-âñjalim,
“dautyen'[20] âgatya, kalyâṇi, kathaṃ sv'-ârtham ih' otsahe? 15
kathaṃ hy aham pratiśrutya devatânâm viśeṣataḥ,
par'-ârthe yatnam ârabhya, kathaṃ sv'-ârtham ih' otsahe[33]? 16
eṣa dharmo, yadi sv'-ârtho mam' âpi bhavitâ tataḥ.
evaṃ sv' ârthaṃ kariṣyâmi, tathâ, bhadre, vidhiyatâm[39].” 17
tato vâṣp'-âkulâṃ vâcaṃ Damayanti śuci-smitâ
pratyâharanti[23] śanakair Nalaṃ râjânam abravit, 18
“upâyo 'yam mayâ dṛiṣṭo[37] nir-apâyo, nar'-eśvara,
yena doṣo na bhavitâ tava, râjan, kathañcana. 19
twâṃ c' aiva hi, nara-śreṣṭha, devâś c' endra-puro-gamâḥ
âyântu[1] sahitâḥ sarve mama yatra swayaṃ-varaḥ 20
tato[6] 'haṃ loka-pâlânâṃ sannidhau tvâṃ, nar'-eśvara,
varayiṣye[4], nara-vyâghra; n' aivaṃ doṣo bhaviṣyati.” 21

evam uktas tu Vaidarbhyâ Nalo râjâ, viśâm pate,
âjagâma punas tatra, yatra devâḥ samâgatâḥ. 22
tam apaśyans[37] tath' âyântaṃ[1] loka-pâlâ mah'-eśvarâḥ
dṛṣṭvâ c' ainaṃ tato 'pṛcchan[12] vṛtt'-ântaṃ[6] sarvam eva tam, 23
"kaccid dṛṣṭâ tvayâ, râjan, Damayanti śuci-smitâ?
kim abravic[14] ca? naḥ sarvân vada[40], bhûmi-pate 'nagha. 24

Nala uvâca,

"bhavadbhir aham âdiṣṭo[38] Damayantyâ niveśanam
praviṣṭaḥ[7] su-mahâ-kakṣaṃ daṇḍibhiḥ sthavirair vṛtam[4]; 25
praviśantaṃ[7] ca mâṃ tatra na kaścid dṛṣṭavân naraḥ,
ṛte tâm pârthiva-sutâm, bhavatâm eva tejasâ, 26
sakhyaś c' âsyâ mayâ dṛṣṭâs, tâbhiś c' âpy upalakṣitaḥ[25],
vismitâś[32] c' âbhavan sarvâ dṛṣṭvâ mâm, vibudh'-eśvarâḥ; 27
varṇyamâneṣu[5] ca mayâ bhavatsu rucir'- ânanâ,
mâm eva gata-saṃkalpâ vṛṇite[4] sâ, sur'-ottamâḥ, 28
abravic c' aiva mâm, bâlâ, 'âyântu[1] sahitâḥ surâḥ
tvayâ saha, nara-vyâghra, mama yatra swayaṃ-varaḥ; 29
teṣâm ahaṃ sannidhau tvâṃ varayiṣyâmi[4], Naiṣadha.
evaṃ tava, mahâ-bâho, doṣo na bhavit',' iti, ha. 30
etâvad eva, vibudhâ, yathâ-vṛttam udâhṛtam[23]
mayâ; śeṣe pramâṇaṃ tu bhavantas, tri-daś'-eśvarâḥ. 31

iti Nal'-opâkhyâne caturthaḥ sargaḥ

1. yâ	8. man	15. bhaj	22. car	29. śru	36. dah
2. vep	9. ni	16. bhuj	23. hṛ	30. iṣ	37. dṛś
3. vac	10. âp	17. kṛ	24. has	31. as	38. diś
4. vṛ	11. plu	18. kṣip	25. lakṣ	32. smi	39. dhâ
5. varṇ	12. pracch	19. khyâ	26. rabh.	33. sah	40. vad
6. vṛt	13. pat	20. gam	27. ṛch	34. sthâ	
7. viś	14. brû	21. gras	28. rudh	35. trai	

V.

Vṛihadaśva uváca,

atha kále śubhe [17] prápte, tithau puṇye, kṣaṇe tathá,
[35] ájuháva mahi-pálán Bhimo rájá svayam-vare. 1
tac [49] chrutvá pṛithivi-páláḥ sarve hṛi-chaya-[20] piḍitáḥ
tvaritáḥ [28] samupájagmur Damayantim [17] abhipsavaḥ 2
kanaka-stambha-ruciraṃ toraṇena [44] virájitam
[7] viviśus te nṛi-pá ran-gam mahá-siṃhá iv' ácalam. 3
tatr' ásaneṣu vividheṣv [50] ásináḥ pṛithivi-kṣitaḥ
su-rabhi-srag-dharáḥ sarve [13] pramṛiṣṭa-maṇi-kuṇḍaláḥ 4
tatra sma piná [61] dṛiśyante báhavaḥ parigh'-opamáḥ
ákára-varṇa-su-ślakṣṇáḥ paṅca-śirṣá iv' ora-gáḥ, 5
su-keś'-ántáni cárúṇi, su-nás'-ákṣi-bhruváṇi ca
mukháni rájnám [48] śobhante nakṣatráṇi yathá divi 6
táṃ rája-samitim puṇyáṃ, nágair Bhogavatim iva,
[18] sampúrṇám puruṣa-vyághrair, vyághrair giri-guhám iva 7
Damayanti tato ran-gam [7] praviveśa śubh'-ánaná
[14] muṣṇanti prabhayá rájnáṃ cakṣuṃṣi ca manáṃsi ca. 8
tasyá gátreṣu [21] patitá teṣáṃ dṛiṣṭir mahá-'tmanám,
tatra, tatr' aiva [54] saktá [23] 'bhún, na [31] cacála ca [61] paśyatám. 9
tataḥ [26] saṃkirtyamáneṣu rájnáṃ námasu, Bhárata,
[61] dadarśa Bhaimi puruṣán paṅca tuly'-ákṛitin atha. 10
tán [27] samikṣya tataḥ sarván nirviśeṣ'-ákṛitin [56] sthitán,
sandehád atha Vaidarbhi n' [34] abhyajánán Nalaṃ nṛi-pam, 11
yaṃ yaṃ hi [61] dadṛiśe teṣám, taṃ tam [10] mene Nalaṃ nṛi-pam.
sá [30] cintayanti buddhyá 'tha [58] tarkayámása bhávini,

“kathaṃ hi deván jániyáṃ[34]? kathaṃ vidyáṃ[9] Nalaṃ nṛi-pam?” 12
evaṃ saṅcintayanti[30] sá Vaidarbhi bhṛiśa-duḥkhitá,
śrutáni[49] deva-lin·gáni tarkayámása, Bhárata. 13
“devánáṃ yáni lin·gáni sthavirebhyaḥ śrutáni me,
tán' iha tiṣṭhatám[56] bhúmáv ekasy' ápi na lakṣaye[38].” 14
sá viniścitya[30] bahudhá, vicárya[32] ca punaḥ, punaḥ,
śaraṇam prati devánám prápta-kálam amanyata[10]; 15
vácá ca manasá c' aiva namas-káram prayujya[3] sá,
devebhyaḥ práñjalir bhútvá vepamán'[5] edam abravit, 16
“haṃsánáṃ vacanaṃ srutvá yathá me Naisadho vṛitaḥ
patitve, tena satyena devás tam pradiśantu[62] me; 17
manasá, vacasá c' aiva yathá n' ábhicarámy[32] aham,
tena satyena vibudhás tam eva pradiśantu me; 18
yathá devaiḥ sa me bhartá vihito[63] Niṣadh'-ádhipaḥ,
tena satyena me devás tam eva pradiśantu me. 19
yath' edaṃ vratam árabdhaṃ[43] Nalasy' árádhane mayá,
tena satyena me devás tam eva pradiśantu me. 20
svaṃ c' aiva rúpaṃ[25] kurvantu loka-pálá mah'-eśvaráḥ,
yathá 'ham abhijániyám[34] Puṇyaślokaṃ nar'-ádhipam.” 21
niśamya Damayantyás tat karuṇam, paridevitam[62],
niścayam paramaṃ tathyam anurágaṃ ca Naiṣadhe, 22
mano-viśuddhim, buddhiṃ ca, bhaktiṃ, rágaṃ ca Naiṣadhe,
yath' oktaṃ cakrire[25] deváḥ sámarthyaṃ lin·ga-dháraṇe; 23
sá 'paśyad[61] vibudhán sarván asvedán, stabdha-locanán;
hṛiṣita-srag-rajo-hinán[37], sthitán aspṛiśataḥ[52] kṣitim. 24
cháyá-dvitiyo, mlána-srag[12], rajaḥ-sveda-samanvitaḥ[1],
bhúmi-ṣṭho Naiṣadhaś c' aiva, nimeṣeṇa ca, súcitaḥ[53]. 25

sà[27] samikṣya tu tàn devàn Puṇyaślokaṃ ca, Bhàrata,
Naıṣadhaṃ varayàmàsa[6] Bhaımi dharmeṇa, Pàṇḍava. 26
vılaȷȷamànà[39] vastr'-ànte ȷagràh'[29] àyata-locanà,[69]
skandha-deśe 'srıȷat[55] tasya srajam parama-śobhanàm; 27
varayàmàsa c' aıv' aınam patıtve vara-varṇıni.
tato "hà h'" etı sahasà muktaḥ[11] sabdo nar'-àdhıpaıḥ, 28
devaır mah'-arṣıbhıs tatra, "sàdhu, sàdhv" ıtı, Bhàrata,
vısmıtaır[51] irıtaḥ śabdaḥ praśaṃsadbhır[47] Nalaṃ nṛı-pam. 29
Damayantiṃ tu, Kauravya, Virasena-suto nṛı-paḥ
àśvàsayad[45] var'-àrohàm prahṛıṣṭen'[37] àntar-àtmanà, 30
"yat tvam bhaȷası,[66] kalyàṇı, pumàṃsaṃ deva-sannıdhau,
tasmàn màṃ vıddhı bhartàram evaṃ te vacane ratam.[41] 31
yàvac ca me dharıṣyantı[67] pràṇà dehe, śucı-smıte,
tàvat tvayı bhavıṣyàmı; satyam etad bravimı te." 32
Damayantiṃ tathà vàgbhır abhınandya kṛıt'-àñȷalıḥ,[16]
tau paras-parataḥ pritau[19] dṛıṣṭvà tv Agnı-puro-gamàn,
tàn eva śaraṇaṃ devàn ȷagmatur[28] manasà tadà. 33
vṛıte[6] tu Naıṣadhe Bhaımyà loka-pàlà mah'-auȷasaḥ
prahṛıṣṭa-manasaḥ[37] sarve Nalày' àṣṭau varàn daduḥ;[59] 34
pratyakṣa-darśanaṃ yaȷne, gatıṃ c' ànuttamàṃ śubhàm
Naiṣadhàya dadau[59] Śakraḥ priyamàṇaḥ Śaci-patıḥ. 35
Agnır àtma-bhavam pràdàd,[59] yatra vàñchatı[4] Naıṣadhaḥ;
lokàn àtma-prabhàṅś c' aıva dadau tasmaı Hutàśanaḥ. 36
Yamas tv anna-rasam pràdàd, dharme ca paramàṃ sthıtım.
apàm patır apàm bhàvaṃ yatra vàñchatı Naıṣadhaḥ; 37
srajaś c' ottama-gandh'-àḍhyàḥ: sarve ca mıthunaṃ daduḥ.
varàn evam pradày'[59] àsya, devàs te trı-dıvaṃ gatàḥ; 38

pàrthıvàś c' ànubhuy'[23] àsya vıvàhaṃ vısmay'-ànvıtàḥ[1]
Damayantyàś ca mudıtàḥ[15] pratıjagmur[28] yathà-'gatam.[28] 39

gateṣu pàrthıv'-endreṣu Bhimaḥ prito[19] mahà-manàḥ
vıvàhaṃ kàrayàmàsa[25] Damayantyà, Nalasya ca. 40

uṣya[8] tatra yathà-kàmaṃ Naıṣadho, dvı-padàṃ varaḥ,
Bhimena samanujnàto[34] jagàma[28] nagaraṃ svakam. 41

avàpya[17] nàri-ratnaṃ tu Puṇyaśloko 'pı pàrthıvaḥ
reme[41] saha tayà, ràjan, Śacy' eva Bala-Vṛıtra-hà. 42

ativa mudıto[15] ràjà bhràjamàno[24] 'ṃśumàn ıva
arañjayat[42] prajà viro dharmeṇa parıpàlayan.[68] 43

ije[2] c' àpy aśva-medhena Yayàtır ıva Nàhuṣaḥ,
anyaıś ca bahubhır dhimàn kratubhıś c' àpta-dakṣıṇaıḥ. 44

punaś ca ramaṇiyeṣu vaneṣ', ùpavaneṣu ca
Damayantyà saha Nalo vıjahàr'[36] àmar'-opamaḥ, 45

janayàmàsa[33] ca Nalo Damayantyà mahà-manàḥ
Indrasenaṃ sutaṃ c' àpı, Indrasenàṃ ca kanyakàm. 46

evaṃ sa yajamànaś[2] ca, vıharaṅś[36] ca nar'-àdhıpaḥ
rarakṣa[69] vasu-sampùrṇàṃ[18] vasu-dhàṃ vasu-dhà-'dhıpaḥ. 47

ıtı Nal'-opàkhyàne pañcamaḥ sargaḥ.

1. ı	13. mṛıj	25. kṛı	37. hṛıṣ	49. śru	61. dṛıś
2. yaj	14. muṣ	26. kṛıt	38. lakṣ	50. às	62. dıś
3. yuj	15. mud	27. ikṣ	39. laj	51. smı	63. dhà
4. vàñch	16. nand	28. gam	40. ir	52. spṛıś	64. dhṛıṣ
5. vep	17. àp	29. grah	41. ram	53. suc	65. yam
6. vṛı	18. pùr	30. cınt	42. rañj	54. saj	66. bhaj
7. vıś	19. pri	31. cal	43. rabh	55. sṛıj	67. dhṛı
8. vas	20. piḍ	32. car	44. ràj	56. sthà	68. pàl
9. vıd	21. pat	33. jan	45. śvas	57. tvar	69. rakṣ
10. man	22. brù	34. jnà	46. śam	58. tark	
11. muc	23. bhù	35. hve	47. śaṃs	59. dà	
12. mlaı	24. bhràj	36. hṛı	48. śubh	60. dev	

VI.

Vṛıhadaśva uvàca,

vṛıte[5] tu Naıṣadhe Bhaımyà, loka-pàlà mah'-aujasaḥ
yànto dadrıśur[28] àyàntaṃ[2] Dvàparaṃ Kalınà saha. 1
ath' àbravit Kalıṃ Śakraḥ samprekṣya[16] Bala-Vṛıtra-hà,
"Dvàpareṇa sahàyena, Kale, brùhı[12] kva yàsyası[2]?" 2
tato 'bravit Kalıḥ Śakraṃ, "Damayantyàḥ svayaṃ-varaṃ;
gatvà hı varayıṣye[5] tàm; mano hı mama tàṃ gatam[17]." 3
tam abravit prahasy'[21] endro, "nıvṛıttaḥ[6] sa svayaṃ-varaḥ.
vṛıtas[5] tayà Nalo ràjà patır, asmat-samipataḥ." 4
evam uktas tu Śakreṇa Kalıḥ, krodha-samanvıtaḥ[1],
devàn àmantrya[9] tàn sarvàn uvàc' edaṃ vacas tadà, 5
"devànàm mànuṣam madhye yat sà patım avındata[3],
tatra tasyà bhaven[13] nyàyyaṃ vıpulaṃ daṇḍa-dhàraṇam." 6
evam ukte tu Kalınà pratyùcus[4] te dıv'-aukasaḥ,
"asmàbhıḥ samanujnàte[18] Damayantyà Nalo vṛıtaḥ. 7
kà ca sarva-guṇ'-opetaṃ n' àśrayeta[25] Nalaṃ nṛı-pam?
yo veda[8] dharmàn akhılàn yathàvac carıta-vrataḥ; 8
yo 'dhite[1] caturo vedàn sarvàn àkhyàna-pañcamàn.
nıtyaṃ tṛıptà[27] gṛıhe yasya devà yajneṣu dharmataḥ; 9
ahıṃsa-nırato[22] yaś ca, satya-vàdi dṛıḍha-vrataḥ;
yasmın satyaṃ, dhṛıtır, dànam, tapaḥ, śaucaṃ, damaḥ, śamaḥ, 10
dhruvàṇı puruṣa-vyàghre loka-pàla-same nṛı-pe.
evaṃ-rùpaṃ Nalaṃ yo vaı kàmayec[15] chapıtuṃ[24], Kale, 11
àtmànaṃ sa śapen[24] mùḍho hañyàd[19] àtmànam àtmanà.
evaṃ-guṇaṃ Nalaṃ yo vaı kàmayec chapıtuṃ, Kale. 12

kṛicchre sa narake majjed[10] agâdhe vipule hrade."
evam uktvâ Kalim devâ Dvâparam ca divam yayuḥ.[2] 13
tato gateṣu deveṣu Kalir Dvâparam abravit,
"saṃhartum[20] n' otsahe[26] kopam; Nale vatsyâmi, Dvâpara; 14
bhraṃśayiṣyâmi tam râjyân, na Bhaimyâ saha raṃsyate.
tvam apy akṣân samâviśya sahayyam kartum arhasi." 15

itı Nal'-opâkhyâne ṣaṣṭhaḥ sargaḥ.

1. i	6. vṛit	11. muh	16. îkṣ	21. has	26. sah
2. yâ	7. vas	12. brû	17. gam	22. ram	27. tṛip
3. vind	8. vid	13. bhû	18. jnâ	23. arh	28. dṛiś
4. vac	9. mantr	14. bhraṃś	19. han	24. śap	
5. vṛi	10. maj	15. kam	20. hṛi	25. śri	

VII.

Vṛihadaśva uvâca,

evam sa samayam kṛitvâ Dvâpareṇa Kaliḥ saha,
âjagâma tatas tatra, yatra râjâ sa Naiṣadhaḥ; 1
sa nityam antara-prepsur[11] Niṣadheṣv avasac[6] ciram.
ath' âsya dvâ-daśe varṣe dadarśa[28] Kalir antaram. 2
kṛitvâ mûtram upaspṛiśya[25] sandhyâm anvâsta[24] Naiṣadhaḥ,
akṛitvâ pâdayoḥ śaucam; tatr' ainam Kalir âviśat.[5] 3
sa samâviśya[5] ca Nalam samipam, Puṣkarasya ca
gatvâ Puṣkaram âh'[19] edam, "ehi, divya[27] Nalena vai; 4
akṣa-dyûte Nalam jetâ[18] bhavân hi sahito mayâ,
Niṣadhân pratipadyasva,[12] jitvâ[18] râjyam Nalam nṛi-pam." 5
evam uktas tu Kalinâ Puṣkaro Nalam abhyayât[2]

Kaliś c' aiva vṛiṣo bhútvá gavám Puṣkaram abhyagát ;   6

ásádya tu Nalaṃ viram Puṣkaraḥ para-vira-há,

"divyáv'" ety abravit bhrátá, "vṛiṣeṇ'" eti, muhur muhuḥ.   7

ná cakṣame tato rájá samáhvánam mahá-manáḥ

Vaidarbhyaḥ prekṣamáṇáyáḥ paṇa-kálam amanyata.   8

hiraṇyasya, suvarṇasya, yána-yugyasya, vásasám,

ávistaḥ Kaliná dyúte jiyate sma Nalas tadá.   9

tam akṣa-mada-sammattaṃ su-hṛidáṃ na tu kaścana

niváraṇe 'bhavac chakto divyámánam arin-damam.   10

tataḥ paura-janáḥ sarve mantribhiḥ saha, Bhárata,

rájánaṃ draṣṭum ágacchan nivárayitum áturam.   11

tataḥ súta upágamya Damayantyai nyavedayat,

"eṣa paura-jano, devi, dvári tiṣṭhati káryaván;   12

nivedyatáṃ Naiṣadháya, 'sarváḥ prakṛitayaḥ sthitáḥ,

amṛiṣyamáṇá vyasanaṃ rájno dharm'-ártha-darśinaḥ.'"   13

tataḥ sá váṣpa-kalayá vácá, duḥkhena karṣitá,

uváca Naiṣadham Bhaimi śok'-opahata-cetaná,   14

"rájan, paura-jano dvári tvám didṛikṣur avasthitaḥ,

mantribhiḥ sahitaḥ sarvai, rája-bhakti-puras-kṛitaḥ.

taṃ draṣṭum arhas'" ity evam punaḥ, punar abháṣata.   15

táṃ tathá rucir'-ápán·gi vilapantiṃ tathá-vidhám

ávistaḥ Kaliná rájá n' ábhyabháṣata kiñcana.   16

tatas te mantriṇaḥ sarve, te c' aiva pura-vásinaḥ

"n' áyam ast'" iti duḥkh'-ártá, vriditá jagmur álayán.   17

tathá tad abhavad dyútam Puṣkarasya, Nalasya ca,

Yudhiṣṭhira, bahún másán Puṇyaślokas tv ajiyata.   18

iti Nal'-opákhyáne saptamaḥ sargaḥ.

1. i	6. vas	11. àp	16. kṣam	21. arh	26. sad
2. yà	7. vid	12. pad	17. gà	22. ard	27. div
3. vṛi	8. man	13. bhù	18. ji	23. śak	28. dṛś
4. vriḍ	9. mṛiṣ	14. kṛiṣ	19. àh	24. às	29. hve
5. viś	10. mad	15. ikṣ	20. lap	25. spṛiś	30. han

VIII.

Vṛihadaśva uvàca,

Damayanti tato dṛiṣṭvà Puṇyaślokaṃ nar'-àdhipam,
unmattavad[6] anunmattà[6] devane gata-cetasam, 1

bhaya-śoka-samàviṣṭà, ràjan, Bhima-sutà tataḥ
cintayàmàsa[13] tat kàryaṃ su-mahat pàrthivam prati; 2
sà śan-kamànà[20] tat-pàpaṃ, cikirṣanti[11] ca tat-priyam;
Nalaṃ ca hṛita-sarva-svam upalabhy'[16] edam abravit 3

Vṛihatsenàm atiyaśàṃ tàṃ dhàtrim paricàrikàm,
hitàṃ[26] sarv'-àrtha-kuśalàm anuraktàṃ[17] subhàṣitàm, 4
“Vṛihatsene, vraj'[3] àmàtyàn ànàyya[7] Nala-śàsanàt,
àcakṣva[14] yad dhṛitaṃ[27] dravyam, avaśiṣṭaṃ ca yad vasu.” 5
tatas te mantriṇaḥ sarve vijnàya[15] Nala-śàsanam,
“api no bhàga-dheyaṃ syàd,” ity uktvà Nalam àvrajan.[3] 6

tàs tu sarvàḥ prakṛitayo dvitiyaṃ samupasthitàḥ
nyavedayad Bhima-sutà; na ca sa pratyanandata.[8] 7
vàkyam apratinandantam[8] bhartàram abhivikṣya[28] sà
Damayanti punar veśma vriḍità[4] praviveśa ha. 8
niśamya[19] satataṃ c' àkṣàn Puṇyaśloka-paran-mukhàn,
Nalaṃ ca hṛita-sarva-svaṃ, dhàtrim punar uvàca ha, 9
“Vṛihatsene, punar gaccha[12] Vàrṣṇeyaṃ, Nala-śàsanàt,

sûtam ânaya[7], kalyâṇi, mahat kâryam upasthitam." 10
Vṛhatsena tu tac chrutvâ Damayantyâ prabhâṣitam,
Vârṣṇeyam ânayâmâsa[7] puruṣair âpta-kâribhiḥ. 11
Vârṣṇeyaṃ tu tato Bhaimi sântvayan[24] ślakṣṇayâ girâ
uvâca deśa-kâla-jnâ prâpta-kâlam anindità[9], 12
"jâniṣe[15] tvaṃ yathâ râjâ samyag-vṛttaḥ sadâ tvayi,
tasya tvaṃ viṣama-sthasya sâhâyyaṃ kartum arhasi. 13
yathâ yathâ hi nṛ-patiḥ Puṣkareṇ' aiva jiyate,
tathâ tathâ 'sya vai dyûte râgo bhûyo 'bhivardhate; 14
yathâ ca Puṣkarasy' âksâḥ patanti vaśa-vartinaḥ,
tathâ viparyayaś c' âpi Nalasy' âkṣeṣu dṛśyate. 15
su-hrit-sva-jana-vâkyâni yathâvan na śṛṇoti ca,
mam' âpi ca tathâ vâkyaṃ n' âbhinandati[8] mohitaḥ[5]. 16
nûnam manye na doṣo 'sti Naiṣadhasya mahâ-'tmanaḥ,
yat tu me vacanaṃ râjâ n' âbhinandati mohitaḥ. 17
śaraṇaṃ tvâm prapannâ 'smi; sârathe, kuru[11] mad-vacaḥ;
na hi me śudhyate[22] bhâvaḥ, kadâcid vinaśed[10] api. 18
Nalasya dayitân aśvân yojayitvâ[2] mano-javân,
idam âropya[18] mithunaṃ Kuṇḍinaṃ yâtum arhasi. 19
mama jnâtiṣu nikṣipya[30] dârakau, syandanaṃ tathâ,
asvâṅś c' emân, yathâ-kâmaṃ vasa vâ, 'nyatra gaccha[12] vâ." 20
Damayantyâs tu tad vâkyaṃ Vârṣṇeyo Nala-sârathiḥ
nyavedayad aśeṣeṇa Nal'-âmâtyeṣu mukhyaśaḥ, 21
taiḥ[1] sametya[13] viniścitya so 'nujnâto[15], mahi-pate,
yayau, mithunam âropya[18] Vidarbhâns tena vâhinâ. 22
hayâns tatra vinikṣipya[30] sûto, ratha-varaṃ ca tam,
Indrasenâṃ ca tâṃ kanyâm, Indrasenaṃ ca bâlakam. 23

âmantrya Bhimaṃ râjânam ârttaḥ śocan Nalaṃ nṛi-pam,
aṭamânas[25] tato 'yodhyâṃ jagâma nagariṃ tadâ. 24
Ṛituparṇaṃ sa râjânam upatasthe su-duḥkhitaḥ,
bhṛitiṃ[29] c' opayayau tasya sârathyena mahi-pateḥ. 25

iti Nal'-opâkhyâne aṣṭamaḥ sargaḥ.

1. i	6. mad	11. kṛi	16. labh	21. śuc	26. dhâ
2. yuj	7. ni	12. gam	17. rañj	22. śudh	27. hṛi
3. vraj	8. nand	13. cint	18. ruh	23. as	28. ikṣ
4. vṛiḍ	9. nind	14. cakṣ	19. śam	24. sântv	29. yâ
5. muh	10. naś	15. jnâ	20. śan·k	25. aṭ	30. kṣip

IX.

Vṛihadaśva uvâca,
tatas tu yâte[2] Vârṣṇeye Puṇyślokasya divyataḥ[43]
Puṣkareṇa hṛitaṃ[30] râjyaṃ, yac c' ânyad vasu kiñcana. 1
hṛita-râjyaṃ Nalaṃ, râjan, prahasan[31] Puṣkaro 'bravit,
"dyûtam pravartatâm[8] bhûyaḥ; pratipâṇo 'sti kas tava? 2
śiṣṭâ te Damayanty ekâ, sarvam anyaj jitam mayâ.
Damayantyâḥ paṇaḥ sadhu vartatâṃ yadi manyase[11]." 3
Puṣkareṇ' aivam uktasya Puṇyaślokasya manyunâ
vyadiryat'[44] eva hṛidayaṃ, na c' ainaṃ kiñcid abravit. 4
tataḥ Puṣkaram âlokya[32] Nalaḥ parama-manyumân,
utsṛijya[38] sarva-gâtrebhyo bhûṣaṇâni mahâ-yaśaḥ, 5
eka-vâsâ[3] hy asaṃvitaḥ[9], su-hṛic-choka-vivardhanaḥ,
niścakrâma[18] tato râjâ tyaktvâ[41] su-vipulâṃ śriyam. 6
Damayanty eka-vastrâ 'tha gacchantam[23] pṛiṣṭhato 'nvagât[22].

sa tayā vāhyataḥ sārddhaṃ tri-rātraṃ Naiṣadho [10]'vasat; 7
[24]Puṣkaras tu, mahā-rāja, ghoṣayāmāsa vai pure,
"Nale yaḥ samyag [39]ātiṣṭhet, sa [23]gacched badhyatām mama." 8
Puṣkarasya tu vākyena tasya, vidveṣaṇena ca
paurā na tasya sat-kāraṃ [17]kṛtavanto, Yudhiṣṭhira. 9
sa tathā nagar'-abhyāśe, sat-kār'-ārho, na sat-kṛtaḥ;
tri-rātram uṣito rājā jala-mātreṇa [8]vartayan, 10
[14]pīḍyamānaḥ kṣudhā tatra phala-mūlāni [19]karṣayan.
[39]prātiṣṭhata tato rājā, Damayantī tam [22]anvagāt. 12
kṣudhayā [14]pīḍyamānas tu Nalo bahutithe 'hani
[45]apaśyac chakunān kāṃścid dhiraṇya-sadṛśac-chadān. 12
sa [26]cintayāmāsa tadā Niṣadh'-ādhipatir bali,
"asti bhakṣyo mam' ādy' āyaṃ, vasu c' edam bhaviṣyati." 13
tatas tān paridhānena vāsasā sa [6]samāvṛṇot;
tasya tad vastram [42]ādāya sarve [23]jagmur vihāyasā; 14
[15]utpatantaḥ kha-gā vākyam etad [28]āhus tato Nalam,
dṛṣṭvā dig-vāsasam, bhūmau [39]sthitaṃ, dīnam, adho-mukham, 15
"vayam akṣāḥ, su-dur-buddhe, tava vāso [30]jihīrṣavaḥ;
[23]āgatā na hi naḥ prītiḥ, savāsasi gate tvayi." 16
tān [20]samīkṣya gatān akṣān, ātmānaṃ ca vivāsasam,
Puṇyaślokas tadā, rājan, Damayantīm ath' ābravīt, 17
"yeṣām prakopād aiśvaryāt [25]pracyuto 'ham, anindite,
prāṇa-yātrāṃ na [4]vinde ca duḥkhitaḥ kṣudhayā [1]'nvitaḥ, 18
yeṣāṃ [17]kṛte na sat-kāram akurvan mayi Naiṣadhāḥ,
ta ime śakunā bhūtvā vāso 'py [30]apaharanti me. 19
vaiṣamyam paramam prāpto, duḥkhito, gata-cetanaḥ,
bharto te 'haṃ, [16]nibodh' edaṃ vacanaṃ [47]hitam ātmanaḥ. 20

ete [23]gacchanti bahavaḥ panthâno dakṣiṇâ-patham,
Avantiṃ, Ṛkṣavantaṃ ca [18]samatikramya parvatam, 21
eṣa Vindhyo mahâ-śailaḥ, Payoṣṇi ca samudra-gâ,
âśramâś ca maha-rsiṇâm bahu-mûla-phal'-[1]ânvitâḥ, 22
eṣa panthâ Vidarbhâṇâm, asau gacchati Kośalân;
ataḥ paraṃ ca deśo 'yaṃ dakṣiṇe dakṣiṇâ-pathaḥ." 23
etad vâkyaṃ Nalo râjâ Damayantiṃ [47]samâhitaḥ,
uvâc', [33]âsakṛd ârto hi Bhaimim [46]uddiśya, Bhârata. 24
tataḥ sâ, vâṣpa-kalayâ vâcâ, duḥkhena [19]karṣitâ,
uvâca Damayanti taṃ Naiṣadhaṃ karuṇaṃ vacaḥ, 25
" [5]udvejate me hṛdayaṃ, [40]sidanty an·gâni sarvaśaḥ,
tava, pârthiva, saṃkalpaṃ [26]cintayantyâḥ punaḥ, punaḥ. 26
hṛta-râjyaṃ, hṛta-dravyaṃ, vivastraṃ, kṣut-tṛṣâ-'nvitam,
katham [38]utsṛjya [23]gaccheyam ahaṃ tvâṃ nirjane vane? 27
[35]śrântasya te [33]kṣudh-ârtasya [26]cintayânasya tat sukham,
vane ghore, mahâ-râja, [12]nâśayiṣyâmy ahaṃ klamam. 28
na ca bhâryâ-samaṃ kiñcid [4]vidyate [11]bhiṣajâm matam
auṣadhaṃ sarva-duḥkheṣu; satyam etad bravimi te." 29

Nala uvâca,

evam etad yathâ [28]'ttha tvaṃ, Damayanti, sumadhyame,
n' âsti bhâryâ-samam mitraṃ narasy' ârtasya bheṣajam 30
na c' âhaṃ [41]tyaktu-kâmas tvâṃ; kim-artham, bhiru, [34]śan·kase?
[41]tyajeyam aham âtmânaṃ, na c' aivaṃ tvâm, anindite. 31

Damayanti uvâca,

yadi mâṃ tvam, mahâ-râja, na [29]vihâtum ih' [36]ecchasi,
tat kim-arthaṃ Vidarbhâṇâm panthâḥ [46]samupadiśyate? 32
avaimi c' âhaṃ, nṛ-pate; na tu mâṃ [41]tyaktum arhasi,

cetasâ tv apakṛṣṭena[19] mâṃ tyajethâ[41], mahi-pate. 33
panthânaṃ hi mam' âbhikṣṇam âkhyâsi[21] ca, nar'-ottama,
ato nimittaṃ śokam me vardhayasy[9], amar'-opama; 34
yadi c' âyam abhiprâyas tava, "jnâtin vrajed[7]," iti,
sahitâv eva gacchâvo Vidarbhân, yadi manyase. 35
Vidarbha-râjas tatra tvâṃ pûjayiṣyati[13], mâna-da;
tena tvam pûjito, râjan, sukhaṃ vatsyasi[10] no gṛhe. 36

iti Nal'-opâkhyâne navamaḥ sargaḥ.

1. i	9. vṛdh	17. kṛi	25. cyu	33. ârd	41. tyaj
2. yâ	10. vas	18. kram	26. cint	34. śan-k	42. dâ
3. vye	11. man	19. kṛṣ	27. ji	35. śram	43. div
4. vind	12. naś	20. ikṣ	28. âh	36. iṣ	44. dṛi
5. vij	13. pûj	21. khyâ	29. hâ	37. as	45. dṛiś
6. vṛi	14. piḍ	22. gâ	30. hṛi	38. sṛij	46. diś
7. vraj	15. pat	23. gam	31. has	39. sthâ	47. dhâ
8. vṛit	16. budh	24. ghuṣ	32. lok	40. sad	

X.

Nala uvâca,

yathâ râjyaṃ tava pitus, tathâ mama na saṃśayaḥ;
na tu tatra gamiṣyâmi viṣama-sthaḥ kathañcana. 1
kathaṃ samṛiddho[33] gatvâ 'haṃ, tava harṣa-vivardhanaḥ[8];
paricyuto[22] gamiṣyâmi, tava śoka-vivardhanaḥ. 2

Vṛihadaśva uvâca,

iti bruvan Nalo râjâ Damayantim punaḥ, punaḥ,
sântvayâmâsa kalyâṇiṃ vâsaso 'rddhena saṃvṛitâm[6]
tâv eka-vastra-saṃvitâv[4] aṭamânâv[43] itas tataḥ,

kṣut-pipàsà[85]-pariśràntau sabhàṃ kàñcid upeyatuḥ[1]. 4
tàṃ sabhàm upasampràpya[13], tadà sa Niṣadh'-àdhipaḥ
Vaidarbhyà sahito ràjà niṣasàda[42] mahi-tale; 5
sa vai vivastro, vikaṭo, malinaḥ, pàṃsu-guṇṭhitaḥ[21],
Damayantyà saha śràntaḥ[35] suṣvàpa[38] dharani-tale. 6
Damayanty api kalyàṇi, nidrayà 'pahṛtà[27] tataḥ,
sahasà duḥkham àsàdya[42] su-kumàri, tapasvini. 7
suptàyàṃ[38] Damayantyàṃ tu Nalo ràjà, viśàm pate,
śok'-onmathita-citt'-àtmà, na sma śete[34] yathà purà. 8
sa tad ràjy'-àpaharaṇaṃ, su-hṛt-tyàgaṃ ca sarvaśaḥ,
vane ca taṃ paridhvaṃsam prekṣya[18] cintàm upeyivàn[1]; 9
"kiṃ nu me syàd[36] idaṃ kṛtvà? kiṃ nu me syàd akurvataḥ[15]?
kiṃ nu me maraṇaṃ śreyaḥ, parityàgo janasya và? 10
màm iyaṃ hy anurakt'[29] aiva duḥkham pràpnoti[13] mat-kṛte;
mad-vihinà[26] tv iyaṃ gacchet kadàcit sva-janam prati. 11
mayi niḥsaṃśayaṃ duḥkhaṃ iyam pràpsyaty[13] anuvratà,
utsarge saṃśayaḥ syàt tu, vindet'[5] àpi sukhaṃ kvacit." 12
sa viniś-citya[23] bahudhà, vicàrya[24] ca punaḥ, punaḥ,
utsargam[9] manyate śreyo Damayantyà nar'-àdhipaḥ. 13
"na c' aiṣà tejasà śakyà kaiścid dharṣayitum[46] pathi,
yaśasvini, mahà-bhàgà, mad-bhakt' eyaṃ pati-vratà." 14
evaṃ tasya tadà buddhir Damayantyàṃ nyavartata[7],
Kalinà duṣṭa-bhàvena Damayantyà visarjane. 15
so 'vastratàm àtmanaś ca, tasyàś c' àpy eka-vastratàm
cintayitvà[23] 'bhyagàd[19] ràjà vastr'-àrddhasy' àvakartanam. 16
"kathaṃ vàso vikarteyaṃ[17], na ca budhyeta[14] me priyà?"

[23]vicinty' aivaṃ Nalo rájá sabhám [24]paryacarat tadá; 17
[45]paridhávann atha Nala itaś c' etaś ca, Bhárata,
[42]ásasáda sabh' oddeśe vikoṣaṃ khaḍgam uttamam. 18
ten' árddhaṃ vásasaś [25]chittvá, nivasya ca paraṃ-tapaḥ,
[38]suptám [41]utsṛjya Vaidarbhim [44]prádravad gata-cetanaḥ. 19
tato, [7]nivṛtta-hṛdayaḥ, punar ágamya táṃ sabhám
Damayantiṃ tadá dṛṣṭvá [32]ruroda Niṣadh'-ádhipaḥ; 20
"yáṃ na váyur, na c' ádityaḥ, purá [47]paśyati me priyám,
s' eyam adya sabhá-madhye [34]śete bhúmáv anáthavat. 21
iyaṃ vastr'-ávakartena [4]saṃvitá, cáru-hásini,
unmatt' eva var'-árohá, katham [14]buddhvá bhaviṣyati? 22
katham eká [36]sati Bhaimi, mayá [31]virahitá, śubhá
[24]cariṣyati vane ghore [37]mṛga-vyála-niṣevite? 23
ádityá, vasavo, rudrá, aśvinau sa-marud-gaṇau,
[30]rakṣantu tvám; mahá-bhága, dharmeṇ' ási [6]samávṛtá." 24
evam uktvá priyám bháryáṃ rúpeṇ' ápratimám bhuvi,
Kaliná [27]'pahṛta-jnáno Nalaḥ prátiṣṭhad [3]udyataḥ. 25
gatvá, gatvá Nalo rájá punar eti sabhám muhuḥ,
[16]ákṛṣyamáṇaḥ Kaliná sauhṛden' [16]ávakṛṣyate. 26
dvidh' eva hṛdayaṃ tasya duḥkhitasy' ábhavat tadá,
dol' eva muhur [2]áyáti, yáti c' aiva sabhám prati. 27
[16]avakṛṣṭas tu Kaliná [10]mohitaḥ [44]prádravan Nalaḥ
[38]suptám [41]utsṛjya tám bháryáṃ [28]vilapya karuṇam bahu. 28
[12]naṣṭ' átmá Kaliná [40]spṛṣṭas, tat tad [20]vigaṇayan nṛ-paḥ,
jagám' aikáṃ vane śúnye bháryám utsṛjya duḥkhitaḥ. 29

iti Nal'-opákhyáne daśamaḥ sargaḥ.

1. i	9. man	17. kṛit	25. chid	33. ṛidh	41. sṛij
2. yā	10. muh	18. ikṣ	26. hā	34. śi	42. sad
3. yam	11. math	19. gā	27. hṛi	35. śram	43. aṭ
4. vye	12. naś	20. gaṇ	28. lap	36. as	44. dru
5. vind	13. āp	21. guṇṭh	29. rañj	37. sev	45. dhāv
6. vṛi	14. budh	22. cyu	30. rakṣ	38. svap	46. dhṛiṣ
7. vṛit	15. kṛi	23. cint	31. rah	39. śantv	47. dṛiś
8. vṛidh	16. kṛiṣ	24. car	32. rud	40. spṛiś	

XI.

Vṛihadaśva uvāca,

[12]apakrānte Nale, rājan, Damayanti gata-klamā
[10]abudhyata var'-ārohā [40]saṃtrastā vijane vane. 1
[41]apaśyamānā bhartāraṃ [1]śoka-duḥkha-samanvitā,
prā[13]krośad uccaiḥ saṃtrastā, "mahā-rāj'" eti Naiṣadham. 2
hā nātha! hā mahā-rāja! hā, svāmin! kiṃ [21]jahāsi mām?
hā! [22]hatā 'smi, [6]vinaṣṭā 'smi, [11]bhitā 'smi, vijane vane. 3
nānu nāma, mahā-rāja, dharma-jnaḥ, satya-vāg asi?
katham uktvā tathā satyaṃ [35]suptām [38]utsṛijya māṃ gataḥ? 4
katham utsṛijya gantā 'si dakṣām bhāryām anuvratām?
viśeṣato 'napakṛite, pareṇ' āpakṛite sati. 5
[30]śakyase tā giraḥ samyak kartum mayi, nar'-eśvara,
yās teṣāṃ loka-pālānāṃ sannidhau kathitāḥ purā? 6
n' ākāle [42]vihito mṛityur martyānām, puruṣa-'ṛṣabha;
yatra kāntā tvay' otsṛiṣṭā muhūrtam api [19]jivati. 7
[7]paryāptaḥ parihāso 'yam etāvān, puruṣa-'ṛṣabha;
[11]bhitā 'ham; atidurdharṣa, [41]darśay' ātmānam, iśvara. 8
[41]dṛiśyase, dṛiśyase, rājann, eṣa dṛiṣṭo 'si, Naiṣadha;

[2]âvârya gulmair âtmânaṃ, kim mâṃ na pratibhâṣase? 9
nṛ-śaṃsa vata râj' endra, yan mâm evaṃ gatâm iha,
vilapantiṃ samâgamya n' [21]âśvâsayasi, pârthiva? 10
na śocâmy aham âtmânaṃ, na c' ânyad api kiñcana.
'kathaṃ nu bhavitâsy eka?' iti tvâṃ nṛ-pa [25]rodimi. 11
kathaṃ nu, râjans, tṛṣitaḥ, kṣudhitaḥ, śrama-karṣitaḥ,
sây'-âhne vṛkṣa-mûleṣu mâm [41]apaśyan, bhaviṣyasi?" 12
tataḥ sâ tivra-śok'-ârtâ, pradipt' eva ca manyunâ,
itaś c' etaś ca [25]rudati [43]paryadhâvata duḥkhitâ; 13
muhur [9]utpatate bâlâ, muhuḥ patati vihvalâ;
muhur [23]âliyate bhitâ, [13]muhuḥ krośati, roditi. 14
ativa [39]śoka-santaptâ, muhur [27]niḥśvasya duḥkhitâ,
uvâca Bhaimi niḥśvasya rudaty atha pati-vratâ, 15
"yasy' âbhiśâpâd duḥkh'-ârto, duḥkhaṃ vindati Naiṣadhaḥ,
tasya bhûtasya no duḥkhâd duḥkham abhyadhikam bhavet! 16
apâpa-cetasam pâpo ya evaṃ kṛtavân Nalam,
tasmâd duḥkhataram prâpya [19]jivatv asukha-jivikâm!" 17
evaṃ tu vilapanti sâ râjno bhâryâ mahâ-'tmanaḥ
[33]anveṣamâṇâ bhartâraṃ vane [34]śvâ-pada-sevite. 18
unmattavad Bhima-sutâ vilapanti tatas tataḥ
"hâ, hâ, râjann," iti, muhur itaś c' etaś ca [43]dhâvati. 19
[44]tâṃ krandamânâm atyarthaṃ kurarim iva [45]vâśatim,
karuṇam bahu śocantiṃ, vilapantim muhur, muhuḥ, 20
sahasâ 'byâgatâm Bhaimim abhyâsa-parivartinim,
[16]jagrâh' âja-garo grâho mahâ-kâyaḥ kṣudhâ-'nvitaḥ. 21
sâ [17]grasyamânâ grâheṇa, śokena ca [8]pariplutâ,
n' âtmânaṃ śocati tathâ, yathâ śocati Naiṣadham 22

"hà nàtha, màm iha vane grasyamànàm anàthavat,
gràheṇ' ànena vijane, kim artham n' ànudhàvasi[43]? 23
katham bhaviṣyasi punar màm anusmṛtya[36], Naiṣadha,
śàpàn muktaḥ[5], punar labdhvà[24] buddhiṃ, ceto, dhanàni ca? 24
śràntasya[31] te kṣudh'-àrtasya, pariglànasya[15], Naiṣadha,
kaḥ śramaṃ, ràja-śàrdùla, nàśayiṣyati[6] te, 'nagha?" 25
tataḥ kaścin mṛga-vyàdho, vicaran gahane vane,
àkrandamànàṃ[44] saṃśrutya, javen' àbhisasàra[37] ha. 26
tàṃ tu dṛṣṭvà tathà grastàm urageṇ' àyat'-ekṣaṇàm,
tvaramàṇo mṛga-vyàdhaḥ samabhikramya[12] vegataḥ, 27
mukhataḥ pàṭayàmàsa[46] śastreṇa niśitena[26] ca.
nirviceṣṭam bhujan-gaṃ taṃ viśasya mṛga-jìvanaḥ[32], 28
mokṣayitvà[2] sa tàṃ vyàdhaḥ, prakṣàlya[14] salilena ca,
samàśvàsya[27] kṛt'-àhàràm atha papraccha, Bhàrata,
"kasya tvam' mṛga-sàv'-àksi, kathaṃ c' abhyàgatà vanam?
kathaṃ c' edam mahat kṛcchram pràptavaty[7] asi, bhàvini?" 30
Damayanti tathà tena pṛcchyamànà, viśàm pate,
sarvam etad yathà-vṛttam[3] àcacakṣe[18] 'sya, Bhàrata. 31
tàm arddha-vastra-saṃvitàm, pìna-śroṇi-payo-dharàm
su-kumàr'-ànavady'-àn-giṃ, pùrṇa-candra-nibh'-ànanàm, 32
aràla-pakṣma-nayanàm, tathà madhura-bhàṣiṇim,
lakṣayitvà mṛga-vyàdhaḥ kàmasya vaśam iyivàn[1]. 33
tàm evaṃ ślakṣṇayà vàcà lubdhako mṛdu-pùrvayà
sàntvayàmàsa[28] kàm'-àrtas: tad abudhyata[10] bhàvini. 34
Damayanty api taṃ duṣṭam upalabhya[24] pati-vratà,
tìvra-roṣa-samàviṣṭà prajajvàl'[20] eva manyunà. 35
sa tu pàpa-matiḥ kṣudraḥ pradharṣayitum[41] àturaḥ,

durdharṣáṃ tarkayámása diptám agni-śıkhám ıva. 36

Damayanti tu duḥkh'-ártá, patı-ráȷya-vıná-kṛıtá,.

[1]atita-vák-pathe kále, [29]śaśáp' aınaṃ rúp'-ánvıtá, 37

"yathá 'haṃ Naıṣadhád anyam manasá 'pı na cıntaye,

tathá 'yam [9]patatáṃ kṣudraḥ par'-ásur mṛıga-ȷivanaḥ." 38

ukta-mátre tu vacane, tathá sa mṛıga-ȷivanaḥ

vyasuḥ [9]papáta medınyám, [47]agnı-dagdha ıva drumaḥ. 39

ıtı Nal'-opákhyána eká-daśaḥ sargaḥ

1. ı	9. pat	17. gras	25. rud	33. eṣ	41. dṛıś
2. vṛı	10. budh	18. cakṣ	26. śı	34. sev	42. dhá
3. vṛıt	11. bhi	19. ȷiv	27. śvas	35. svap	43. dháv
4. mokṣ	12. kram	20. ȷval	28. sántv	36. smṛı	44. krand
5. muc	13. kruś	21. há	29. śap	37. sṛı	45. váś
6. naś	14. kṣal	22. han	30. śak	38. sṛıȷ	46. paṭ
7. áp	15. glaı	23. li	31. śram	39. tap	47. dah
8. plu	16. grah	24. labh	32. śas	40. tras	

XII.

Vṛıhadaśva uváca,

sá nıhıtya mṛıga-vyádham pratasthe kamal'-ekṣaṇá

vanam pratıbhayaṃ śúnyaṃ ȷhıllıká-gaṇa-nádıtam, 1

sıṃha-dvipı-ruru-vyághra-mahıṣa-'rkṣa-gaṇaır yutaṃ,

náná-pakṣı-gaṇ'-ákirṇam, mleccha-taskara-sevıtam, 2

śála-veṇu-dhav'-áśvattha-tınduk'-en-guda-kıṃśukaıḥ,

arȷun'-ārıṣṭa-sañchannaṃ, syandanaıś ca sa-śalmalaıḥ, 3

ȷambv'-ámra-lodhra-khadıra-śála-vetra-samákulam,

padmak'-ámalaka-plakṣa-kadamb'-oḍumbar'-ávṛıtam, 4

vadari-vılva-saṃchannaṃ, nyágrodhaıś ca samákulam,

priyâla-tâla-kharjûra-haritaka-vibhitakaiḥ, 5
nânâ-dhâtu-śatair naddhân vividhân api c' âcalân
nikuñjân parisaṃghuṣṭân, dariś c' âdbhuta-darśanâḥ, 6
nadiḥ sarâṃsi, vâpiś ca, vividhâṅś ca mṛga-dvijân
sâ bahûn bhima-rûpâṅś ca piśâc'-oraga-râkṣasân, 7
palvalâni, taḍâgâni, giri-kûṭâni sarvaśaḥ
sarito nirjharâṅś c' aiva dadarś' adbhuta-darśanân. 8
yûthaśo dadṛśe c' âtra Vidarbh'-âdhipa-nandini
mahiṣâṅś ca, varâhâṅś ca, ṛkṣâṇś ca, vana-pan-na-gân. 9
tejasâ, yaśasâ, lakṣmyâ, sthityâ ca parayâ yutâ
Vaidarbhi vicaraty ekâ, Nalam anveṣati tadâ. 10
n' âbibhyat sâ nṛ-pa-sutâ Bhaimi tatr' âtha kasyacit,
dâruṇâm aṭavim prâpya bhartri-vyasana-piḍitâ; 11
Vidarbha-tanayâ, râjan, vilalâpa su-duḥkhitâ,
bhartri-śoka-parit'-ân·gi, śilâ-talam ath' âśritâ. 12
Damayanty uvâca,
vyûḍh'-oraska, mahâ-bâho, Naiṣadhânâṃ jan'-âdhipa,
kva nu, râjan, gato 's' iha, tyaktvâ mâṃ vijane vane? 13
aśva-medh'-âdibhir, vira, kratubhir bhûri-dakṣiṇaiḥ
katham iṣṭvâ, nara-vyâghra, mayi mithyâ pravartase? 14
yat tvay' oktaṃ, nara-śreṣṭha, mat-samakṣam, mahâ-dyute,
smartum arhasi, kalyâṇa, vacanam, pârthiva-ṛṣabha. 15
yac c' oktam viha-gair haṃsaiḥ samipe tava, bhûmi-pa,
mat-samakṣaṃ yad uktaṃ ca, tad avekṣitum arhasi. 16
catvâra ekato vedâḥ s'-ân·g'-opân·gâḥ savistarâh,
sv-adhitâ, Manu-ja-vyâghra satyam ekaṃ kil' aikataḥ; 17
tasmâd arhasi śatru-ghna, satyaṃ kartuṃ, nar'-eśvara,

uktaván asi yad, vira, mat-sakáśe, purá vacaḥ. 18
há vira na nu nám' áham iṣṭá kila tav', ánagha?
asyám aṭavyáṃ ghoráyáṃ kim máṃ na pratibháṣase? 19
bhakṣayaty eṣa máṃ raudro vyátt'-ásyo dáruṇ'-ákritiḥ
araṇya-ráṭ kṣudh-áviṣṭaḥ; kim máṃ na trátum arhasi? 20
"na me tvad anyá kácid dhi priyá 'st'" ity abraviḥ sadá;
táṃ ṛitáṃ kuru, kalyáṇa, pur'-oktám bháratiṃ, nṛi-pa. 21
unmattáṃ vilapantim mám bháryám iṣṭám, nar'-ádhipa,
ipsitám ipsito, nátha, kim máṃ na pratibháṣase? 22
kṛiśáṃ, dináṃ, vivarṇáṃ ca, malináṃ, vasu-dhá-'dhipa,
vastr'-árddha-právṛitám ekáṃ vilapantim anáthavat, 23
yútha-bhraṣṭám iv' aikám máṃ hariṇim, pṛithu-locana,
na mánayasi mám, árya, rudatim, ari-karṣaṇa. 24
mahá-rája, mahá-'raṇye aham ekákini sati,
Damayanty abhibháṣe tvám; kim máṃ na pratibháṣase? 25
kula-śil'-opasampanna, cáru-sarv'-áṅga-śobhana,
n' ádya tvám pratipaśyámi giráv asmin, nar'-ottama. 26
vane c' ásmin mahá-ghore, siṃha-vyághra-niṣevite,
śayánam, upaviṣṭaṃ vá, sthitaṃ vá, Niṣadh'-ádhipa, 27
prasthitaṃ vá, nara-śreṣṭha, mama śoka-vivardhana?
kaṃ nu pṛicchámi duḥkh'-ártá tvad-arthe śoka-karṣitá, 28
"kaccid dṛiṣṭas tvayá 'raṇye saṃgaty' eha Nalo nṛi-paḥ?"
ko nu me vá 'tha praṣṭavyo vane 'smin prasthitaṃ Nalam? 29
abhirúpam, mahá-'tmanam, para-vyúha-vináśanam,
"yam anveṣasi, rájánaṃ Nalam padma-nibh'-ekṣaṇam. 30
ayaṃ sa," iti, kasy' ádya śroṣyámi madhuráṃ giram?
araṇya-ráḍ ayaṃ śrimáñś, catur-daṃṣṭro, mahá-hanuḥ, 31

śârdûlo 'bhimukho 'bhyeti; vrajâmy enam asaṅkitâ.
bhavân mṛgâṇâm adhipas; tvam asmin kânane prabhuḥ; 32
Vidarbha-râja-tanayâṃ "Damayant'" iti viddhi mâm,
Niṣadh'-âdhipater bhâryâṃ Nalasy' âmitra-ghâtinaḥ, 33
patim anveṣatim ekâṃ kṛpaṇâṃ, śoka-karṣitâm,
âśvâsaya, mṛg'-endr', eha, yadi dṛṣṭas tvayâ Nalaḥ; 34
atha vâ, 'raṇya-nṛ-pate, Nalaṃ yadi na śaṃsasi,
mâṃ khâdaya, mṛga-śreṣṭha, duḥkhâd asmâd vimocaya. 35
śrutvâ 'raṇye vilapitam mam' aiṣa mṛga-râṭ svayam
yâty etâm mṛṣṭa-salilâm âpa-gâṃ sâgaram-gamâm. 36
imaṃ śil'-occayam puṇyaṃ śṛṅgair bahubhir ucchritaiḥ,
virâjadbhir, divi-spṛgbhir, n' aika-varṇair, mano-haraiḥ, 37
nânâ-dhâtu-samâkirṇaṃ, vividh'-opala-bhuṣitam
asy' âraṇyasya mahataḥ ketu-bhûtam iv' otthitam, 38
siṃha-śârdûla-mâtaṅga-varâha-'rkṣa-mṛg'-âyutam,
patatribhir bahu-vidhaiḥ samantâd anunâditam, 39
kiṃśuk'-âśoka-vakula-punnâgair upaśobhitam
karṇikâra-dhava-plakṣaiḥ su-puṣpair upaśobhitam 40
saridbhiḥ sa-vihaṃ-gâbhiḥ, śikharaiś ca samâkulam
giri-râjam imaṃ tâvat pṛcchâmi nṛ-patim prati; 41
bhagavann, acala-śreṣṭha, divya-darśana, viśruta,
śaraṇya, bahu-kalyâṇa, namas te 'stu, mahi-dhara; 42
praṇame tvâ 'bhigamy' âhaṃ; râja-putriṃ nibodha mâm,
râjnaḥ snuṣâṃ, râja-bhâryâṃ, "Damayant' iti viśrutâm. 43
râjâ Vidarbh'-âdhipatiḥ pitâ mama, mahâ-rathaḥ,
Bhimo nâma kṣiti-patiś câtur-varṇyasya rakṣitâ; 44
râja-sûy'-âśva-medhânâṃ kratûnâṃ dakṣiṇâvatâm

àhartà pàrthıva-śreṣṭhaḥ pṛthu-càrv-añcıt'-ekṣaṇaḥ. 45
brahmaṇyaḥ, sàdhu-vṛttaś ca, satyavàg, anasùyakaḥ,
śilavàn, virya-sampannaḥ, pṛthu-śrir, dharma-vıc, chucıḥ, 46
samyag goptà Vıdarbhàṇàṃ, nırȷıt'-àrı-gaṇaḥ prabhuḥ,
tasya màṃ vıddhı tanayàm, bhagavans, tvàm upasthıthàm. 47
Nıṣadheṣu mahà-ràȷaḥ śvaśuro me nar'-ottamaḥ
gṛhita-nàmà, vıkhyàto "Virasena" ıtı, sma ha; 48
tasya ràȷnaḥ suto viraḥ, śrimàn, satya-paràkramaḥ
krama-pràptam pıtuḥ svaṃ yo ràȷyaṃ samanuśàstı ha, 49
Nalo nàm' àrı-hà, śyàmaḥ, Puṇyaśloka ıtı śrutaḥ
brahmaṇyo, veda-vıd, vàgmi, puṇya-kṛt, soma-po 'gnımàn 50
yaṣṭà, dàtà ca, yoddhà ca, samyak c' aıva praśàsıtà;
tasya màm, acala-śreṣṭha, vıddhı bhàryàm ıh' àgatàm, 51
tyakta-śrıyam, bhartṛı-hinàm, anàthàṃ, vyasan'-ànvıtàm,
anveṣamàṇàm bhartàraṃ, taṃ vaı nara-var'-ottamam; 52
kham ullıkhadbhır etaır hi tvayà śṛṅga-śataır nṛı-paḥ
kaccıd dṛṣṭo, 'cala-śreṣṭha, vane 'smın dàruṇe Nalaḥ? 53
gaȷ'-endra-vıkramo, dhimàn, dirgha-bàhur, amarṣaṇaḥ,
vıkràntaḥ, satya-vàg, viro, bhartà mama mahà-yaśàḥ? 54
Nıṣadhànàm adhıpatıḥ kaccıd dṛṣṭas tvayà Nalaḥ?
kım màṃ vılapantim ekàm, parvata-śreṣṭha, vıhvalàm 55
gırà n' àśvàsayasy adya, svàṃ sutàm ıva duḥkhıtàm?
vira, vıkrànta, dharma-ȷna, satya-sandha, mahi-pate, 56
yady asy asmın vane, ràȷan, darśay' atmànam àtmanà.
kadà su-snıgdha-gambhiràṃ ȷimùta-svana-sannıbhàm 57
śroṣyàmı Naıṣadhasy' àhaṃ vàcaṃ tàm amṛıt'-opamàm,
"Vaıdarbh'" ity eva vıspaṣṭàṃ śubhàṃ ràȷno mahà-'tmanaḥ 58

ámnáya-sárıṇim, ṛıddhám mama śoka-vınáśınim?
bhitám áśvásayata máṃ, nṛı-pate, dharma-vatsala." 59
ıtı sá taṃ gırı-śreṣṭham uktvá párthıva-nandıni,
Damayanti tato bhúyo ȷagáma dıṣam uttarám. 60
sá gatvá trin aho-rátrán dadarśa param'-án-ganá
tápas'-áraṇyam atulaṃ dıvya-kánana-darśanam, 61
Vaśıṣṭha-Bhṛıgv-Atrı-samaıs tápasaır upaśobhıtam,
nıyataıḥ, saṃyat'-áháraır, dama-śauca-samanvıtaıḥ, 62
ab-bhakṣair, váyu-bhakṣaıś ca, parṇ'-áháraıs tath' aıva ca
ȷıt'-endrıyaır, mahá-bhágaıḥ, svarga-márga-dıdṛıkṣubhıḥ, 63
valkal'-áȷına-saṃvitaır munıbhıḥ saṃyat'-endrıyaıḥ.
tápas'-ádhyuṣıtaṃ ramyaṃ dadarś' áśrama-maṇḍalam 64
náná-mṛıga-gaṇaır ȷuṣṭaṃ, śákhá-mṛıga-gaṇ'-áyutam
tápasaıḥ samupetaṃ ca, sá dṛıṣṭv' aıva samáśvasat. 65
su-bhrúḥ, su-keśi, su-śroṇi, su-kucá, su-dvı-ȷ'-ánaná,
varcasvıni, su-pratıṣṭhá, sv-asıt'-áyata-locaná, 66
sá vıveś' áśrama-padaṃ Virasena-suta-prıyá,
yoṣıd-ratnam, mahá-bhágá Damayanti tapasvıni. 67
sá 'bhıvádya tapo-vṛıddhán vınayá 'vanatá sthıtá.
"sv-ágataṃ ta," ıtı proktá taıḥ sarvaıs tápasaıś ca sá; 68
púȷáṃ c' ásyá yathá-nyáyaṃ kṛıtvá tatra tapo-dhanáḥ,
"ásyatám" ıty ath' ocus te, "brúhı kıṃ karavámahaı?" 69
tán uváca var'-árohá, "kaccıd bhagavatám ıha
tapasy, agnıṣu, dharmeṣu, mṛıga-pakṣıṣu c', ánagháḥ, 70
kuśalaṃ vo, mahá-bhágáḥ, sva-dharm'-ácaraṇeṣu ca?"
taır uktá, "kuśalam, bhadre, sarvatr'," etı, "yaśasvını, 71
brúhı, sarv'-ánavady'-án-gı, ká tvam? kıṃ ca cıkirṣası?

dṛıṣṭv' aıva te paraṃ rûpaṃ, dyutıṃ ca paramâṃ ıha. 72
vısmayo naḥ samutpannaḥ; samâśvasıhı, mâ śucaḥ.
asy' âraṇyasya devi tvam, utâho 'sya mahi-bhṛıtaḥ, 73
asyâś ca nadyâḥ? kalyâṇı, vada satyam, anındıte."
sâ 'bravit tân ṛıṣin, "n' âham araṇyasy' âsya devatâ, 74
na c' âsya gırer, vıprâ, n' aıva nadyâś ca devatâ.
mânuṣim mâṃ vıjânita yûyaṃ sarve, tapo-dhanâḥ. 75
vıstareṇ' âbhıdhâsyâmı; tan me śṛıṇuta sarvaśaḥ.
Vıdarbheṣu mahi-pâlo Bhimo, nâma mahi-patıḥ; 76
tasya mâṃ tanayâṃ sarve jânita, dvı-ja-sattamâḥ;
Nıṣadh'-âdhıpatır dhimân Nalo nâma mahâ-yaśâḥ, 77
viraḥ saṃgrâma-jıd, vıdvân, mama bhartâ vıśâm patıḥ,
devat'-âbhyarcana-paro, dvı-jâtı-jana-vatsalaḥ, 78
goptâ Nıṣadha-vaṃśasya, mahâ-tejâ, mahâ-balaḥ,
satya-vâg, astra-vıt, prâjnaḥ, satya-sandho, 'rı-mardanaḥ, 79
brahmaṇyo, daıvata-paraḥ, śrimân, para-purañ-jayaḥ,
Nalo nâma, nṛı-pa-śreṣṭho, deva-râja-sama-dyutıḥ, 80
mama bhartâ vıśâl'-âkṣaḥ, pûrṇ'-endu-vadano, 'rı-hâ,
âhartâ kratu-mukhyânâm, veda-ved'-âṅ-ga-pâragaḥ, 81
sa-patnânâṃ mṛıdhe hantâ, ravı-soma-sama-prabhaḥ.
sa kaıścın nıkṛıtı-prajnaır, anâryaır, akṛıt'-âtmabhıḥ, 82
âhûya pṛıthıvi-pâlaḥ, satya-dharma-parâyaṇaḥ,
devane kuśalaır, jıhmaır, jıto râjyaṃ, vasûnı ca. 83
tasya mâm avagacchadhvam bhâryâṃ râja-ṛṣabhasya vaı
'Damayant,' 'itı, vıkhyâtâm bhartur darśana-lâlasâm, 84
sâ vanânı, gıriṅś c' aıva, sarâṃsı, sarıtas tathâ,
palvalânı ca sarvânı, tathâ 'raṇyânı sarvaśaḥ, 85

anveṣamàṇà bhartàraṃ Nalaṃ raṇa-vıśàradam,
mahà-'tmànaṃ, kṛıt'-àstraṃ ca vıcaràm' iha duḥkhıtà. 86
kaccıd bhagavatàṃ ramyaṃ tapo-vanam ıdaṃ nṛı-paḥ
bhavet pràpto Nalo nàma Nıṣadhànàṃ ȷan'-àdhıpaḥ? 87
yat-kṛıte 'ham ıdaṃ durgam prapannà bhṛıśa-dàruṇam
vanam pratıbhayaṃ, ghoraṃ, śàrdùla-mṛıga-sevıtam, 88
yadı kaıścıd aho-ràtraır na drakṣyàmı Nalaṃ nṛi-pam,
àtmànam śreyasà yokṣye dehasy' àsya vımocanàt. 89
ko nu me ȷivıten' àrthas taṃ ṛıte puruṣa-ṛṣabham?
katham bhavıṣyàmy ady' àham bhartṛı-śok'-àbhıpiḍıtà?" 90
tathà vılapantim ekàm araṇye Bhima-nandınim
Damayantim ath' ocus te tàpasàḥ satya-darśınaḥ, 91
"udarkas tava, kalyàṇı, kalyàṇo bhavıtà, subhe,
vayam paśyàmas tapasà, kṣıpraṃ drakṣyası Naıṣadham, 92
Nıṣadhànàm adhıpatıṃ Nalaṃ, rıpu-nıpàtınam,
Bhaımı, dharma-bhṛıtàṃ śreṣṭhaṃ drakṣyase vıgata-ȷvaram, 93
vımuktaṃ sarva-pàpebhyaḥ sarva-ratna-samanvıtam,
tad eva nagaram bhùyaḥ praśàsatam arıṃ-damam, 94
dvıṣatàm bhaya-kartàraṃ, su-hṛıdaṃ śoka-nàśanam,
patıṃ drakṣyası, kalyàṇı, kalyàṇ'-àbhıȷanaṃ nṛı-pam." 95
evam uktvà Nalasy' eṣṭàm mahıṣim, pàrthıv'-àtma-ȷàm,
tàpasà 'ntar-hıtàḥ sarve, s'-àgnı-hotr'-àśramàs tadà. 96
sà dṛıṣṭvà mahad àścaryaṃ vısmıtà hy abhavat tadà
Damayanty, anavady'-àn·gi, Virasena-nṛı-pa-snuṣà; 97
"kıṃ nu svapno mayà dṛıṣṭaḥ? ko 'yaṃ vıdhır ıh' àbhavat?
kva nu te tàpasàḥ sarve? kva tad àśrama-maṇḍalam? 98
kva sà puṇya-ȷalà, ramyà nadi dvi-ȷa-nıṣevıtà?

kva nu te ha nagâ hṛıdyâḥ, phala-puṣp'-opaśobhıtâḥ?" 99
dhyâtvâ cıram Bhima-sutâ Damayanti śucı-smıtâ,
bhartṛı-śoka-parâ, dinâ, vıvarṇa-vadanâ 'bhavat. 100
sâ gatvâ 'th' âparâm bhûmıṃ vâṣpa-sandıgdhayâ gırâ
vılalâp' âśru-pûrṇ'-âkṣi dṛıṣṭvâ 'śoka-taruṃ tataḥ 101
upagamya taru-śreṣṭham aśokam puṣpıtaṃ vane
pallav'-âpiḍıtaṃ hṛıdyam vıhaṃ-gaır anunâdıtam, 102
"aho vat' âyam agamaḥ śrimân asmın van'-ântare,
âpiḍaır bahubhır bhâtı śrimân parvata-râḍ ıva, 103
vıśokâṃ kuru mâṃ kṣıpram, aśoka prıya-darśana.
vita-soka, bhay'-âbâdhaṃ kaccıt tvaṃ dṛıṣṭavân nṛı-pam 104
Nalaṃ nâm' ârı-mardanaṃ, Damayantyâḥ prıyam patım?
Nıṣadhânâm adhıpatıṃ dṛıṣṭavân ası me prıyam, 105
eka-vastr'-ârddha-saṃvitaṃ, su-kumâra-tanu-tvacam,
vyasanen' ârdıtaṃ viram, araṇyam ıdam âgatam? 106
yathâ vıśokâ gaccheyam, aśoka-naga, tat kuru,
satya-nâmâ bhav', âsoka, aśokaḥ, śoka-nâśanaḥ." 107
evaṃ sâ 'śoka-vṛıkṣaṃ tam ârtâ vaı parıgamya ha,
jagâma dâruṇataraṃ deśam Bhaımi var'-ân-ganâ. 108
sâ dadarśa nagân n'-aıkân, n'-aıkâś ca sarıtas tathâ,
n'-aıkâṅś ca parvatân ramyân, n'-aıkâṅś ca mṛıga-pakṣıṇaḥ, 109
kandarâṅś ca, nıtambâṅś ca, nadiś c' âdbhuta-darśanâḥ,
dadarśa sâ Bhima-sutâ patım anveṣati tadâ. 110
gatvâ prakṛıṣṭam adhvânaṃ, Damayanti śucı-smıtâ,
dadarś' âtha mahâ-sârthaṃ, hasty-aśva-ratha-saṃkulam, 111
uttarantaṃ nadiṃ ramyâm, prasanna-salılâṃ, śubhâm
su-śânta-toyâṃ vıstirṇâṃ, hradınim, vetasaır vṛıtâm, 112

prodghuṣṭàṃ krauñca-kuraraiś, cakra-vàk'-opakùjitàm
kùrma-gràha-jhaṣ'-àkirṇàm, pulina-dvipa-śobhitàm. 113
sà dṛṣṭv' aiva mahà-sàrthaṃ Nala-patni yaśasvini,
upasarpya var'-àrohà jana-madhyam viveśa ha, 114
unmatta-rùpà, śok'-àrtà, tathà vastr'-àrddha-saṃvṛtà,
kṛśà, vivarṇà, malinà, pàṃśu-dhvasta-śiro-ruhà. 115
tàṃ dṛṣṭvà tatra manu-jàḥ, kecid bhitàḥ pradudruvuḥ,
kecic cintà-paràs tasthuḥ, kecit tatra pracukruśuḥ, 116
prahasanti sma tàṃ kecid, abhyasùyanti c' àpare,
akurvata dayàṃ kecit, papracchuś c' àpi, Bhàrata, 117
"kà 'si? kasy' àsi, kalyàṇi? kiṃ và mṛgayase vane?
tvàṃ dṛṣṭvà vyathitàḥ sm' eha; kaccit tvam asi mànuṣi? 118
vada satyam; vanasy' àsya, parvatasy', àtha và diśaḥ
devatà tvaṃ hi, kalyàṇi, tvàṃ vayaṃ śaraṇaṃ gatàḥ. 119
yakṣi và, ràkṣasi và, tvam utàho 'si sur'-àn-ganà?
sarvathà kuru naḥ sv-asti, rakṣa c' àsmàn, anindite; 120
yathà 'yaṃ sarvathà sàrthaḥ kṣemi śighram ito vrajet;
tathà vidhatsva, kalyàṇi, yathà śreyo hi no bhavet." 121
tath' oktà tena sàrthena Damayanti nṛ-p'-àtma-jà
pratyuvàca tataḥ sàdhvi, bhartṛ-vyasana-piḍità, 122
sàrtha-vàhaṃ ca, sàrthaṃ ca, janà ye tatra kecana,
yuva-sthavira-bàlàś ca, sàrthasya ca puro-gamàḥ, 123
"mànuṣim màṃ vijànita, manu-j'-àdhipateḥ sutàm,
nṛ-pa-snuṣàṃ, ràja-bhàryàm, bhartṛ-darśana-làlasàm; 124
Vidarbha-ràḍ mama pità; bhartà ràjà ca Naiṣadhaḥ,
Nalo nàma, mahà-bhàgas, tam màrgàmy aparàjitam 125
yadi jànitha nṛ-patiṃ kṣipraṃ, śaṃsata me priyam,

Nalam, puruṣa-śârdûlam, amıtra-gaṇa-sûdanam." 126
tâm uvâc' ânavady-ân-gim sârthasya mahataḥ prabhuḥ,
sârtha-vâhaḥ, Śucır nâma, "śṛṇu, kalyâṇı, mad-vacaḥ; 127
ahaṃ sârthasya netâ vaı sârtha-vâhaḥ, śuci-smıte,
manuṣyaṃ Nala-nâmânaṃ na paśyâmı, yaśasvını. 128
kuñjara-dvipı-mahıṣa-śârdûla-ṛkṣa-mṛgân api
paśyâmy asmın vane kṛtsne hy amanuṣya-nıṣevıte, 129
ṛte tvâm mânuṣim martyaṃ na paśyâmı mahâ-vane.
tathâ no yakṣa-râḍ adya Maṇıbhadraḥ prasidatu." 130
sâ 'bravit banıjaḥ sarvân, sârtha-vâhaṃ ca taṃ tataḥ,
"kva nu yâsyatı sârtho 'yam? etad âkhyâtum arhası." 131
sârtha-vâha uvâca,
sârtho 'yaṃ Cedı-râjasya Subâhoḥ, satya-darśınaḥ,
kṣıpraṃ jana-padaṃ gantâ lâbhâya, manu-j'-âtma-je. 132
ıtı Nal'-opâkhyâne dva-daśaḥ sargaḥ.

XIII.

sâ tac chrutvâ 'navady'-ân-gi sârtha-vâha-vacas tadâ,
jagâma saha ten' aıva sârthena patı-lâlasâ. 1
atha kâle bahutıthe vane mahatı dâruṇe,
taḍâgam sarvato bhadram padma-saugandhıkam mahat 2
dadṛıśur banıjo ramyam, prabhûta-yavas'-endhanam,
bahu-puṣpa-phal'-opetaṃ, nânâ-pakṣı-nıṣevıtam; 3
nırmala-svâdu-salılam, mano-hârı, su-śitalam;
su-parıśrânta-vâhâs te nıveśâya mano dadhuḥ; 4
sammate sârtha-vâhasya vıvıśur vanam uttamam.

uvâsa sârthaḥ sa mahân velâm âsâdya paścimâm. 5
ath' ârddha-râtra-samaye niḥśabda-stimite tadâ,
supte sârthe pariśrânte, hasti-yûtham upâgamat 6
pâniy'-ârthaṃ giri-nadim, mada-prasravaṇ'-âvilâm,
ath' âpaśyata sârthaṃ taṃ, sârtha-jân su-bahûn gajân; 7
te tân grâmya-gajân dṛṣṭvâ sarve vana-gajâs tadâ,
samâdravanta vegena jighâṃsanto mad'-otkaṭâḥ. 8
teṣâm âpatatâṃ vegaḥ kariṇâṃ duḥsaho 'bhavat,
nag'-âgrâd iva śirṇânâṃ śṛṅ-gâṇâṃ patatâṃ kṣitau; 9
syandatâm api nâgânâm mârgâ naṣṭâ van'-odbhavaiḥ
mârgaṃ saṃrudhya saṃsuptam padminyâḥ sârtham uttamam; 10
te tam mamarduḥ sahasâ ceṣṭamânam mahi-tale.
hâ-hâ-kâram pramuñcantaḥ sârthikâḥ śaraṇ'-ârthinaḥ, 11
vana-gulmâṅś ca dhâvanto nidrâ-'ndhâ bahavo 'bhavan,
kecid dantaiḥ, karaiḥ kecit, kecit padbhyâṃ hatâ gajaiḥ. 12
nihat'-oṣṭrâś ca bahulâḥ, padâti-jana-saṃkulâḥ,
bhayâd âdhâvamânâś ca paras-para-hatâs tadâ, 13
ghorân nâdân vimuñcanto nipetur dharaṇi-tale,
vṛkṣeṣv âruhya saṃrabdhâḥ patitâ, viṣameṣu ca. 14
evam prakârair bahubhir daiven' âkramya hastibhiḥ,
râjan, vinihataṃ sarvaṃ samṛddhaṃ sârtha-maṇḍalam. 15
ârâvaḥ su-mahâṅś c' âsit trai-lokya-bhaya-kârakaḥ,
"eṣo 'gnir utthitaḥ kaṣṭas; trâyadhvaṃ, dhâvat' âdhunâ 16
ratna-râśir viśirṇo 'yaṃ; gṛhṇidhvaṃ kim pradhâvatha?
sâmânyam etad draviṇam; na mithyâ-vacanam mama." 17
evam ev'-âbhibhâṣanto vidravanti bhayât tadâ,
"punar ev' âbhidhâsyâmi, cintayadhvaṃ, sa-kâtarâḥ." 18

tasmins tathâ vartamâne dâruṇe jana-saṃkṣaye,
Damayantî ca bubudhe bhaya-santrasta-mânasâ, 19
apaśyad vaiśasaṃ tatra sarva-loka-bhayaṃ-karam.
adṛṣṭa-pûrvaṃ tad dṛṣṭvâ bâlâ padma-nibh'-ekṣaṇâ, 20
saṃsakta-vadan'-âśvâsâ uttasthau bhaya-vihvalâ.
ye tu tatra vinirmuktâḥ sârthât kecid avikṣatâḥ, 21
te 'bruvan sahitâḥ sarve, "kasy' edaṃ karmaṇaḥ phalam?
nûnaṃ na pûjito 'smâbhir Maṇibhadro mahâ-yaśâḥ? 22
tathâ yakṣ'-âdhipaḥ śrîmân na vai Vaiśravaṇaḥ prabhuḥ?
na pûjâ vighna-kartṛṇâm atha vâ prathamaṃ kṛtâ? 23
śakunânâm phalaṃ vâ 'tha viparîtam idaṃ dhruvam?
grahâ na viparîtâs tu? kim anyad idam âgatam?" 24
apare tv abruvan dînâ, jnâti-dravya-vinâkṛtâḥ,
"yâ 'sâv adya mahâ-sârthe nârî hy unmatta-darśanâ, 25
praviṣṭâ vikṛt'-âkârâ, kṛtvâ rûpam amânuṣam,
tay' eyam vihitâ pûrvam mâyâ parama-dâruṇâ, 26
râkṣasî vâ dhruvaṃ yakṣî, piśâcî vâ bhayaṃ-karî;
tasyâḥ sarvam idam pâpaṃ; n' âtra kâryâ vicâraṇâ. 27
yadi paśyema tâm pâpâṃ, sârtha-ghnîṃ n'-aika-duḥkha-dâm,
loṣṭabhiḥ, pâṃśubhiś c' aiva tṛṇaiḥ, kâṣṭhaiś ca muṣṭibhiḥ, 28
avaśyam eva hanyâma sârthasya kila kṛtyakâm."
Damayantî tu tac chrutvâ vâkyaṃ teṣâṃ su-dâruṇam, 29
hrîtâ, bhîtâ ca saṃvignâ prâdravad yatra kânanam.
âśan-kamânâ tat pâpam âtmânam paryadevayat, 30
"aho mam' opari vidheḥ saṃrambho dâruṇo mahân;
n' ânubadhnâti kuśalaṃ; kasy' edaṃ karmaṇaḥ phalam? 31
na smarâmy aśubhaṃ kiñcit kṛtaṃ kasyacid aṇv api;

karmaṇà, manasà, vàcà, kasy' edaṃ karmaṇaḥ phalam? 32
nùnaṃ janm'-àntara-kṛıtaın pàpam àpatıtam mahat;
apaścımàm ımàṃ kaṣṭàm àpadam pràptavaty aham. 33
bhartṛı-ràjy'-àpaharaṇaṃ, sva-janàc ca paràjayaḥ;
bhartrà saha vıyogaś ca, tanayàbhyàṃ ca vıcyutıḥ, 34
nırnàthatà, vane vàso bahu-vyàla-nıṣevıte."
ath' àpare-dyuḥ sampràpte, hata-śıṣṭà janàs tadà 35
deśàt tasmàd vınıṣkramya śocante vaıśasaṃ kṛıtaın;
bhràtaram, pıtaram, putraṃ, sakhàyaṃ ca, nar-àdhıpa; 36
aśocat tatra Vaıdarbhi, "kıṃ nu me duṣkrıtaṃ kṛıtam?
yo 'pı me nırjane 'raṇye sampràpto 'yaṃ jan'-àrṇavaḥ, 37
sa hato hastı-yùthena manda-bhàgyàd mam' aıva tat
pràptavyaṃ sucıraṃ duḥkhaṃ nùnam ady' àpı vaı mayà; 38
'n' apràpta-kàlo mrıyate,' śrutaṃ vṛıddh'-ànuśàsanam;
yad n' àham adya mṛıdıtà hastı-yùthena duḥkhıtà, 39
na hy adaıvaṃ kṛıtaṃ kıñcın naràṇàm ıha vıdyate,
na ca me bàla-bhàve 'pı kıñcıt pàpa-kṛıtaṃ kṛıtam, 40
karmaṇà, manasà, vàcà, yad ıdaṃ duḥkham àgatam.
manye svayaṃ-vara-kṛıte loka-pàlàḥ samàgatàh, 41
pratyàkhyàtà mayà tatra Nalasy' àrthàya devatàḥ,
nùnaṃ teṣàm prabhàvena vıyogam pràptavaty aham." 42
evam-àdını duḥkhàrtà sà vılapya var'-àṅ-ganà,
pralàpànı tadà tànı Damayanti patı-vratà, 43
hata-śeṣaıḥ saha tadà bràhmaṇaır veda-pàra-gaıḥ,
agacchad, ràja-śàrdùla, candra-lekh' eva śàradi. 44
gacchanti sà cıràd bàlà puram àsàdayad mahat
sày'-àhne Cedı-ràjasya Subàhoḥ satya-darśınaḥ. 45

atha vastr'-ârddha-saṃvitâ pravıveśa pur'-ottamam.
tâṃ vıhvalâṃ, kṛśâṃ, dinâm, mukta-keśim, amârȷıtâm, 46
unmattâm ıva gacchantiṃ dadṛśuḥ pura-vâsınaḥ;
pravıśantiṃ tu tâṃ dṛṣṭvâ Cedı-râȷa-puriṃ tadâ 47
anuȷagmus tatra bâlâ grâmı-putrâḥ kutûhalât.
sâ taıḥ parıvṛtâ 'gacchat samipaṃ râȷa-veśmanaḥ. 48
tâm prâsâda-gatâ 'paśyad râȷa-mâtâ ȷanaır vṛtâm,
dhâtrim uvâca, "gacch' aınâm ânay' eha mam' ântıkam. 49
ȷanena klıśyate bâlâ duḥkhıtâ śaraṇ' ârthıni;
tâdṛg rûpaṃ ca paśyâmı vıdyotayatı me gṛham, 50
unmatta-veśâ kalyâṇi Śrir ıv' âyata-locanâ."
sâ ȷanaṃ vârayıtvâ tam prâsâda-talam uttamam 51
âropya vısmıtâ, râȷan, Damayantim apṛcchata,
"evam apy asukh'-âvıṣṭâ bıbharṣı paramaṃ vapuḥ, 52
bhâsı vıdyud ıv' âbhreṣu; śaṃsa me, kâ 'sı, kasya vâ;
na hı te mânuṣaṃ rûpam, bhûṣaṇaır apı varȷıtam; 53
asahâyâ narebhyaś ca n' odvıȷasy, amara-prabhe."
tac chrutvâ vacanaṃ tasyâ Bhaımi vacanam abravit, 54
"mânuṣim mâṃ vıȷânihı bhartâraṃ samanuvratâm
saırandhriṃ, ȷâtı-sampannâm, bhuȷıṣyâm, kâma-vâsınim; 55
phala-mûl'-âśanâm ekâṃ yatra-sâyam-pratıśrayâm.
asaṃkhyeya-guṇo bhartâ, mâṃ ca nıtyam anuvrataḥ, 56
bhaktâ 'ham apı taṃ viraṃ chây' ev' ânugatâ pathı.
tasya daıvât prasaṅgo 'bhûd atımâtraṃ sma devane; 57
dyûte sa nırȷıtaś c' aıva vanam eka upeyıvân;
tam eka-vasanaṃ viram unmattam ıva vıhvalam, 58
âśvâsayanti bhartâram aham apy agamaṃ vanam.

sa kadácıd vane virah kasmıńścıt káran'-ántare,   59
kṣut-parıtas tu vımanás tad apy ekaṃ vyasarjayat.

tam eka-vasaná nagnam, unmattavad acetasam,   60
anuvrajanti bahulá na svapámı nıśás tadá;
tato bahutıthe kále suptám utsrıjya máṃ kvacıt,   61
vásaso 'rddham parıcchıdya tyaktaván mám anágasam.

tam márgamáná bhartáraṃ dahyamáná dıvá-nıśam   62
sá 'haṃ kamala-garbh'-ábham apaśyanti hrıdı prıyam,
na vındámy amara-prakhyam prıyam prán'-eśvaram prabhum."   63
tám aśru-parıpúrn'-ákṣim, vılapantiṃ tathá bahu,
rája-mátá 'bravid ártám Bhaımim ártatará svayam,   64
"vasasva mayı, kalyánı; prıtır me paramá tvayı.

mrıgayıṣyantı te, bhadre, bhartáram puruṣá mama;   65
apı vá svayam ágacehet parıdhávann ıtas-tataḥ,
ıh' aıva vasati, bhadre, bhartáram upalapsyase."   66
rája-mátur vacaḥ śrutvá, Damayanti vaco 'bravit,
"samayen' otsahe vastuṃ tvayı, vira-prajáyınī,   67
ucchıṣṭaṃ n' aıva bhuñjīyáṃ, na kuryám páda-dhávanam,
na c' áham puruṣán anyán prabháṣeyaṃ kathańcana;   68
prárthayed yadı máṃ kaścıd, dandyas te sa pumán bhavet;
badhyaś ca te 'sakrın manda, ıtı me vratam áhıtam;   69
bhartur anveṣan'-ártham tu paśyeyam bráhmanán aham:
yady evam ıha kartavyaṃ vatsyámy aham asaṃśayam;   70
ato 'nyathá na me váso vartate hrıdaye kvacıt."
tám prahrıṣṭena manasá rája-mát' edam abravit,   71
"sarvam etat karıṣyámı dıṣṭyá te vratam idrıśam."
evam uktvá tato Bhaımiṃ rája-mátá, vıśám pate,   72

uvâc' edaṃ duhitaraṃ Sunandâṃ nâma, Bhârata,
"sairandhrim abhijânişva, Sunande, deva-rûpiṇim; 73
vayasâ tulyatâm prâptâ sakhi tava bhavatv iyam;
etayâ saha modasva nirudvigna-manâḥ sadâ." 74
tataḥ parama-saṃhṛṣṭâ Sunandâ gṛham âgamat,
Damayantim upâdâya sakhibhiḥ parivâritâ. 75

iti Nal'-opâkhyâne trayo-daśaḥ sargaḥ.

XIV.

Vṛhadaśva uvâca,
utsṛjya Damayantiṃ tu Nalo râjâ, viśâm pate,
dadarśa dâvam dahyantam mahântam gahane vane, 1
tatra śuśrâva śabdaṃ vai madhye bhûtasya kasyacit,
"abhidhâva, Nal'" ety uccaiḥ, "Puṇyaślok'" eti c' âsakṛt. 2
"mâ bhair," iti, Nalaś c' oktvâ, madhyam agneḥ praviśya tam
dadarśa nâga-râjânaṃ śayânaṃ, kuṇḍali-kṛtam. 3
sa nâgaḥ, prâñjalir bhûtvâ, vepamâno Nalaṃ tadâ
uvâca, "mâṃ viddhi, râjan, nâgaṃ Karkoṭakaṃ, nṛ-pa; 4
mayâ pralabdho maha-ṛṣir Nâradaḥ sa mahâ-tapâḥ;
tena manyu-paritena sapto 'smi, manu-j'-âdhipa; 5
'tiṣṭha tvaṃ sthâvara iva, yâvad eva Nalaḥ kvacit
ito netâ; hi tatra tvaṃ śâpâd mokṣyasi mat-kṛtât.' 6
tasya śâpâd na śakto 'smi padâd vicalitum padam;
upadekṣyâmi te śreyas trâtum arhati mâm bhavân; 7
sakhâ ca te bhaviṣyâmi, mat-samo n' âsti pan-na-gaḥ;
laghuś ca te bhaviṣyâmi śighram âdâya gaccha mâm." 8

evam uktvâ sa nâg'-endro babhûv' an-gusṭha-mâtrakaḥ;
taṃ gṛhitvâ Nalaḥ prâyâd deśaṃ dâva-vivarjitam. 9
âkâśa-deśam âsâdya vimuktaṃ kṛṣṇa-vartmanâ,
utsraṣṭu-kâmaṃ taṃ nâgaḥ punaḥ Karkoṭako 'bravit, 10
"padâni gaṇayan gaccha svâni, Naiṣadha, kânicit;
tatra te 'ham, mahâ-bâho, śreyo dhâsyâmi yat param." 11
tataḥ saṃkhyâtum ârabdham adaśad daśame pade;
tasya daṣṭasya tad-rûpaṃ kṣipram antar-adhiyata. 12
sa dṛṣṭvâ vismitas tasthâv âtmânaṃ vikṛtaṃ Nalaḥ.
sva-rûpa-dhâriṇaṃ nâgaṃ dadarśa ca mahi-patiḥ; 13
tataḥ Karkoṭako nâgaḥ sântvayan Nalam abravit,
"mayâ te 'ntar-hitaṃ rûpaṃ na tvâṃ vidyur janâ iti; 14
yat-kṛte c' âsi nikṛto duḥkhena mahatâ, Nala,
viṣeṇa sa madiyena tvayi duḥkhaṃ nivatsyati. 15
viṣeṇa saṃvṛtair gâtrair yâvat tvâṃ na vimokṣyati,
tâvat tvayi, mahâ-râja, duḥkhaṃ vai sa nivatsyati. 16
anâgâ yena nikṛtas tvam anarho, jan'-âdhipa,
krodhâd asûyayitvâ taṃ rakṣâ me bhavataḥ kṛtâ. 17
na te bhayaṃ, nara-vyâghra, daṃṣṭribhyaḥ, śatruto 'pi vâ,
brahma-ṛṣibhyaś ca bhavitâ mat-prasâdâd, nar'-âdhipa. 18
râjan, viṣa-nimittâ ca na te piḍâ bhaviṣyati;
saṃgrâmeṣu ca, râj'-endra, śaśvaj jayam avâpsyasi. 19
gaccha, râjann, itaḥ, sûto Vâhuko 'ham', iti, bruvan
samipaṃ Ṛtuparṇasya; sa hi ved'-âkṣa-naipuṇam; 20
Ayodhyâṃ nagariṃ ramyâm adya vai, Niṣadh'-eśvara;
sa te 'kṣa-hṛdayaṃ dâtâ râj' âśva-hṛdayena vai: 21
Ikṣvâku-kula-jaḥ śrimân mitraṃ c' aiva bhaviṣyati.

bhavıṣyası yadâ 'kṣa-ȷnaḥ śreyasâ yokṣyase tadâ, 22
sameṣyası ca dâraıs tvam, mâ sma soke manaḥ kṛıthâḥ,
râȷyena, tanayâbhyâṃ ca; satyam etad bravimı te: 23
sva-rûpaṃ ca yadâ draṣṭum ıcchethâs tvaṃ, nar'-âdhıpa,
saṃsmartavyas tadâ te 'haṃ, vâsaś c' edaṃ nıvâsayeḥ; 24
anena vâsasâ 'cchannaḥ sva-rûpam pratıpatsyase."
ıty uktvâ pradadau tasmaı dıvyaṃ vâso-yugaṃ tadâ; 25
evaṃ Nalaṃ ca sandıśya, vâso datvâ ca, Kaurava,
nâga-râȷas tato, raȷans, tatr' aıv' antar-adhiyata. 26

ıtı Nal' opâkhyâne catur-daśaḥ sargaḥ.

XV.

Vṛıdhaśva uvâca,

tasmınn antar-hıte nâge, prayayau Naıṣadho Nalaḥ,
Ṛıtuparṇasya nagaram prâvıśad daśame 'hanı. 1
sa râȷânam upâtıṣṭhad, "Vâhuko 'ham," ıtı, bruvan,
"aśvânâṃ vâhane yuktaḥ, pṛıthıvyâṃ n' âstı mat-samaḥ; 2
artha-kṛıcchreṣu c' aıv' âham praṣṭavyo, naıpuneṣu ca;
anna-saṃskâram apı ca ȷânâmy anyaır vıśeṣataḥ. 3
yânı śılpânı loke 'smın, yac c' ânyat su-duṣkaram,
sarvaṃ yatıṣye tat kartuṃ; Ṛıtuparṇa, bharasva mâm." 4
Ṛıtuparṇa uvâca,
vasa, Vâhuka, bhadraṃ te; sarvam etat karıṣyası;
śighra-yâne sadâ buddhır dhrıyate me vıśeṣataḥ; 5
sa tvam âtıṣṭha yogaṃ taṃ, yena śighrâ hayâ mama
bhaveyur; aśv'-âdhyakṣo 'sı; vetanaṃ te śataṃ śatâḥ. 6

tvȧm upasthȧsyataṡ c' aıva nıtyaṃ Vȧrṣṇeya-Jivalau;
etȧbhyȧṃ raṃsyase sȧrddhaṃ: vasa vaı mayı, Vȧhuka." 7
evam ukto Nalas tena nyavasat tatra pu̇ȷıtaḥ,
Ṛıtuparṇasya nagare saha-Vȧrṣneya-Jivalaḥ. 8
sa vaı tatr' ȧvasad rȧȷȧ Vaıdarbhim anucıntayan,
sȧyaṃ, sȧyaṃ sadȧ c'emaṃ ṡlokam ekaṃ ȷagȧda ha, 9
"kva nu sȧ kṣut-pıpȧs'-ȧrtȧ, ṡrȧntȧ, ṡete tapasvıni,
smaranti tasya mandasya, kaṃ vȧ sȧ 'dy' opatıṣṭhatı?" 10
evam bruvantaṃ rȧȷȧnaṃ nıṡȧyȧṃ Jivalo 'bravit, 11
"kȧm ımȧṃ ṡocase nıtyaṃ, ṡrotum ıcchȧmı, Vȧhuka;
ȧyuṣman, kasya vȧ nȧri, yȧm evam anuṡocası." 12
tam uvȧca Nalo rȧȷȧ, "manda-praȷnasya kasyacıt
ȧsid bahumatȧ nȧri tasy' ȧdṛıḍhataraṃ vacaḥ; 13
sa vaı kenacıd arthena tayȧ mando vyayuȷyata,
vıprayuktaḥ sa, mand'-ȧtmȧ bhramaty asukha-piḍıtaḥ, 14
dahyamanaḥ sa ṡokena dıvȧ-rȧtram atandrıtaḥ,
nıṡȧ-kȧle smarans tasyȧḥ ṡlokam ekam sma gȧyatı. 15
sa vıbhraman mahiṃ sarvȧṃ kvacıd ȧsȧdya kıṅcana,
vasaty anarhas tad duḥkham bhu̇ya ev' ȧnusaṃsmaran. 16
sȧ tu tam puruṣaṃ nȧri kṛıcchre 'py anugatȧ vane,
tyaktȧ ten' ȧlpa-puṇyena duṣkaraṃ yadı ȷivatı. 17
ekȧ bȧlȧ 'nabhıȷnȧ ca mȧrgȧṇȧm a-tath'-ocıtȧ,
kṣut-pıpȧsȧ-parit'-ȧn·gi duṣkaraṃ yadı ȷivatı. 18
svȧ-pad'-ȧcarıte nıtyaṃ vane mahatı dȧruṇe
tyaktȧ ten' ȧlpa-bhȧgyena manda-praȷnena, mȧrıṣa." 19
ıty evam Naıṣadho rȧȷȧ Damayantim anusmaran,
aȷnȧta-vȧsaṃ nyavasad rȧȷnas tasya nıveṡaṇe. 20
ıtı Nal'-opȧkhyȧne paṅca-daṡaḥ sargaḥ.

XVI.

Vṛıhadaśva uvâca,

hṛıta-râȷye Nale, Bhimaḥ, sa-bhârye preṣyatâṃ gate,
dvıȷân prasthâpayâmâsa Nala-darśana-kân·kṣayâ 1
saṃdıdeśa ca tân Bhimo vasu datvâ ca puṣkalam,
"mṛıgayadhvaṃ Nalaṃ yûyaṃ, Damayantiṃ ca me sutâm. 2
asmın karmaṇı sampanne, vıȷnâte Nıṣadh'-âdhıpe,
gavâṃ sahasraṃ dâsyâmı yo vas tâv ânayıṣyatı. 3
agrahârâṅś ca dâsyâmı grâmaṃ nagara-sammıtam;
na cec chakyâv ıh' ânetuṃ Damayanti, Nalo 'pı vâ, 4
ȷnâta-mâtre 'pı dâsyâmı gavâṃ daśa śataṃ dhanam."
ıty uktâs te yayur hṛıṣṭâ brâhmaṇâḥ sarvato dıśam, 5
pura-râstrâṇı cınvanto Naıṣadhaṃ saha bhâryayâ;
n'aıva kv' âpı prapaśyantı Nalaṃ, vâ Bhima-putrıkâm. 6
tataś Cedı-puriṃ ramyâṃ Sudevo nâma vaı dvıȷaḥ,
vıcınvâno 'tha Vaıdarbhim apaśyad râȷa-veśmanı, 7
puṇy-âha-vâcane râȷnaḥ Sunandâ-sahıtâṃ sthıtâm.
mandam prakhyâyamânena rûpeṇ' âpratımena tâm,
nıbaddhâṃ dhûma-ȷâlena prabhâm ıva vıbhâvasoḥ. 8
tâṃ samikṣya vıśâl'-âkṣim, adhıkam malınâṃ, krıśâm,
tarkayâmâsa, "Bhaımi" 'tı, kâraṇaır upapâdayan. 9

Sudeva uvâca,

yath' eyam me purâ dṛıṣṭâ, tathâ-rûp' eyam an·ganâ
krıt'-ârtho 'smy adya dṛıṣṭv' emâṃ loka-kântâm ıva śrıyam, 10
pûrṇa-candra-nıbhâṃ, śyâmâṃ câru-vṛıtta-payo-dharâm,

kurvantim prabhayâ devim̤ sarvâ vıtımırâ dıśaḥ, 11
câru-padma-vıśâl'-âkṣim, Manmathasya Ratim ıva;
ıṣṭâm samasta-lokasya pûrṇa-candra-prabhâm ıva. 12
Vıdarbha-sarasas tasmâd daıva-doṣâd ıv' oddhṛıtâm,
mala-pan·k'-ânulıpt'-ân·gim mṛıṇâlim ıva c'oddhṛıtâm 13
paurṇa-mâsim ıva nıśâm̤ râhu-grasta-nıśâ-karâm,
patı-śok'-âkulâm̤ dinâm̤ śuṣka-srotâm̤ nadim ıva; 14
vıdhvasta-parṇa-kamalâm̤, vıtrâsıta-vıhan·-gamâm
hastı-hasta-parâmṛıṣṭâm̤ vyâkulâm ıva padmınim. 15
su-kumârim, su-jât'-ân·gim̤, ratna-garbha-gṛıh'-ocıtâm,
dahyamânâm ıv' ârkeṇa mṛıṇâlim ıva c'oddhṛıtâm. 16
rûp'-audârya-guṇ'-opetâm, maṇḍan'-ârhâm, amaṇḍıtâm,
candra-lekhâm ıva navâm̤ vyomnı nil'-âbhra-sam̤vṛıtâm. 17
kâma-bhogaıḥ prıyaır hinâm̤, hinâm, bandhu-janena ca,
deham̤ dhârayatim̤, dinâm, bhartṛı-darśana-kân·kṣayâ. 18
bhartâ nâma param̤ nâryâ bhûṣaṇam bhûṣaṇaır vınâ;
eṣâ hı rahıtâ tena śobhamânâ na śobhate. 19
duṣkaram̤ kurute 'tyantam̤ hino yad anayâ Nalaḥ
dhârayaty âtmano deham̤ na śoken' âvasidatı. 20
ımâm asıta-keś'-ântâm̤, śata-patr'-âyat'-ekṣaṇâm
sukh'-ârhâm̤ duḥkhıtâm̤ dṛıṣṭvâ mam' âpı vyathate manaḥ. 21
kadâ nu khalu duḥkhasya pâram̤ yâsyatı vaı śubhâ,
bhartuḥ samâgamât sâdhvi Rohıṇi śaśıno yathâ? 22
asyâ nûnam punar-lâbhâd Naıṣadhaḥ pritım eṣyatı,
râjâ râjya-parıbhraṣṭaḥ, punar labdhvâ ca medınim; 23
tulya-śila-vayo-yuktâm̤, tuly'-âbhıjana-sam̤vṛıtâm,
Naıṣadho 'rhatı Vaıdarbhim̤, tam̤ c' eyam asıt'-ekṣaṇâ. 24

yuktaṃ tasy' âprameyasya, virya-sattvavato mayâ
samâśvâsayıtum bhâryâm patı-darśana-lâlasâm. 25
aham âśvâsayâmy enâm pûrṇa-candra-nıbh'-ânanâm
adṛṣṭa-pûrvâm duḥkhasya duḥkh'-ârtâṃ dhyâna-tat-parâm. 26
Vṛhadaśva uvâca,
evaṃ vımṛıśya vıvıdhaıḥ kâraṇaır, lakṣaṇaıś ca tâm,
upâgamya tato Bhaımiṃ Sudevo brâhmaṇo 'bravit, 27
"ahaṃ Sudevo, Vaıdarbhı, bhrâtus te dayıtaḥ sakhâ,
Bhimasya vacanâd râȷnas tvâm anveṣṭum ıh' âgataḥ. 28
kuśali te pıtâ, râȷnı, ȷanani, bhrâtaraś ca te,
âyuṣmantau kuśalınau tatra-sthau dârakau ca tau. 29
tvat-kṛıte bandhu-vargâś ca gata-sattvâ ıv' âsate;
anveṣṭâro brâhmaṇâś ca bhramantı śataśo mahim." 30
abhıȷnâya Sudevaṃ taṃ Damayanti, Yudhısthıra,
paryaprıcchata tân sarvân krameṇa su-hṛıdaḥ svakân. 31
ruroda ca bhṛıśaṃ, râȷan, Vaıdarbhi śoka-karṣıtâ,
dṛıṣṭvâ Sudevaṃ sahasâ bhrâtur ıṣṭaṃ dvı-ȷ'-ottamam. 32
tato rudantiṃ tâṃ dṛıṣṭvâ Sunandâ śoka-karṣıtâm
Sudevena sah' aık'-ânte kathayantiṃ ca, Bhârata, 33
ȷanıtryâḥ kathayâmâsa, "saırandhri rodıt'" itı, "vaı
brâhmaṇena samâgamya tâm vettha yadı manyase." 34
atha Cedı-pater mâtâ râȷnaś c' ântaḥ-purât tadâ,
ȷagâma yatra sâ bâlâ brâhmaṇena sah' âbhavat. 35
tataḥ Sudevam ânâyya râȷa-mâtâ, vıśâm pate,
papraccha, "bhâryâ kasy' eyaṃ? sutâ vâ kasya bhâvıni? 36
kathaṃ ca bhraṣṭâ ȷnâtıbhyo, bhartur vâ vâma-locanâ?
tvayâ ca vıdıtâ, vıpra, katham evaṃ-gatâ sati? 37

etad icchâmy aham̲ śrotum̲ tvattaḥ sarvam aśeṣataḥ;
tattvena hi mam' âcakṣva pṛcchantyâ deva-rûpinim." 38
evam uktas tayâ, râjan, Sudevo, dvi-ja-sattamaḥ,
sukh'-opaviṣṭa âcaṣṭe Damayantyâ yathâ-tatham. 39

iti Nal'-opâkhyâne ṣo-ḍaśaḥ sargaḥ.

XVII.

Sudeva uvâca,

Vidarbha-râjo dharm'-âtmâ Bhimo nâma mahâ-dyutiḥ.
sut' eyam̲ tasya kalyâṇi Damayanti 'ti viśrutâ; 1
râjâ tu Naiṣadho nâma Virasena-suto Nalaḥ,
bhâry' eyam̲ tasya kalyâṇi Puṇyaślokasya, dhimatah. 2
sa dyûte nirjito bhrâtrâ hṛta-râjyo mahi-patiḥ;
Damayantyâ gataḥ sârddham̲ na prâjnâyata karhicit. 3
te vayam̲ Damayanty-arthe carâmaḥ pṛthivim imâm;
s' eyam âsâditâ bâlâ tava putra-niveśane. 4
asyâ rûpeṇa sadṛśi mânuṣi na hi vidyate;
asyâ hy eṣa bhruvor madhye sahajaḥ piplur uttamaḥ 5
śyâmâyâḥ padma-san·kâśo lakṣito 'ntar-hito mayâ,
malena sam̲vṛto hy asyâś channo 'bhreṇ' eva candra-mâḥ. 6
cihna-bhûto vibhûty-artham ayam̲ dhâtrâ vinirmitaḥ
pratipat-kaluṣasy' endor lekhâ n' âtivirâjate. 7
na c'âsyâ naśyate rûpam̲ vapur mala-samâcitam,
asam̲skṛtam api vyaktam bhâti kâñcana-sannibham. 8
anena vapuṣâ bâlâ pipluṇâ 'nena sûcitâ,
lakṣit' eyam mayâ devi, nibhṛto 'gnir iv' oṣmaṇâ." 9

Vṛıhadaṡva uvȧca,

tac chrutvȧ vacanaṃ tasya Sudevasya, vıṡȧm pate,
Sunandȧ ṡodhayȧmȧsa pıplu-pracchȧdanam malam. 10
sa malen' ȧpakṛıṣṭena pıplus tasyȧ vyarocata
Damayantyȧs, tadȧ vyabhre nabhas' iva nıṡȧ-karaḥ. 11
pıpluṃ dṛıṣṭvȧ Sunandȧ ca, rȧȷa-mȧtȧ ca, Bhȧrata,
rudantyau tȧm parıṣvaȷya, muhu̇rtam ıva tasthatuḥ. 12
utsṛıȷya vȧṣpaṃ ṡanakaı, rȧȷa-mȧt' edam abravit,
"bhagınyȧ duhıtȧ me 'sı, pıplunȧ 'nena su̇cıtȧ; 13
ahaṃ ca, tava mȧtȧ ca rȧȷnas tasya mahȧ-'tmanaḥ
sute Daṡȧrṇ'-ȧdhıpateḥ Sudȧmnaṡ, cȧru-darṡane; 14
Bhimasya rȧȷnaḥ sȧ dattȧ, Virabȧhor aham punaḥ;
tvaṃ tu ȷȧtȧ mayȧ dṛıṣṭȧ Daṡȧrṇeṣu pıtur gṛıhe. 15
yath' aıva te pıtur gehaṃ, tath'aıva mama, bhȧvını;
yath' aıva ca mam' aıṡvaryaṃ, Damayantı, tathȧ tava." 16
tȧm prahṛıṣṭena manasȧ Damayanti, vıṡȧm pate,
praṇamya mȧtur bhagınim ıdaṃ vacanam abravit, 17
"aȷnȧyamȧnȧ 'pı sati sukham asmy uṣıtȧ tvayı,
sarva-kȧmaıḥ su-vıhıtȧ rakṣyamȧṇȧ sadȧ tvayȧ. 18
sukhȧt sukhataro vȧso bhavıṣyatı na saṃṡayaḥ;
cıra-vıproṣıtȧm, mȧtar, mȧm anuȷnȧtum arhası, 19
dȧrakau ca hı me nitau vasatas tatra bȧlakau,
pıtrȧ vıhinau ṡok'-ȧrtau, mayȧ c' aiva kathaṃ nu tau! 20
yadı c' ȧpı prıyaṃ kıñcıd mayı kartum ıh' ecchası,
Vıdarbhȧn yȧtum ıcchȧmı, ṡighram me yȧnam ȧdıṡa." 21
"vȧḍham," ıty eva tȧm uktvȧ hṛıṣṭȧ mȧtṛı-ṣvasȧ, nṛı-pa.
guptȧm balena mahatȧ, putrasy' ȧnumate tataḥ, 22

pràsthàpayad ràȷa-màtà śrimatiṃ, nara-vàhınà
yànena, Bharata-śreṣṭha, hy anna-pàna-parıcchadàm. 23
tataḥ sà na-cıràd eva Vıdarbhàn agamat punaḥ;
tàṃ tu bandhu-ȷanaḥ sarvaḥ prahṛıṣṭaḥ samapùȷayat; 24
sarvàn kuśalıno dṛıṣṭvà bàndhavàn, dàrakau ca tau,
màtaram, pıtaraṃ c' obhau, sarvaṃ c'aıva sakhi-ȷanam. 25
devatàḥ pùȷayàmàsa, bràhmaṇàṅś ca yaśasvıni
pareṇa vıdhınà devi Damayanti, vıśàm pate. 26
atarpayat Sudevaṃ ca go-sahasreṇa pàrthıvaḥ,
prito dṛıṣṭv' aıva tanayàṃ, gràmeṇa, dravıṇena ca. 27
sà vyuṣṭà raȷaniṃ tatra pıtur veśmanı bhàvıni,
vıśràntà màtaram, ràȷann, ıdaṃ vacanam abravit, 28
"màṃ ced ıcchası ȷivantim, màtaḥ, satyam bravimı te,
nara-virasya c'aıtasya Nalasy' ànayane yata." 29
Damayantyà tath' oktà tu, sà devi bhṛıśa-duḥkhıtà
vàṣpeṇ' àpıhıtà, ràjan, n'ottaraṃ kıñcıd abravit. 30
tad-avasthàṃ tu tàṃ dṛıṣṭvà sarvam antaḥ-puraṃ tadà
hà-hà-bhùtam atiṿ' àsid, bhṛıśaṃ ca praruroda ha. 31
tato Bhimam mahà-ràȷam bhàryà vacanam abravit,
"Damayanti tava sutà bhartàram anuśocatı; 32
apakṛıṣya ca laȷȷàṃ sà svayam uktavati, nṛı-pa,
'prayatantu tava preṣyàḥ Puṇyaślokasya màrgaṇe.'" 33
tayà pradeśıto ràȷà bràhmaṇàn vaśa-vartınaḥ
pràsthàpayad dıśaḥ sarvà, "yatadhvaṃ Nala-màrgaṇe." 34
tato Vıdarbh'-àdhıpater niyogàd bràhmaṇàs tadà,
Damayantim atho sṛıtvà, 'prasthıtàḥ sm' ety,' ath' àbruvan. 35
atha tàn abravid Bhaımi, "sarva-ràṣṭreṣv ıdaṃ vacaḥ

brûyâsta ȷana-saṃsatsu, tatra tatra punaḥ punaḥ: 36
'kva nu tvaṃ, kıtava, cchıttvâ vastr'-ârddham prasthıto mama,
utsrıȷya vıpıne suptâm anuraktâm prıyâm, prıya? 37
sâ vaı yathâ samâdıṣṭâ, tathâ 'ste tvat-pratikṣıṇi.
dahyamânâ bhṛıśam bâlâ vastr'-ârddhen' âbhısaṃvṛıtâ. 38
tasyâ rudantyâḥ satataṃ tena śokena, pârthıva.
prasâdaṃ kuru vaı, vira, pratıvâkyaṃ vadasva ca.' 39
evam anyac ca vaktavyaṃ, kṛıpâṃ kuryâd yathâ mayı,
(vâyunâ dhûyamâno hı vanaṃ dahatı pâvakaḥ,) 40
'bhartavyâ, rakṣaṇiyâ ca patni hı patınâ sadâ.
tan naṣṭam ubhayaṃ kasmâd dharma-ȷnasya satas tava? 41
khyâtaḥ prâȷnaḥ, kulinaś ca s'-ânukrośo bhavân sadâ.
saṃvṛıtto nıranukrośaḥ, śan-ke, mad-bhâgya-san-kṣayât. 42
tat kuruṣva, nara-vyâghra, dayâm mayı, nar'-eśvara.
ânṛı-saṃsyam paro dharmas, tvatta eva mayâ śrutaḥ.' 43
evam bruvâṇân yadı vaḥ pratıbrûyâd dhı kaścana,
sa naraḥ sarvathâ ȷneyaḥ, kaś c' âsau, kva ca vartate. 44
yaś c' aıvaṃ vacanaṃ śrutvâ brûyât pratıvaco naraḥ,
tad âdâya vacas tasya mam' âvedyaṃ, dvıȷ'-ottamâh; 45
yathâ ca vo na ȷâniyâd bruvato mama śâsanât,
punar âgamanaṃ c' aıva, tathâ kâryam atandrıtaıḥ, 46
yadı vâ' sau samṛıddaḥ syâd, yadı vâ 'py adhano bhavet,
yadı vâ 'py artha-kâmaḥ syâȷ, ȷneyaṃ tasya cıkirṣıtam." 47
evam uktâs tv agacchaṃs te brâhmaṇâḥ sarvato dıśaḥ,
Nalam mṛıgayıtuṃ, râȷaṃs, tadâ vyasanınaṃ tathâ. 48
te purâṇı sa-râṣṭrâṇı, grâmân, ghoṣâṃs, tathâ 'śramân,
anveṣanto Nalaṃ, râȷan, n' âdhıȷagmur dvıȷâtayaḥ. 49

tac ca vâkyam tathâ sarve tatra tatra, viśâm pate,
śrâvayâṅ-cakrire viprâ Damayantyâ yath' eritam. 50

iti Nal'-opâkhyâne sapta-daśaḥ sargaḥ.

XVIII.

Vṛihadaśva uvâca,

atha dirghasya kâlasya Parṇâdo nâma vai dvijaḥ
pratyetya nagaram, Bhaimim idaṃ vacanam abravit, 1
"Naiṣadham mṛigayânena, Damayanti, mayâ Nalam,
Ayodhyâm nagarim gatvâ Bhâṅ-gâsurir upasthitaḥ, 2
śrâvitaś ca mayâ vâkyaṃ tvadiyaṃ sa, mahâ-mate,
Ṛituparṇo mahâ-bhâgo yath'-oktaṃ, vara-varṇini, 3
tac chrutvâ n' âbravit kiṇcid Ṛituparṇo nar'-âdhipaḥ,
na ca pâriṣadaḥ kaścid bhâṣyamâṇo mayâ 'sakṛit. 4
ânujnâtaṃ tu mâṃ râjnâ vijane kaścid abravit
Ṛituparṇasya puruṣo, Vâhuko nâma nâmataḥ, 5
sûtas tasya nar'-endrasya virûpo hrasva-bâhukaḥ,
śighra-yâneṣu kuśalo, miṣṭa-kartâ ca bhojane: 6
sa viniḥśvasya bahuśo, ruditvâ ca punaḥ, punaḥ,
kuśalaṃ c' aiva mâm pṛiṣṭvâ, paścâd idam abhâṣata, 7
'vaiṣamyam api samprâptâ gopâyanti kula-striyaḥ
âtmânam âtmanâ satyo, jita-svargâ na saṃśayaḥ; 8
rahitâ bhartṛibhis c' aiva na krudhyanti kadâcana
prâṇâṃś câritra-kavacân dhârayanti vara-striyaḥ. 9
viṣama-sthena mûḍhena, paribhraṣṭa-sukhena ca
yat sâ tena parityaktâ tatra na kroddhum arhati. 10

prâna-yâtrâm pariprepsoḥ, śakunaır hṛıta-vâsasaḥ,

âdhıbhır dahyamânasya śyâmâ na kroddhum arhatı ;   11

sat-kṛıtâ 'sat-kṛıtâ vâ 'pı patıṃ dṛıṣṭvâ tathâ-gatam

bhraṣṭa-râjyaṃ, śrıyâ hinaṃ, kṣudhıtaṃ, vyasan'-âplutam.'   12

tasya tad vacanaṃ śrutvâ tvarıto 'ham ıh' âgataḥ ;

śrutvâ pramâṇam bhavati, râjnaś c'aıva nıvedaya."   13

etac chrutvâ 'śru-pûrṇ'-âkṣi Parṇâdasya, vıśâm pate,

Damayanti raho 'bhyetya mâtaram pratyabhâṣata,   14

"ayam artho na saṃvedyo Bhime, mâtaḥ, kathaṅcana ;

tvat-sannıdhau nıyokṣye 'haṃ Sudevaṃ dvıja-sattamam.   15

yathâ na nṛı-patır Bhimaḥ pratıpadyeta me matım,

tathâ tvayâ prayattavyam, mama cet prıyam ıcchası,   16

yathâ c'âhaṃ samânitâ Sudeven' âśu bândhavân,

ten' aıva man·galen' âśu Sudevo yâtu mâ-cıram,   17

samânetuṃ Nalam, mâtar, Ayodhyâṃ nagarim ıtaḥ."   18

vıśrântam tu tataḥ paścât Parṇâdaṃ dvıja-sattamam

arcayâmâsa Vaıdarbhi dhanen' âtiva bhâvını.

"Nale c' eh' âgate, vıpra, bhûyo dâsyâmı te vasu ;   19

tvayâ hı me bahu kṛıtaṃ, yathâ n' ânyaḥ karıṣyatı,

yad bhartrâ 'haṃ sameṣyâmı śighram eva, dvıj'-ottama."   20

evam ukto 'th' âśvâsya tâm âśir-vâdaıḥ sa-man·galaıḥ,

gṛıhân upayayau c' âpı kṛıt'-ârthaḥ su-mahâ-manâḥ.   21

tataḥ Sudevam âbhâṣya Damayanti, Yudhıṣṭhıra,

abravit sannıdhau mâtur duḥkha-śoka-samanvıtâ,   22

"gatvâ, Sudeva, nagarim Ayodhyâ-vâsınaṃ nṛı-pam

Ṛıtuparṇaṃ vaco brûhı, sampatann ıva kâma-gaḥ,   23

'âsthâsyatı punar Bhaımi Damayanti svaṃ-varam,

tatra gacchantı ráȷáno, ráȷa-putráś ca sarvaśaḥ; 24
tathá ca gaṇıtaḥ kálaḥ śvo-bhúte sa bhavıṣyatı;
yadı sambhávaníyas te, gaccha śíghram, arın-dama. 25
súry'-odaye dvıtíyaṃ sá bhartáraṃ varayıṣyatı;
na hı sa ȷnáyate víro Nalo ȷívatı vá na vá.'" 26
evaṃ tayá yath'-okto vaı gatvá ráȷánam abravít
Ṛıtuparṇam, mahá-ráȷa, Sudevo bráhmaṇas tadá. 27

ıtı Nal'-opákhyáne aṣṭá-daśaḥ sargaḥ.

XIX.

Vṛıhadaśva uváca,

śrutvá vacaḥ Sudevasya Ṛıtuparṇo nar'-ádhıpaḥ
sántvayan ślakṣṇayá vácá Váhukam pratyabháṣata, 1
"Vıdarbhám yátum ıcchámı Damayantyáḥ svayaṃ-varam
ek'-áhná, haya-tattva-ȷna, manyase yadı, Váhuka." 2
evam uktasya, Kaunteya, tena ráȷná Nalasya ha
vyadíryata mano duḥkhát, pradadhyau ca mahá-manáḥ, 3
"Damayantí vaded etat, kuryád duḥkhena mohıtá?
asmad-arthe bhaved vá 'yam upáyaś cıntıto mahán? 4
nṛı-śaṃsaṃ vata Vaıdarbhí kartu-kámá tapasvını,
mayá kṣudreṇa nıkṛıtá kṛıpaṇá pápa-buddhıná. 5
strí-sva-bhávaś calo loke, mama doṣaś ca dáruṇaḥ.
syád evam apı kuryát sá vıvásád gata-sauhṛıdá, 6
mama śokena saṃvıgná naırásyát tanu-madhyamá:
n'aıvaṃ sá karhıcıt kuryát, s'-ápatyá ca vıśeṣataḥ. 7
yad atra satyaṃ vá 'satyaṃ, gatvá vetsyámı nıścayam;

Ṛituparṇasya vai kâmam âtm'-ârthaṃ ca karomy aham." 8
iti niścitya manasâ Vâhuko dina-mânasaḥ,
kṛit'-âñjalir uvâc' edam Ṛituparṇaṃ nar'-âdhipam, 9
"pratijânâmi te vâkyaṃ, gamiṣyâmi, nar'-âdhipa,
ek'-âhnâ, puruṣa-vyâghra Vidarbha-nagariṃ nṛi-pa." 10
tataḥ parikṣâm aśvânâm cakre, râjan, sa Vâhukaḥ,
aśva-śâlâm upâgamya Bhân-gâsuri-nṛi-p'-âjnayâ. 11
sa tvaryamâṇo bahuśa Ṛituparṇena Vâhukaḥ
aśvân jijnâsamâno vai vicârya ca punaḥ, punaḥ, 12
adhyagacchat kṛiśân aśvân samarthân, adhvani kṣamân,
tejo-bala-samâyuktân, kula-śila-samanvitân, 13
varjitâl lakṣaṇair hinaiḥ, prithu-prothân, mahâ-hanûn,
śuddhân daśabhir âvartaiḥ, Sindhu-jân, vâta-raṃhasaḥ. 14
dṛiṣṭvâ tân abravid râjâ kiñcit kopa-samanvitaḥ,
"kim idam prârthitaṃ kartum pralabdhavyâ na te vayam? 15
katham alpa-bala-prâṇâ vakṣyant' ime hayâ mama?
mahad-adhvânam api ca gantavyaṃ katham idṛiśaiḥ? 16
Vâhuka uvâca,
eko lalâṭe, dvau mûrdhni, dvau dvau pârśv'-opapârśvayoḥ,
dvau dvau vakṣasi vijneyau, prayâṇe c' aika eva tu; 17
ete hayâ gamiṣyanti Vidarbhân, n' âtra saṃśayaḥ·
yân anyân mânyase, râjan, brûhi, tân yojayâmi te. 18
Ṛituparṇa uvâca,
tvam eva haya-tattva-jnaḥ kuśalo hy asi, Vâhuka,
yân manyase samarthâṃs tvaṃ, kṣipraṃ tân eva yojaya. 19
Vṛihadaśva uvâca,
tataḥ sad-aśvâṃś caturaḥ kula-śila-samanvitân,

yojayámása kuśalo java-yuktán rathe Nalaḥ. 20
tato yuktaṃ rathaṃ rájá samárohat tvará-'nvitaḥ,
atha paryapatan bhúmau jánubhis te hay'-ottamáḥ. 21
tato nara-varaḥ śrímán Nalo rájá, viśám pate,
sántvayámása tán aśváṃs tejo-bala-samanvitán, 22
raśmibhiś ca samudyamya Nalo yátum iyeṣa saḥ
sútam áropya Várṣṇeyaṃ javam ásthaya vai param. 23
te codyamáná vidhivad Váhukena hay'-ottamáḥ
samutpetur ath' ákáśam rathinam mohayann iva. 24
tathá tu dṛṣṭvá tán aśván vahato váta-raṃhasaḥ,
Ayodhyá-'dhipatiḥ śrímán vismayam paramaṃ yayau. 25
ratha-ghoṣaṃ tu taṃ śrutvá, haya-saṅ-grahaṇaṃ ca tat,
Várṣṇeyaś cintayámása Váhukasya haya-jnatám, 26
"kiṃ nu syád Mátalir ayaṃ deva-rájasya sárathiḥ?
tathá tal-lakṣaṇaṃ víre Váhuke dṛśyate mahat. 27
Śálihotro 'tha kiṃ nu syád dhayánáṃ kula-tattva-vit,
mánuṣaṃ samanupŕápto vapuḥ parama-śobhanam? 28
utáho svid bhaved rájá Nalaḥ para-puraṅ-jayaḥ?
so 'yaṃ nṛ-patir áyáta," ity eva samacintayat. 29
"atha vá yáṃ Nalo veda vidyáṃ, tám eva Váhukaḥ;
tulyaṃ hi lakṣaye jnánaṃ Váhukasya Nalasya ca; 30
api c'edaṃ vayas tulyaṃ Váhukasya, Nalasya ca.
n'áyam Nalo mahá-víryas, tad-vidyaś ca bhaviṣyati. 31
pracchanná hi mahá-'tmánaś caranti pṛthivím imám;
daivena vidhiná yuktáḥ, pracchannáś c'ápi rúpataḥ. 32
bhavet tu mati-bhedo me gátra-vairúpyatám prati,
pramáṇát parihínas tu bhaved iti matir mama. 33

vayaḥ-pramāṇaṃ tat tulyaṃ, rûpeṇa tu vıparyayaḥ,
Nalaṃ sarva-guṇaır yuktam manye Vâhukam antataḥ." 34
evaṃ vıcârya bahuśo Vârṣṇeyaḥ paryacıntayat,
hṛıdayena, mahâ-râȷa Puṇyaślokasya sârathıḥ. 35
Ṛıtuparṇas tu râȷ'-endro Vâhukasya haya-ȷnatâm
cıntayan mumude râȷâ saha-Vârṣṇeya-sârathıḥ. 36
aıkâgryaṃ ca tath' otsâhaṃ, haya-san·grahaṇe ca tat,
paraṃ yatnaṃ ca samprekṣya parâm mudam avâpa ha. 37

ıtı Nal'-opâkhyâne nava-daśaḥ sargaḥ.

XX.

Vṛıhadaśva uvâca,
sa nadîḥ parvatâṃś c'aıva, vanânı ca, sarâṃsı ca
acıreṇ' âtıcakrâma khe-caraḥ khe carann ıva. 1
tathâ prayâte tu rathe tadâ Bhân·gâsurır nṛı-paḥ
uttarîyam adho 'paśyad bhraṣṭam para-purañ-ȷayaḥ; 2
tataḥ sa tvaramâṇas tu paṭe nıpatıte tadâ,
grahiṣyam' itı taṃ râȷâ Nalam âha mahâ-manâḥ, 3
"nıgrıhṇiṣva, mahâ-buddhe, hayân etân mahâ-ȷavân,
Vârṣṇeyo yâvad etam me paṭam ânayatâm ıha." 4
Nalas tam pratyuvâc' âtha, "dûre bhraṣṭaḥ paṭas tava
yoȷanaṃ samatıkrânto n' âhartum śakyate punaḥ." 5
evam ukto Nalen' âtha tadâ Bhân·gâsurır nṛı-paḥ
âsasâda vane, râȷan, phalavantam vıbhîtakam. 6
taṃ dṛıṣṭvâ, Vâhukaṃ râȷâ tvaramâṇo 'bhyabhâṣata,
"mam' âpı, sûta, paśya tvaṃ san·khyâne paramam balam. 7

sarvaḥ sarvaṃ na ȷânâtı, sarva-ȷno n'âstı kaścana;
n' aıkatra parıṇıṣṭhâ 'stı ȷnânasya puruṣe kvacıt. 8
vṛkṣe 'smın yânı parṇânı, phalâny apı ca, Vâhuka,
patıtâny apı yâny atra, tatr' aıkam adhıkaṃ śatam. 9
ekam atr' âdhıkam patram, phalam ekaṃ ca, Vâhuka.
pañca-koṭyo 'tha patrâṇâṃ dvayor apı ca śâkhayoḥ. 10
pracınuhy asya śâkhe dve, yâś c 'âpy anyâḥ praśâkhıkâḥ
âbhyâm phala-sahasre dve pañc'-onaṃ śatam eva ca." 11
tato ratham avasthâpya râȷânaṃ Vâhuko 'bravit,
"paro-'kṣam ıva me, râȷan, katthase, śatru-karṣaṇa, 12
pratyakṣam etat kartâsmı śâtayıtvâ vıbhitakam;
ath' âtra gaṇıte, râȷan, vıdyate na paro-'kṣatâ. 13
pratyakṣaṃ te, mahâ-râȷa, śâtayiṣye vıbhitakam.
ahaṃ hı n' âbhıȷânâmı bhaved evaṃ na v' etı ca. 14
saṅ-khyâsyâmı phalâny asya, paśyatas te, ȷan'-âdhıpa;
muhûrtam apı Vârṣṇeyo raśmin yacchatu vâȷınâm." 15
taṃ abravin nṛı-paḥ sûtaṃ, "n' âyaṃ kâlo vılambıtum."
Vâhukas tv abravid enam paraṃ yatnaṃ samâsthıtaḥ, 16
"pratikṣasva muhûrtaṃ tvam, atha vâ tvarate bhavân;
eṣa yâtı śıvaḥ panthâ; yâhı Vârṣṇeya-sârathıḥ." 17
abravid Ṛıtuparṇas tu sântvayan, kuru-nandana,
"tvam ıva yantâ n' ânyo 'stı pṛıthıvyâm apı, Vâhuka. 18
tvat-kṛıte yâtum ıcchâmı Vıdarbhân, haya-kovıda,
śaraṇaṃ tvâm prapanno 'smı, na vıghnaṃ kartum arhası; 19
kâmaṃ ca te karıṣyâmı, yan mâṃ vakṣyası, Vâhuka,
Vıdarbhân yadı yâtvâ 'dya sûryaṃ darṣayıtâsı me." 20
ath' âbravid Vâhukas, "taṃ saṅ-khyâya ca vıbhitakam,

tato Vıdarbhán yásyámı, kuruṣv' aıvaṃ vaco mama." 21
akáma ıva taṃ ráȷá "gaṇayasv" ety uváca ha,
eka-deśaṃ ca śákháyáḥ samádıṣṭam mayá, 'nagha, 22
gaṇayasv' ásya, tattva-ȷna, tatas tvam prítım ávaha."
so 'vatírya rathát túrṇam śátayámása taṃ drumam. 23
tataḥ sa vısmay'-ávıṣṭo ráȷánam ıdam abravít,
"gaṇayıtvá yath' oktánı távanty eva phalánı ca; 24
atyadbhutam ıdaṃ, ráȷan, dṛṣṭaván asmı te balam,
śrotum ıcchámı táṃ vıdyám, yay' aıtaȷ ȷnáyate, nṛ-pa." 25
tam uváca tato ráȷá, tvarıto gamane nṛ-pah,
vıddhy akṣa-hṛdaya-ȷnam máṃ, san-khyáne ca vıśára-dam." 26
Váhukas tam uvác' átha, "dehı vıdyám ımám mama,
matto 'pı c' áśva-hṛdayaṃ gṛhánṇa, puruṣa-'rṣabha." 27
Ṛtuparṇas tato ráȷá Váhukaṃ kárya-gauravát,
haya-ȷnánasya lobhác ca tath' ety ev' ábravid vacaḥ, 28
"yath' oktaṃ tvaṃ gṛhán' edam akṣáṇáṃ hṛdayam param
nıkṣepo me, 'śva-hṛdayaṃ tvayı tıṣṭhatı, Váhuka." 29
evam uktvá dadau vıdyáṃ Ṛtuparṇo Naláya vaı.
tasy' ákṣa-hṛdaya-ȷnasya śarírád nıḥsṛtaḥ Kalıḥ,
Karkoṭaka-vıṣaṃ tíkṣṇam mukhát satatam udvaman. 30
Kales tasya tad-ártasya śáp'-ágnıḥ sa vınıḥsṛtaḥ.
sa tena karṣıto ráȷá dírgha-kálam anátmaván. 31
tato vıṣa-vımukt'-átmá svam rúpam akarot Kalıḥ;
taṃ śaptum aıcchat kupıto Nıṣadh'-ádhıpatır Nalaḥ. 32
tam uváca Kalır bhíto, vepamánaḥ, kṛt'-áñȷalıḥ,
"kopaṃ saṃyaccha, nṛ-pate, kírtıṃ dásyámı te parám; 33
Indrasenasya ȷananí kupıtá má 'śapat purá,

yadà tvayà parityaktà, tato 'ham bhṛiśa-piḍitaḥ 34
avasaṃ tvayi, ràj'-endra, su-duḥkham, aparàjita,
viṣeṇa nàga-ràjasya dahyamàno divà-niśam; 35
śaraṇaṃ tvàm prapanno 'smi, śṛiṇu c' edaṃ vaco mama,
ye ca tvàm manu-jà loke kìrtayiṣyanty atandritàḥ, 36
mat-prasùtam bhayaṃ teṣàṃ na kadàcid bhaviṣyati,
bhay'-àrtaṃ śaraṇaṃ yàtaṃ yadi màṃ tvaṃ na śapsyase." 37
evam ukto Nalo ràjà nyayacchat kopam àtmanaḥ,
tato bhitaḥ Kaliḥ kṣipram praviveśa vibhitakam. 38
Kalis tv anyena n' àdṛiśyata kathayan Naiṣadhena vai.
tato gata-jvaro ràjà Naiṣadhaḥ para-vira-hà, 39
sampraṇaṣṭe Kalau, ràjan, san-khyàya ca phalàny uta,
mudà paramayà yuktas, tejasà 'tha pareṇa ca, 40
ratham àruhya tejasvi prayayau javanair hayaiḥ.
vibhitakaś c' àpraśastaḥ saṃvṛittaḥ Kali-saṃśrayàt. 41
hay'-ottamàn utpatato dvi-jàn iva punaḥ, punaḥ
Nalaḥ saṃcodayàmàsa prahṛiṣṭen' àntar-àtmanà 42
Vidarbh'-àbhimukho ràjà prayayau sa mahà-yaśàḥ.
Nale tu samatikrànte Kalir apy agamad gṛiham. 43
tato gata-jvaro ràjà Nalo 'bhùt pṛithivi-patiḥ,
vimuktaḥ Kalinà, ràjan, rùpa-màtra-viyojitaḥ. 44

iti Nal'-opàkhyàne viṃśatitamaḥ sargaḥ.

XXI.

Vṛihadaśva uváca,

tato Vidarbhán sampráptaṃ sáyáhne satya-vikramam
Ṛituparṇaṃ janá rájne Bhímáya pratyavedayan. 1
sa Bhíma-vacanád rájá Kuṇḍinam právisat puram,
nádayan ratha-ghoṣeṇa sarváḥ savidiśo diśaḥ. 2
tatas taṃ ratha-nirghoṣaṃ Nal'-áśvás tatra śuśruvuḥ;
śrutvá tu samáhṛiṣyanta pur' eva Nala-sannidhau. 3
Damayantí tu śuśráva ratha-ghoṣaṃ Nalasya tam,
yathá meghasya nadato gambhíraṃ jala-d'-ágame. 4
paraṃ vismayam ápanná śrutvá nádam mahá-svanam
Nalena san-gṛihíteṣu pur' eva Nala-vájiṣu; 5
sadṛiśaṃ haya-nirghoṣam mene Bhaimí, tathá hayáḥ,
prásáda-stháś ca śikinaḥ, śálá-stháś c' aiva váraṇaḥ,
hayáś ca śuśruvus tasya ratha-ghoṣam mahí-pateḥ. 6
te śrutvá ratha-nirghoṣaṃ váraṇáḥ, śikhinas tathá.
praṇedur unmukhá, rájan, megha-náda iv' otsukáḥ 7
Damayanty uváca,
yathá 'sau ratha-nirghoṣaḥ púrayann iva mediním
mam' áhládayate ceto; Nala eṣa mahí-patiḥ. 8
adya candr'-ábha-vaktraṃ taṃ na paśyámi Nalaṃ yadi,
asan-khyeya-guṇaṃ víraṃ vinakṣyámi, na saṃśayaḥ. 9
yadi c' aitasya vírasya báhvor n' ády' áham antaram
praviśámi sukha-sparśaṃ, na bhaviṣyámy asaṃśayam. 10
yadi mám megha-nirghoṣo n' opagacchati Naiṣadhaḥ,
adya cámíkara-prakhyam pravekṣyámi hut'-áśanam. 11

yadı màṃ sıṃha-vıkrànto, matta-vàrana-vıkramaḥ,
n' àbhıgacchatı ràj'-endro vınakṣyàmı na saṃśayaḥ. 12
na smaràmy anṛıtaṃ kıṅcın, na smaràmy apakàratàm,
na ca paryuṣıtaṃ vàkyaṃ svaıreṣv apı kadàcana. 13
prabhuḥ, kṣamàvàn, viraś ca, dàtà c' abhyadhıko nṛı-paiḥ,
raho 'nic'-ànuvarti ca klivavad mama Naıṣadhaḥ. 14
guṇàns tasya smarantyà me tat-paràyà dıvà-nıśam
hṛıdayaṃ diryata ıdaṃ śokàt prıya-vınà-kṛıtaṃ." 15
evaṃ vılapamànà sà, naṣṭa-saṅjn' eva, Bhàrata,
àruroha mahad veśma Puṇyaśloka-dıdṛıkṣayà, 16
tato madhyama-kakṣàyàṃ dadarśa ratham àsthıtam
Ṛıtuparṇam mahi-pàlaṃ saha-Vàrṣṇeya-Vàhukam. 17
tato 'vatirya Vàrṣṇeyo, Vàhukaś ca rath'-ottamàt,
hayàns tàn avamucy' àtha sthàpayàmàsa vaı ratham. 18
so 'vatirya rath'-opasthàd Ṛıtuparṇo nar'-àdhıpaḥ,
upatasthe mahà-ràjam Bhimam bhima-paràkramam. 19
tam Bhimaḥ pratıjagràha pùjayà parayà tataḥ,
akasmàt sahasà pràptaṃ, stri-mantraṃ na sma vındatı. 20
"kıṃ kàryam? sv-àgataṃ te 'stu," ràjnà pṛıṣṭaḥ sa, Bhàrata;
n' àbhıjajne sa nṛı-patır duhıtr-arthe samàgatam. 21
Ṛıtuparṇo 'pı ràjà sa dhimàn, satya-paràkramaḥ,
ràjànam, ràja-putraṃ và na sma paśyatı kaṅcana, 22
n' aıva svayaṃ-vara-kathàṃ, na ca vıpra-samagàmam,
tato vıgaṇayan ràjà manasà Kośal'-àdhıpaḥ, 23
"àgato 'sm,' ity, uvàc' aınam, "bhavantam abhıvàdakaḥ."
ràjà 'pı ca smayan Bhimo manasà samacıntayat, 24
"adhıkaṃ yojana-śataṃ tasy' àgamana-kàraṇam,

grámán bahún atıkramya n' ádhyagacchad yathá-tatham; 25
alpa-káryaṃ vınırdıṣṭaṃ tasy' ágamana-káraṇam;
paścád udarke ȷnásyámı káraṇam yad bhavıṣyatı; 26
n' aıtad." evaṃ sa nṛı-patıs taṃ sat-krıtya vyasarȷayat;
"vıśrámyatám," ıty uváca, "klánto s' itı, punaḥ, punaḥ. 27
sa sat-kṛıtaḥ prahṛıṣṭ'-átmá pritaḥ pritena párthıvaḥ,
raȷa-preṣyaır anugato dıṣṭaṃ veśma samávıśat. 28
Ṛıtuparṇe gate, rájan, Várṣṇeya-sahıte nṛı-pe,
Váhuko ratham ádáya ratha-śálám upágamat. 29
sa mocayıtvá tán aśván, upacarya ca śástrataḥ,
svayaṃ c' aıtán samáśvásya, rath'-opastha upávıśat. 30
Damayanti tu śok'-ártá dṛıṣṭvá Bhán-gásurıṃ nṛı-pam,
súta-putraṃ ca Várṣṇeyaṃ, Váhukaṃ ca tathá-vıdham, 31
cıntayámása Vaıdarbhi, "kasy' aıṣa ratha-nısvanaḥ?
Nalasy' eva mahán ásin, na ca paśyámı Naıṣadham. 32
Várṣṇeyena bhaven núnaṃ vıdyá s' aıv' opaśıkṣıtá?
ten' ádya ratha-nırghoṣo Nalasy' eva mahán abhút, 33
áhosvıd Ṛıtuparṇo 'pı yathá rájá Nalas tathá?
tathá 'yam ratha-nırghoṣo Naıṣadhasy' eva lakṣyate." 34
evaṃ sá tarkayıtvá tu Damayanti, vıśám pate,
dútim prasthápayámása Naıṣadh'-ánvesaṇe śubhá. 35

ıtı Nal'-opákhyáne eka-vıṃśatıtamaḥ sargaḥ.

XXII.

Damayanty uvàca,

gaccha, Keśini, jànihi ka eṣa ratha-vàhakaḥ,
upaviṣṭo rath'-opasthe vikṛto hrasva-bàhukaḥ. 1
abhyetya kuśalam, bhadre, mṛdu-pùrvaṃ samàhità,
pṛcchethàḥ puruṣaṃ hy enaṃ yathà-tattvam, anindite. 2
atra me mahati śan-kà bhaved eṣa Nalo nṛ-paḥ,
yathà ca manasas tuṣṭir, hṛdayaśya ca nirvṛtiḥ. 3
brùyàś c' ainaṃ kathà-'nte tvam Parṇàda-vacanaṃ yathà,
prativàkyaṃ ca, su-śroṇi, budhyethàs tvam, anindite. 4

Vṛhadaśva uvàca,

tataḥ samàhità gatvà dùti Vàhukam abravit,
Damayanty api kalyàṇi pràsàda-sthà hy upaikṣata. 5

Keśiny uvàca,

sv-àgataṃ te, manuṣy'-endra, kuśalaṃ te bravimy aham:
Damayantyà vacaḥ sàdhu nibodha, puruṣa-'rṣabha; 6
"kadà vai prasthità yùyaṃ? kim artham iha c' àgatàḥ?"
tat tvam brùhi yathà-nyàyaṃ, Vaidarbhi śrotum icchati. 7

Vàhuka uvàca,

śrutaḥ svayaṃ-varo ràjnà Kauśalena mahà-'tmanà
dvitiyo Damayantyà vai bhavità śva iti dvijàt. 8
śrutv' aitat prasthito ràjà śata-yojana-yàyibhiḥ
hayair vàta-javair mukhyair, aham asya ca sàrathiḥ. 9

Keśiny uvàca,

atha yo 'sau tṛtiyo vaḥ, sa kutaḥ? kasya và punaḥ?

tvaṃ ca kasya? kathaṃ c' edaṃ tvayı karma samâhıtam? 10
Vâhuka uvâca,
Puṇyaślokasya vaı sûto Vârṣṇeya ıtı vıśrutaḥ;
sa Nale pradrute, bhadre, Bhâṅgâsurım upasthıtaḥ. 11
aham apy aśva-kuśalaḥ, sûtatve ca pratıṣṭhıtaḥ,
Ṛıtuparṇena sârathye, bhoȷane ca vṛıtaḥ svayam. 12
Keśıny uvâca,
atha ȷânâtı Vârṣṇeyaḥ kva nu râȷâ Nalo gataḥ?
kathaṃ ca tvayı c' aıtena kathıtaṃ syât tu, Vâhuka? 13
Vâhuka uvâca,
ıh' aıva putrau nıkṣıpya Nalasy' âśubha-karmaṇaḥ,
gatas tato yathâ-kâmaṃ n' aıṣa ȷânâtı Naıṣadham, 14
na c' ânyaḥ puruṣaḥ kaścın Nalaṃ vettı, yaśasvını.
gûḍhas caratı loke 'smın naṣṭa-rûpo mahi-patıḥ. 15
âtm' aıva tu Nalaṃ vettı, yâ c' âsya tad-anantarâ,
na hı vaı svânı lıṅgânı Nalaḥ śaṃsatı karhıcıt. 16
Keśıny uvâca,
yo 'sav Ayodhyâm prathamaṃ gatavân brâhmaṇas tadâ,
ımânı nâri-vâkyânı kathayânaḥ punaḥ punaḥ, 17
"kva nu tvaṃ, kıtava, cchıttvâ vastr'-ârddham prasthıto mama,
utsṛıȷya vıpıne suptâm anuraktâm prıyâm, prıya? 18
sâ vaı yathâ samâdıṣṭâ tathâ 'ste, tvat-pratikṣıṇi,
dahyamânâ dıvâ-râtraṃ vastr'-ârddhen' âbhısaṃvṛıtâ. 19
tasyâ rudantyâḥ satataṃ tena duḥkhena, pârthıva,
prasâdaṃ kuru vaı, vira, pratıvâkyaṃ vadasva ca." 20
tasyâs tat prıyam âkhyânam pravadasva, mahâ-mate;
tad eva vâkyaṃ Vaıdarbhi śrotum ıcchaty anındıtâ, 21

etac chrutvà pratıvacas tasya dattaṃ tvayà kıla,
yat purà, tat punas tvatto Vaıdarbhi śrotum ıcchatı. 22

Vṛıhadaśva uvàca,

evam uktasya Keśınyà Nalasya, Kuru-nandana,
hṛıdayaṃ vyathıtaṃ c' àsid, aśru-pùrṇe ca locane. 23
sa nıgṛıhy' àtmano duḥkhaṃ dahyamàno mahi-patıḥ,
vàṣpa-sandıgdhayà vàcà punar ev' edam abravit, 24

Vàhuka uvàca,

vaıṣamyam apı sampràptà gopàyantı kula-strıyaḥ
àtmànam àtmanà satyo, jıta-svargà na saṃśayaḥ; 25
rahıtà bhartṛıbhıś c' àpı na krudhyantı kadàcana,
pràṇàṅś càrıtra-kavacàn dhàrayantı vara-strıyaḥ. 26
vıṣama-sthena, mùḍhena, parıbhraṣṭa-sukhena ca,
yat sà tena parıtyaktà, tatra na kroddhum arhatı. 27
pràṇa-yàtràm parıprepsoḥ śakunaır hṛıta-vàsasaḥ
àdhıbhır dahyamànasya śyàmà na kroddhum arhatı. 28
sat-kṛıtà, 'sat-kṛıtà và 'pı patıṃ dṛıṣṭvà tathà-gatam
bhraṣṭa-ràjyaṃ, śrıyà hinaṃ, ksudhıtaṃ, vyasan'-àplutam." 29
evam bruvàṇas tad vàkyaṃ Nalaḥ parama-duḥkhıtaḥ,
na vàṣpam aśakat soḍhum prarurod' àtha, Bhàrata. 30
tataḥ sà Keśıni gatvà Damayantyaı nyavedayat
tat sarvaṃ kathıtaṃ c' aıva, vıkàraṃ c' aıva tasya tam. 31

ıtı Nal'-opàkhyàne dvà-vıṃśatıtamaḥ sargaḥ.

XXIII.

Vṛıhadaśva uvàca,

Damayanti tu tac chrutvà bhṛıśaṃ śoka-paràyaṇà
śan·kamànà Nalaṃ taṃ va Keśınim ıdam abravit. 1
"gaccha, Keśını bhùyas tvam parikṣàṃ kuru Vàhuke,
abruvàṇà samipa-sthà carıtàny asya lakṣaya; 2
yadà ca kıñcıt kuryàt sa kàraṇaṃ tatra, bhàvını,
tatra sañceṣṭamànasya lakṣayanti vıceṣṭıtam. 3
na c' àsya pratıbandhena deyo 'gnır apı, Keśını,
yàcate na ȷalaṃ deyaṃ sarvathà tvaramàṇayà; 4
etat sarvaṃ samikṣya tvaṃ carıtam me nıvedaya,
nımıttaṃ yat tvayà dṛıṣṭaṃ Vàhuke daıva-mànuṣaṃ.
yac c' ànyad apı paśyethàs, tac c' àkhyeyaṃ tvayà mama." 5
Damayanty' aıvam uktà sà ȷagàm' àtha ca Keśıni,
nıśamy' àtha haya-ȷnasya lın·gànı punar àgamat. 6
sà tat sarvaṃ yathà-vṛıttaṃ Damayantyaı nyavedayat,
nımıttaṃ yat tayà dṛıṣṭaṃ Vàhuke dıvya-mànuṣam. 7

Keśıny uvàca,

dṛıḍhaṃ sucy-upacàro 'sau; na mayà mànuṣaḥ kvacıt
dṛıṣṭa-pùrvaḥ, śruto và 'pı, Damayantı, tathà-vıdhaḥ. 8
hrasvam àsàdya saṃcàraṃ n' àsau vınamate kvacıt,
taṃ tu dṛıṣṭvà yathà-san·gam utsarpatı yathà-sukham. 9
Ṛıtuparṇasya c' àrthàya bhoȷaniyam anekaśaḥ
preṣıtam tatra ràȷnà tu màṃsam bahu ca pàśavam. 10
tasya prakṣ-àlan'-àrthàya kumbhàs tatr' opakalpıtàḥ,
te ten' àvekṣıtàḥ kumbhàḥ pùrṇà ev' àbhavaṃs tataḥ. 11

tataḥ prakṣâlanaṃ kṛıtvâ, samadhıśrıtya Vâhukaḥ
tṛıṇa-muṣṭıṃ samâdâya savıtus taṃ samâdadhat, 12
atha praȷvalıtas tatra sahasâ havya-vâhanaḥ.
tad adbhutatamaṃ dṛıṣṭvâ vısmıtâ 'ham ıh' âgatâ. 13
anyac ca tasmın su-mahad âścaryaṃ lakṣıtam mayâ,
yad agnım apı saṃspṛıśya n' aıv' âsau dahyate, śubhe, 14
chandena c' odakaṃ tasya vahaty âvarȷıtaṃ drutam;
ativa c' ânyat su-mahad âścaryaṃ dṛıṣṭavaty aham, 15
yat sa puṣpâny upâdâya hastâbhyâm mamṛıde śanaıḥ,
mṛıdyamânânı pâṇıbhyâṃ tena puṣpâṇı tâny atha, 16
bhûya eva su-gandhını hṛıṣıtânı bhavantı hı.
etâny adbhuta-lın·gânı dṛıṣṭvâ 'haṃ drutam âgatâ. 17
Vṛıhadaśva uvâca,
Damayanti tu tac chrutvâ Puṇyaślokasya ceṣṭıtam
amanyata Nalam prâptaṃ karma-ceṣṭ'-âbhısûcıtam. 18
sâ śan·kamânâ bhartâraṃ Nalaṃ Vâhuka-rûpıṇam,
Keśınıṃ ślakṣṇayâ vâcâ rudati punar abravit, 19
"punar gaccha pramattasya Vâhukasy'-opasaṃskṛıtam
mahâ-nasâc chṛıtam mâṃsaṃ samâdây' aıhı, bhâvını." 20
sâ gatvâ Vâhukasy' âgre tan mâṃsam apakṛıṣya ca
atyuṣṇam eva tvarıtâ tat-kṣaṇât prıya-kârıṇi
Damayantyaı tataḥ prâdât Keśıni, Kuru-nandana. 21
s' ocıtâ Nala-sıddhasya mâṃsasya bahuśaḥ purâ,
prâśya matvâ Nalaṃ sûtam, prâkrośad bhṛıśa-duḥkhıtâ, 22
vaıklavyam paramaṃ gatvâ, prakṣâlya ca mukhaṃ tataḥ,
mıthunam preṣayâmâsa Keśınyâ saha, Bhârata. 23
Indrasenâṃ saha bhrâtrâ samabhıȷnâya Vâhukaḥ,

abhıdrutya tato râȷâ parıṣvaȷy' ân·kam ânayat; 24
Vâhukas tu, samâsâdya sutau sura-sut'-opamau,
bhṛıśaṃ duḥkha-parit'-âtmâ su-svaram praruroda ha. 25
Naıṣadho darśayıtvâ tu vıkâram asakṛıt tadâ,
utsṛıȷya sahasâ putrau, Keśınim ıdam abravit, 26
"ıdaṃ su-sadṛıśam, bhadre, mıthunam mama putrayoḥ,
ato dṛıṣṭv' aıva sahasâ vâṣpam utsṛıṣṭavân aham; 27
bahuśaḥ sampatantiṃ tvâṃ ȷanaḥ śan·keta doṣataḥ,
vayaṃ ca deś'-âtıthayo; gaccha, bhadre, yathâ-sukham. 28

ıtı Nal'-opâkhyâne trayo-vıṃśatıtamaḥ sargaḥ.

XXIV.

Vṛıhadaśva uvâca,
sarvaṃ vıkâraṃ dṛıṣṭvâ tu Puṇyaślokasya dhimataḥ,
âgatya Keśıni kṣıpraṃ Damayantyaı nyavedayat. 1
Damayanti tato bhûyaḥ preṣayâmâsa Keśınim
mâtuḥ sakâśaṃ duḥkhârtâ Nala-darśana-kân·kṣayâ. 2
"parikṣito me bahuśo Vâhuko Nala-śan·kayâ
rûpe me saṃśayas tv ekaḥ svayam ıcchâmı vedıtum. 3
sa vâ praveśyatâm, mâtar, mâṃ vâ 'nuȷnâtum arhası;
vıdıtaṃ vâ, 'tha vâ 'ȷnâtam pıtur me saṃvıdhiyatâm." 4
evam uktâ tu Vaıdarbhyâ sâ devi Bhimam abravit,
duhıtus tam abhıprâyam anvaȷânât sa pârthıvaḥ. 5
sâ vaı pitrâ 'bhyanuȷnâtâ, mâtrâ ca, Bharata-ṛṣabha,
Nalam praveśayâmâsa yatra tasyâḥ pratıśrayaḥ. 6
tâṃ sma dṛıṣṭv' aıva sahasâ Damayantiṃ Nalo nṛı-paḥ,

âvıṣṭaḥ śoka-duḥkhâbhyâm babhûv' âśru-parîplutaḥ.   7

taṃ tu dṛıṣṭvâ tathâ-yuktaṃ Damayanti Nalaṃ tadâ

tivra-śoka-samâvıṣṭâ babhûva vara-varṇını.   8

tataḥ kâṣâya-vasanâ jaṭılâ mala-pan·kıni,

Damayanti, mahâ-râja, Vâhukâṃ vâkyam abravit,   9

"pûrvaṃ dṛıṣṭas tvayâ kaścıd dharma-jno nâma, Vâhuka,

suptâm utsṛıjya vıpıne gato yaḥ puruṣaḥ strıyam?   10

anâgasam prıyâm bhâryâṃ vıjane śrama-mohıtâm.

apahâya tu kó gacchet Puṇyaślokam ṛıte Nalam?   11

kıṃ nu tasya mayâ bâlyâd aparâddham mahi-pate,

yo mâm utsṛıjya vıpıne gatavân nıdrayâ hṛıtâm?   12

sâkṣâd devân apahâya vṛıto yaḥ sa mayâ purâ

anuvratâṃ sâbhıkâmâm putrıṇıṃ tyaktavân katham?   13

agnau pâṇıṃ gṛıhitvâ tu devânâm agratas tathâ

'bhavıṣyâṃ' ıtı', satyaṃ tu pratıśrutya, kva tad gatam?"   14

Damayantyâ bruvantyâs tu sarvam etad, arın-dama,

śoka-jaṃ vârı netrâbhyâm asukham prâsravad bahu.   15

ativa kṛıṣṇa-sârâbhyâṃ rakt'-ântâbhyâṃ jalaṃ tu tat

parısravad Nalo dṛıṣṭvâ śok'-ârtâm ıdam abravit,   16

"mama râjyam praṇaṣṭaṃ yad, n' âhaṃ tat kṛıtavân svayam,

Kalınâ tat kṛıtam, bhiru; yac ca tvâm aham atyajam.   17

tvayâ tu pâpaḥ kṛıcchreṇa śâpen' âbhıhataḥ purâ

vanasthayâ, duḥkhıtayâ, śocantyâ mâṃ dıvâ-nıśam,   18

sa mac-charire tvac-châpâd dahyamâno 'vasat Kalıḥ,

tvac-châpa-dagdhaḥ satataṃ so 'gnâv agnır ıv' âhıtaḥ,   19

mama ca vyavasâyena, tapasâ, c' aıva nırjıtaḥ;

duḥkhasy' ântena c' ânena bhavıtavyaṃ hı nau, śubhe.   20

vımucya mȧṃ gataḥ pȧpas, tato 'ham ıha c' ȧgataḥ,
tvad-arthaṃ, vıpula-śroṇı; na hı me 'nyat prayojanam. 21
kathaṃ tu nȧri bhartȧram anuraktam, anuvratam,
utsṛjya varayed anyaṃ yathȧ tvam, bhiru, karhıcıt? 22
du̇tȧś carantı pṛthıviṃ kṛtsnȧṃ nṛ-patı-śȧsanȧt,
"Bhaımi kıla sma bhartȧraṃ dvıtiyaṃ varayıṣyatı, 23
svaıra-vṛttȧ, yathȧ-kȧmam, anuru̇pam ıv' ȧtmanaḥ;'
śrutv' aıva c' aıtat tvarıto Bhȧn-gȧsurır upasthıtaḥ." 24
Damayanti tu, tac chrutvȧ Nalasya parıdevıtam,
prȧñjalır, vepamȧnȧ ca, bhitȧ ca Nalam abravit, 25
"na mȧm arhası, kalyȧṇa, doṣeṇa parıśan-kıtum;
mayȧ hı devȧn utsṛjya vṛtas tvaṃ, Nıṣadh'-ȧdhıpa, 26
tav' ȧdhıgaman'-ȧrthaṃ tu sarvato brȧhmaṇȧ gatȧḥ,
vȧkyȧnı mama gȧthȧbhır gȧyamȧnȧ dıśo daśa. 27
tatas tvȧṃ brȧhmaṇo vıdvȧn Parṇȧdo nȧma, pȧrthıva,
abhyagacchat Kośalȧyȧm Ṛtuparṇa-nıveśane. 28
tena vȧkye kṛte samyak pratıvȧkye tathȧ 'hṛte,
upȧyo 'yam mayȧ dṛṣṭo, Naıṣadh', ȧnayane tava. 29
tvȧm ṛte na hı loke 'nya ek'-ȧhnȧ, pṛthıvi-pate,
samartho yojana-śataṃ gantum aśvaır, nar'-ȧdhıpa. 30
spṛśeyaṃ tena satyena pȧdȧv etau, mahi-pate,
yathȧ n' ȧsat-kṛtaṃ kıñcıd manasȧ 'pı carȧmy aham. 31
ayaṃ caratı loke 'smın bhu̇ta-sȧkṣi sadȧ-gatıḥ,
eṣa me muñcatu prȧṇȧn, yadı pȧpaṃ carȧmy aham; 32
tathȧ caratı tıgm'-ȧṃśuḥ pareṇa bhuvanaṃ sadȧ,
sa muñcatu mama prȧṇȧn, yadı pȧpaṃ carȧmy aham; 33
candra-mȧḥ sarva-bhu̇tȧnȧm antaś-caratı sȧkṣıvat,

sa muñcatu mama prâṇân, yadı pâpaṃ carâmy aham. 34
ete devâs trayaḥ kṛtsnaṃ traı-lokyaṃ dhârayantı vaı,
vıbruvantu yathâ-satyam, ete vâ 'dya tyaȷantu mâm." 35
evam uktas tayâ vâyur antar-ikṣâd abhâṣata,
"n' aıṣâ kṛtavati pâpaṃ, Nala, satyam bravimı te; 36
râȷan, śila-nıdhıḥ sphito Damayantyâ su-rakṣıtaḥ,
sâkṣıṇo rakṣıṇaś c' âsyâ vayaṃ trin parıvatsarân. 37
upâyo vıhıtaś c' âyaṃ tvad-artham atulo 'nayâ,
na hy ek'-âhnâ śataṃ gantâ, tvâm ṛte 'nyaḥ pumân ıha. 38
upapannâ tvayâ Bhaımi, tvaṃ ca Bhaımyâ, mahi-pate,
n' âtra śan·kâ tvayâ kâryâ san·gaccha saha bharyayâ." 39
tathâ bruvatı vâyau tu puṣpa-vṛṣṭıḥ papâta ha
deva-dundubhayo nedur, vavau ca pavanaḥ śıvaḥ. 40
tad adbhutatamaṃ dṛṣṭvâ Nalo râȷâ 'tha, Bhârata,
Damayantyâṃ vıśan·kâṃ tâṃ vyapâkarṣad, arın-dama, 41
tatas tad vastram araȷaḥ prâvṛṇod vasu-dhâ-'dhıpaḥ
saṃsmṛtya nâga-râȷaṃ taṃ, tato lebhe svakaṃ vapuḥ. 42
sva-rûpıṇaṃ tu bhartâraṃ dṛṣṭvâ Bhima-sutâ tadâ,
prâkrośad uccaır âlin·gya Puṇyaślokam anındıtâ. 43
Bhaımimı apı Nalo râȷâ bhrâȷamâno yathâ purâ
sasvaȷe, sva-sutau c' âpı yathâvat pratyanandata. 44
tataḥ sv'-orası vınyasya vaktraṃ tasya śubh'-ânanâ
paritâ tena duḥkhena nıśaśvâs' âyat'-ekṣaṇâ. 45
tath' aıva mala-dıgdh'-ân·gim parıṣvaȷya śucı-smıtâm,
su-cıram puruṣa-vyâghras tasthau śoka-parıplutaḥ. 46
tataḥ sarvaṃ yathâ-vṛttaṃ Damayantyâ, Nalasya ca,
Bhimây' âkathayat prityâ Vaıdarbhi-ȷanani, nṛ-pa. 47

tato 'bravid mahà-ràjaḥ, "kṛta-śaucam ahaṃ Nalam
Damayantyà sah' opetaṃ kalyaṃ draṣṭà sukh'-oṣitam." 48
Vṛhadaśva uvàca,
tatas tau sahitau ràtriṃ kathayantau puràtanam
vane vicaritaṃ sarvam ùṣatur muditau, nṛ-pa, 49
gṛhe Bhimasya nṛ-pateḥ paras-para-sukh-aiṣiṇau
vasetàṃ hṛṣṭa-san-kalpau, Vaidarbhi ca, Nalaś ca ha. 50
sa caturthe tato varṣe san-gamya saha bhàryayà
sarva-kàmaiḥ su-siddh'-àrtho labdhavàn paramàm mudam. 51
Damayanty api bhartàram àsàdy' àpyàyità bhṛiśam
arddha-sañjàta-śasy' eva toyam pràpya vasun-dharà, 52
s' aivaṃ sametya vyapaniya tandràṃ śànta-jvarà harṣa-vivṛiddha-
sattvà,
raràja Bhaimi samavàpta-kàmà śit'-àṃśunà ràtrir iv' oditena. 53
iti Nal' opàkhyàne catur-viṃśatitamaḥ sargaḥ.

XXV.

Vṛihadaśva uvàca,
atha tàṃ vyuṣito ràtriṃ Nalo ràjà sv-alan-kṛitaḥ
Vaidarbhyà sahitaḥ kàle dadarśa vasu-dhà-'dhipam. 1
tato 'bhivàdayàmàsa prayataḥ śvaśuraṃ Nalaḥ.
tato 'nu Damayanti ca vavande pitaraṃ śubhà. 2
tam Bhimaḥ pratijagràha putravat parayà mudà
yathà-'rham pùjayitvà ca samàśvàsayata prabhuḥ
Nalena sahitàṃ tatra Damayantim pati-vratàm. 3
tàm arhaṇàṃ Nalo ràjà pratigṛihya yathà-vidhi
paricaryàṃ svakàṃ tasmai yathàvat pratyavedayat. 4

tato babhúva nagare su-mahán harṣa-ȷaḥ svanaḥ
ȷanasya samprahṛıṣṭasya Nalaṃ dṛıṣṭvá tathá-gatam. 5
aśobhayanta nagaram patáká-dhvaȷa-málınam.
sıktáḥ su-mṛıṣṭa-puṣp'-áḍhyá ráȷa-margáḥ sv-alan-kṛıtáḥ, 6
dvárı, dvárı ca pauráṇám puṣpa-bhan-gaḥ prakalpıtaḥ,
arcıtánı ca sarváṇı devat'-áyatanánı ca, 7
Ṛıtuparṇo 'pı śuśráva Váhuka-cchadminaṃ Nalam
Damayantyá samáyuktaṃ, ȷahṛıṣe ca nar'-ádhıpaḥ. 8
tam ánáyya Nalo ráȷá kṣamayámása párthıvam,
sa ca taṃ kṣamayámása hetubhır buddhı-sammıtaıḥ. 9
sa sat-kṛıto mahi-pálo Naıṣadhaṃ vısmıt'-ánanaḥ,
"dıṣṭyá sameto dáraıḥ svaır bhaván," ıty abhyanandata, 10
"kaccıt tu n' áparádhaṃ te kṛıtaván asmı, Naıṣadha,
aȷnáta-vásaṃ vasato mad-gṛıhe, vasu-dhá-'dhıpa? 11
yadı vá buddhı-púrváṇı yady abuddhyá 'pı kánıcıt
mayá kṛıtány akáryáṇı, tánı tvaṃ kṣantum arhası." 12
Nala uváca,
na me 'parádhaṃ kṛıtaváns tvaṃ sv-alpam apı, párthıva;
kṛıte 'pı ca na me kopaḥ; kṣantavyaṃ hı mayá tava. 13
púrvaṃ hy apı sakhá me 'sı sambandhi ca, ȷan'-ádhıpa;
ata úrddhvaṃ tu bhúyas tvam pritım áhartum arhası. 14
sarva-kámaıḥ su-vıhıtaıḥ sukham asmy uṣıtas tvayı;
na tathá sva-gṛıhe, ráȷan, yathá tava gṛıhe sadá. 15
ıdaṃ c' aıva haya-ȷnánaṃ tvadiyam mayı tıṣṭhatı,
tad upákartum ıcchámı manyase yadı, párthıva." 16
evam uktvá dadau vıdyám Ṛıtuparṇáya Naıṣadhaḥ,
sa ca tám pratıȷagráha vıdhı-dṛıṣṭena karmaṇá. 17

gṛhitvà c' àśva-hṛdayaṃ, ràȷan, Bhàn-gàsurır nṛı-paḥ,
Nıṣadh'-àdhıpateś c' àpı dattvà 'kṣa-hṛdayaṃ nṛı-paḥ,
sùtam anyam upàdàya yayau sva-puram eva ha. 18
Ṛıtuparṇe gate, ràȷan, Nalo ràȷà, vıśàm pate,
nagare Kuṇḍıne kàlam n' àtıdirgham ıv' àvasat. 19

ıtı Nal'-opàkhyàne pañca-vıṃśatıtamaḥ sargaḥ.

XXVI.

Vṛhadaśva uvàca,

sa màsam uṣya, Kaunteya, Bhimam àmantrya Naıṣadhaḥ,
puràd alpa-parivàro ȷagàma Nıṣadhàn pratı. 1
rathen' aıkena śubhreṇa dantıbhıḥ parı-ṣo-ḍaśaıḥ,
pañcàśadbhır hayaıś c' aıva, ṣaṭ-śataıś ca padàtıbhıḥ, 2
sa kampayann ıva mahiṃ tvaramàṇo mahi-patıḥ,
praviveśa su-saṃrabdhas taras' aıva mahà-manàḥ. 3
tataḥ Puṣkaram àsàdya Virasena-suto Nalaḥ
uvàca, "divyàva punar, bahu vıttam mayà 'rȷıtam; 4
Damayanti ca yac c' ànyad mama kıñcana vıdyate,
eṣa vaı mama sannyàsas, tava ràȷyaṃ tu, Puṣkara: 5
punaḥ pravartatàṃ dyùtam," ıtı, "nıścıtà matıḥ,
paṇen' aıkena, bhadraṃ te, pràṇayoś ca paṇàvahe. 6
ȷıtvà para-svam àhṛtya, ràȷyaṃ và, yadı và vasu,
pratıpàṇaḥ pradàtavyaḥ, paramo dharma ucyate. 7
na ced vàñchası dyùtaṃ tvaṃ yuddha-dyùtam pravartatàm,
dvaı-rathen' àstu śàntıs tava và, mama và, nṛı-pa. 8
vaṃśa-bhoȷyam ıdaṃ ràȷyam arthıtavyaṃ yathà-tathà,

yena ken' àpy upàyena vṛddhànàm iti śàsanam, 9
dvayor ekatare buddhiḥ kriyatàm adya, Puṣkara,
kaitaven' àkṣavatyàṃ và, yuddhe và nàmyatàṃ dhanuḥ." 10
Naiṣadhen' aivam uktas tu Puṣkaraḥ prahasann iva,
dhruvam àtma-jayam matvà pratyàha pṛthivi-patim, 11
"diṣṭyà tvayà 'rjitaṃ vittam pratipàṇàya, Naiṣadha!
diṣṭyà ca duṣkaraṃ karma Damayantyàḥ kṣayaṃ gatam! 12
diṣṭyà ca dhriyase, ràjan, sa-dàro 'dya, mahà-bhuja!
dhanen' ànena vai Bhaimi jitena samalan-kṛtà, 13
màm upasthàsyàti, vyaktaṃ divi Śakram iv' àpsaràḥ.
nityaśo hi smaràmi tvàm pratikṣe 'pi ca, Naiṣadha; 14
devanena mama pritir na bhavaty asuhṛd-gaṇaiḥ,
jitvà tv adya var'-àrohàṃ Damayantim aninditàm, 15
kṛta-kṛtyo bhaviṣyàmi, sà hi me nityaśo hṛdi."
śrutvà tu tasya tà vàco bahv-abaddha-pralàpinaḥ, 16
iyeṣa sa śiraś chettuṃ khaḍgena kupito Nalaḥ,
smayans tu roṣa-tàmr'-àkṣas tam uvàca tato Nalaḥ, 17
"paṇàvaḥ; kiṃ vyàharase? jito, na vyàhariṣyasi."
tataḥ pràvartata dyùtam Puṣkarasya, Nalasya ca, 18
eka-pàṇena vireṇa Nalena so paràjitaḥ,
sa ratna-koṣa-nicayaiḥ pràṇena paṇito 'pi ca. 19
jitvà ca Puṣkaràṃ ràjà prahasann idam abravit,
"mama sarvam idaṃ ràjyam avyagraṃ, hata-kaṇṭakam. 20
Vaidarbhi na tvayà śakyà, ràj'-àpasada, vikṣitum,
tasyàs tvaṃ sa-parivàro, mùḍha, dàsatvam àgataḥ. 21
na tvayà tat kṛtaṃ karma, yen' àhaṃ vijitaḥ purà,
Kalinà tat kṛtaṃ karma, tvaṃ ca, mùḍha, na budhyase. 22

n' áham para-kṛıtaṃ doṣaṃ tvayy ádhásye kathañcana.
yathá-sukhaṃ vaı ȷiva tvam, práṇán avasrıȷámı te, 23
tath' aıva sarva-sambháraṃ svam aṃśaṃ vıtarámı te.
taṭh' aıva ca mama pritıs tvayı, vira, na saṃśayaḥ, 24
sauhárdaṃ c' ápı me tvatto na kadácıt prahásyatı.
Puṣkara, tvaṃ hı me bhrátá, sañȷiva śaradaḥ śatam!" 25
evaṃ Nalaḥ sántvayıtvá bhrátaraṃ satya-vıkramaḥ,
sva-puram preṣayámása parıśvaȷya punaḥ, punaḥ. 26
sántvıto Naıṣadhen' aıvam Puṣkaraḥ pratyuváca ha,
Puṇyaślokaṃ tadá, ráȷann, abhıvádya kṛıt'-áñȷalıḥ, 27
"kirtır astu tav' ákṣayyá, ȷiva varṣ'-áyutaṃ sukhi,
yo me vıtarası práṇán, adhıṣṭhánaṃ ca, párthıva." 28
sa tathá sat-kṛıto ráȷná másam uṣya tadá nṛı-paḥ
prayayau sva-puraṃ hṛıṣṭaḥ Puṣkaraḥ sva-ȷan'-ávṛıtaḥ, 29
mahatyá senayá sárddhaṃ vınitaıḥ parıcárakaıḥ,
bhráȷamána ıv' ádıtyo vapuṣá, Bharata-'rṣabha. 30
prasthápya Puṣkaraṃ ráȷá vıttavantam anámayam
pravıveśa puriṃ śrimán atyartham upaśobhıtám,
pravıśya sántvayámása pauráñś ca Nıṣadh'-ádhıpaḥ. 31
paura-ȷána-padáś c' ápı samprahṛıṣṭa-tanú-ruháḥ,
úcuḥ práñȷalayaḥ sarve sámátya-pramukhá ȷanáḥ, 32
"adya sma nırvṛıtá, ráȷan, pure, ȷana-pade 'pı ca,
upásıtum punaḥ práptá devá ıva śata-kratum." 33
praśánte tu pure hṛıṣṭe, sampravṛıtte mah'-otsave,
mahatyá senayá ráȷá Damayantim upánayat. 34
Damayantim apı pıtá sat-kṛıtya para-vira-há
prásthápayad amey'-átmá Bhimo bhima-parákramaḥ. 35

âgatâyâṃ tu Vaidarbhyâṃ sa-putrâyâṃ Nalo nṛi-paḥ
vartayâmâsa mudito deva-râḍ iva Nandane. 36
tataḥ prakâśatâṃ yâto Jambudvipe sa râjasu,
punaḥ śaśâsa tad râjyam pratyâhṛitya mahâ-yaśâḥ,
ije ca vividhair yajnair vidhivac c' âpta-dakṣiṇaiḥ. 37

iti Nal' opâkhyâṇaṃ samâptam.

VOCABULARY TO NALA.

a

atas, *adv.* hence. ataḥ-param, beyond this.

atra, *adv.* here.

atha, *conj.* *used generally at the beginning of a sentence;* and, now.

atha vâ, *conj.* or.

adya[1], *adv.* to-day, now.

aṃśa, *m.* a share, portion; a shoulder.

aṃśu, *m.* a ray of light.

aṃśumat, *adj.* having rays, radiant: *m.* the sun.

akṣa[2], *m.* an eye; dice; a wheel; a chariot.

akṣa-jna, *adj.* dice-knowing.

akṣa-dyuta, *m. n.* a game at dice.

akṣa-naipuṇya, *n.* skill at dice.

akṣa-priya, *adj.* dice-loving.

akṣa-mada-sammanna, *adj.* maddened- by madness- for dice.

akṣavati, *f.* a game at dice.

akṣi, *n.* an eye.

akṣauhiṇi, *f.* an army.

adhyakṣa, *m.* an overseer, a chief.

antar-ikṣa[3], *n.* the air, sky.

antar-ikṣa-ga, *m.* (sky-goer,) a bird.

ikṣ, 1. *m.* ikṣate, ikṣâñcakre, ikṣitâ, ikṣiṣyate, aikṣiṣṭa: see. ava-, behold, examine.

ikṣaṇa, *n.* sight; an eye.

parikṣâ, *f.* inspection.

parokṣa, *adj.* out of sight, invisible.

parokṣatâ, *f.* invisibility.

pratyakṣa, *adj.* within sight, visible.

samakṣam, *adv.* in the presence *of.*

sâkṣât, *adv.* in sight.

sâkṣin, *m.* an eye-witness.

sâkṣivat, *adv.* as an eye-witness.

ag, 1. *a.* go tortuously.

an-g, 1. *a.* an-gati; ânan-ga: go. 10. *a.* an-gayati, mark.

agni[4], *m.* fire; the god of fire, Agni.

agni-dagdha, *adj.* consumed by fire.

akâma	kam	akliṣṭa	kliṣ	agama	gam
akârya	kṛi	akṣaya	kṣi	agâdha	gâdh
akâla	kal	akhila	khan	acala	cal
akṛitâtman	kṛi	aga	gam	acira	ci

[1] *Pali,* ajja; *Hindustani,* âj.

[2] οκκο; oculus; *Gothic,* augo; *German,* auge; *Anglo-Saxon,* eâge; *Russian,* oko.

[3] *Pal.* antalika.

[4] ignis; *Rus.* ogon'.

agni-puro-gama, *adj.* whom Agni precedes.
agnimat, *adj.* having fire, fire-worshipping.
agni-śikhà, *f.* a flame of fire.
agni-hotra, *n.* a sacred fire.
agra, *adj.* chief: the top, summit. agre, *adv.* in front.
agra-ja, *adj.* elder-born.
agratas, *adv.* in front.
agrahàra, *m.* an endowment of lands and villages.
an·ga, *n.* a limb; a body: help: *the name of six sacred books.*
an·gana, *n.* a court yard.
an·ganà, *f.* a woman.
an·gustha[1], *m.* a thumb.
an·gustha-màtraka, *adj.* having the size of a thumb.
anàgas, *adj.* sinless.
apàn·ga, *n.* the outer corner of an eye.
avyagra, *adj.* undisturbed.
àgas, *n.* sin.
ekàgra, *adj.* having but one end, eager, intent.
aikàgrya, *n.* eagerness.
vyagra, *adj.* troubled.
sàgnika, *adj.* together with Agni.
agh, 10. *a.* sin.
agha, *n.* sin.
anagha, *adj.* sinless.
an·k, 1. *m.* and 10. *a.* mark.
an·ka, *m.* a mark; the flank, *the part above the hips.*
ac, *and* añc, 1. *a. m.* añcati, -te; ànañca, -ce; añcità; *prec.* añcyàt, acyàt: *p.* añcyate *and* acyate. go, honour. añc, 10. *a.* añcayati: speak distinctly.
añcita, *adj.* erect, *of the hair from delight.*
aparàn·-mukha, *adj.* with unaverted face.
nyagrodha, *m.* the Indian figtree, ficus indica.
paràc, *adj.* going elsewhere, averted.
paràn·-mukha, *adj.* with averted face.
pratyac, *adj.* western.
pràk, *adv.* previously; eastward.
pràc, *adj.* eastern.
samyak, *adv.* together; at once; wholly; rightly.
aj, 1. *a.* go; throw. añj, 7. *and* 10. *a.* anakti; ànañja; añjità, *and* an·ktà; añjiṣyati, *and* an·kṣyati; àñjit; añjitvà, an·ktvà, *and* aktvà; akta. go; shine; anoint[2]. vi-, show.
aja, *m.* ajà, *f.* a goat[3].
aja-gara, *m.* a goat-eater, a boa.
ajina, *n.* a goat's skin, *used as a seat.*
añjali, *m.* the hollow formed by putting the hands together, as if to hold water: the hands thus joined are carried to the head, as a respectful salutation.
abhivyakta, *adj.* distinct.
avyakta, *adj.* indistinct.
kṛit'-àñjali, *adj.* having the hands joined in an añjali.

acetana	cit	atimàtra	mà	adina	di
acyuta	cyu	atiyaśas	yaś	adbhuta	bhù
atandrita	tandrà	atula	tul	adya	a
atidurdharṣa	dhṛiṣ	aditi	diti	adhigamana	gam

[1] *Persian*, anguṣt. [2] ungere. [3] αἰξ, αἰγος.

pràñjali, *adj. id.*
vyakta, *p. p. p.* manifest, distinct.
aṭ, 1. *a. m.* aṭati, -te; àṭa; aṭità; aṭiṣyati; àṭit: go; walk.
aṭavi, *f.* a forest.
aṇ, 1. *a.* aṇiti; àṇa; aṇità: sound.
aṇu, *adj.* small.
aṇḍa, *n.* an egg.
aṇḍa-ja, *adj.* egg-born; *m.* a bird.
at, 1. *a.* atati; àta; atità; atiṣyati; àtit: go continuously.
ati-, *insep. part.* beyond; very.
atithi, *m.* a visitor, guest.
ativa, *adv.* very.
ad[1], 2. *a.* atti; 1 *pret.* àdat; àda (2 *s.* àditha); attà; atsyati: *p.* adyate; anna: eat.
anna, *p. p. p.* eaten: *n.* food.
danta, *m.* a tooth[2].
dantin, *adj.* toothed; tusked: *m.* an elephant.
svàd, 1. *m.* be pleasant to the taste.
svàdu, *adj.* sweet[3].
adas, *n.* asau, *m. f. pron.* this; that.
adha.
adhama, *adj.* lowest; very mean, very vile.
adhara, *adj.* lower: the lower lip.
adhas, *adv.* below, down; *prp. w. g.* under.
adhastàt, *prp. w. g.* under.
adhi-, *insep. part.* over, upon.
adhika, *adj.* more; greater.
adhunà, *adv.* now.
adhvan, *m.* a way, road.
an-, *and before consonants,* a-, not, in-, un-[4].
an, 2. *a.* aniti; 1 *pret.* anit, *and* ànat; anitu; anyàt; àna; anità; aniṣyati; ànit; anitum: *p.* anyate: breathe; live[5].
anas, *n.* a cart: breath, life; a mother; birth: boiled rice.
àna, *m.* the breath.
ànana, *n.* the mouth; the face.
pràṇa[6], *m. pl.* the breath, life.
pràṇa-yàtrà, *f.* the means of living.
mahà-'nasa, *m. n.* (having much food;) a kitchen.
anu, *prp. sep. and insep.* after according to.
ant, 1. *a.* antati: bind.
aty-antam, *adv.* exceedingly.
anantara, *adj.* immediate.
anta, *m. n.* an end; the end; death.
anta-kara, *m.* (the end-maker), the god of death.
antar[7], *prp. insep.* within; under.
antara, *n.* the inner part, middle; an interval; the difference; an opportunity.
antavat, *adj.* finite.
anti, *adv.* near.

adhipa	pà	anagha	agh	anàthavat	ni
adhiṣṭhàna	sthà	anabhijna	jnà	anàmaya	am
adhyakṣa	akṣ	anavadya	vad	anùttama	ut
adhyàya	i	anasùyaka	as	anupama	mà

[1] ἐδειν; edere; *Go.* itan; *A. S.* etan; *Ge.* essen; *Rus.* yest'.
[2] ὀδους; dens; *Pers.* dandàn; *Go.* tunθus; *Ge.* zahn; Welsh, dant.
[3] suàvis.
[4] ἀν-, in-.
[5] ἀνεμος, animus.
[6] *Pal.* pàṇa.
[7] inter; *Pers.* andar.

antıka, *n.* neighbourhood.
abhyadhıka, *adj.* superior.
ekànta, *adj.* excessive: private.
tad-anantara, *adj.* next to him *or* it.
samanta, *adj.* all; entire: *m.* limit; boundary.
andha, *adj.* blind.
anya[1], *adj.* other.
anyatama, *adj.* any one out of several.
anyatra, *adv.* elsewhere.
anyathà, *adv.* otherwise.
anyadà, *adv.* at another time.
anyo-'nya, *adj.* each other.
ap[2], *f.* water.
ap-saras, *f.* a water-dweller, nymph.
ab-bhakṣa, *adj.* feeding on water.
abhra[3], *n.* (= ab-bhara, water bearing,) a cloud.
àpa-gà, *f.* a river.
dvipa, *m.* an island.
dvipın, *m.* an islander; a leopard, *from its spots.*
vyabhra, *adj.* cloudless.
samipa, *m.* (confluence;) neighbourhood.
apa-[4], *prp. insep.* from, away.
apı-[5], *prp. insep.* upon: *conj.* also, even.
abhı-, *prp. insep. and sep.* unto, towards.
am, 10. *a.* àmayatı: be sick.
anàmaya, *m.* health.
àmaya, *m.* sickness.
àmra, *m.* a mango tree.
amà, *prp.* with.
amàtya, *and* àmàtya, *m.* a councillor.
aràla, *adj.* curved.
ark, 10. *a.* arkayatı: burn; praise.
arka[6], *m.* the sun.
udarka, *m.* sun-rise; future time.
arc, 1. *a.* arcatı; ànarca; arcıtà; arcıṣyatı; àrcit: honour, salute.
arcana[7], *n.* the act of honouring.
arȷ, 1. *a.* arȷatı; ànarȷa; arȷıtà: gain by toil; get; do.
araṇya, *n.* a forest.
arth, 10. *m.* arthayate: ask; demand.
aty-artha, *adj.* beyond reason.
artha, *m.* any thing; wealth; profit; cause, reason. *Used adverbially in acc. dat. inst. and loc.* for the sake of.
arthın, *adj.* asking, desiring; needy.
samartha, *adj.* able, fit; powerful.
sàmarthya, *n.* ability, fitness, power.
sàrtha, *m.* a multitude of travelling merchants, a caravan.
sàrthaka, *m.* a merchant.
sàrtha-vàha, *m.* the leader of a caravan.

anumata	man	anuśàsana	śàs	antaḥpura	pṛi
anuvrata	vṛı	anṛıta	ṛı	antarikṣa	akṣ
anuràga	rañȷ	anṛıśaṃsa	nṛı	anvıta	ı
anuvartın	vṛıt	aneka	eka	anveṣṭṛı	ıṣ

[1] *Rus.* ėnόı; αλλος; alıus; *Go.* anthar.
[2] *Pers.* àb; *Wel.* afon; aqua; amnis.
[3] *Pal.* abbha; *Pers.* abr.
[4] απο, ab; *Go.* af.
[5] επι.
[6] *Hind.* ark.
[7] *Hind.* arcanà.

ard, 1. *a.* ardatı ; ànarda ; ardıtà ; ardıṣyatı ; àrdit ; àrta : go ; ask ; injure, annoy.
àrta, *p. p. p.* injured, pained.
arh, 1. *a.* arhatı ; ànarha : arhıtà ; arhıṣyatı ; àrhit : be worthy ; deserve ; be equal, fit ; be able ; ought ; honour.
arha, *adj.* worthy.
arhana, *n.* the act of honouring ; worship.
yathà-'rham, *adv.* worthily, fitly.
al, 1. *a.* alatı ; àla ; alıtà ; alıṣyatı ; àlit : repel ; suffice ; adorn.
alan-kṛıta, *p. p. p.* adorned.
alam, *indec.* an ornament : *int.* enough ! no more !
alpa, *adj.* small, little.
samalan-kṛıta, *p. p. p.* fully adorned.
sv-alan-kṛıta, *p. p. p. id.*
sv-alpa, *adj.* very small.
ava-, *prp. insep.* down.
aś, 9. *a.* aśnàtı ; àśa ; aśıtà ; aśıṣyatı ; àśit : eat, enjoy. 5. *m.* aśnute ; ànaśe, (2. *s.* ànaśıse *and* ànakṣe, *pl.* ànaśıdhve, ànaḍḍhve ;) aśıtà *and* aṣṭà ; aśıṣyate *and* akṣyate ; àśıṣṭa *and* àṣṭa. pervade, occupy ; heap.
aśana, *adj.* -eating.
aśru, *n.* a tear. *See* daṃś.
aśvattha, *m.* the holy fig-tree ; its fruit.
aṣṭan[1], *num.* eight.
aṣṭama, *adj.* eighth.
àśà[2], *f.* hope.
àśıs, *f.* hope ; a benediction.
àśir-vàda, *m.* a benediction.
nıràśın, *adj.* hopeless.
naıràśya, *n.* hopelessness.
as[3], 2. *a.* astı, (2 *s.* ası ;) *pot.* syàt ; *imp.* astu, (2 *s.* edhı ;) *impf.* àsit ; 2 *pret.* àsa : *part pres.* sat : be.
asatya, *adj.* untrue.
asu, *n. s.* thought, feeling : *m. pl.* asavas, breath.
paràsu, *adj.* dead.
vyasu, *adj. id.*
sat, *part. pres.* being ; true ; good.
sat-kàra, *m.* hospitality ; respect, honour.
sattama, *adj. sup.* best.
sattva, *n.* mind ; an animal ; a sentient being.
satya, *adj.* true : *n.* truth.
satya-vàdın, *adj.* truth-speaking.
svastı, *ind.* welfare ; a benediction.
as, 4. *a.* asyatı ; àsa ; asıtà ; asıṣyatı ; àsthat ; asıtvà, *and* astvà : *p.* asyate ; àsı ; asta : throw, send.
anasùyaka, *adj.* unenvious.
asana, *n.* the act of throwing *or* sending.
abhyàsa, *m.* neighbourhood.
asùyaka, *adj.* envious.
asùyatı, -te, makes angry, slanders, envies.
astra, *n.* a weapon.
àsa, *m.* a bow.
kṛıtàstra, *adj.* skilful in weapons.

apakàratà	kṛı	aparàdha	ràdh	apaharaṇa	hṛı
apakṛıta	,,	aparedyus	dıv	apan-ga	an-g
apara	pṛi	apaścıma	paśca	apàya	ı
aparàjıta	jı	apasada	sad	apraja	jan

[1] *Pal.* aṭṭha ; *Pers.* hast ; *Hind.* àṭh ; οκτω ; octo ; *Go.* ahtau ; *Rus.* osm'.

[2] *Hind. ıd.*

[3] εσεσθαι, esse.

nyåsa, *m.* the act of throwing down; a deposit.
vyasana, *n.* a calamity, misfortune.
sannyåsa, *m.* a renunciation; a deposit, stake.
ah, *v. used only in the 2nd pret.* åha, åttha, åha, åhatus, åhathus,—åhus: said.
akṛıt'-åtman, *adj.* unrestrained.
asmat, *pron. crude form of the first person.*
aham[1], *pron.* I.
åtma-ȷa, *m.* a son.
åtman, *m.* the mind, soul, self.
åtma-bhåva, *m.* self-existence.
åtma-bhů, *adj.* self-existent, *applied to Brahmå, Vıṣṇu, Śıva, and Kåma.*
åtmavat, self-possessed.
kṛıt'-åtman, *adj.* self-restrained.
mat-, *px.* my-.
madiya, *adj.* mine.
aho, *int. denoting wonder.*
ahovat, alas!
ahosvıt, *conj.* or.
å-, *prp. insep.* unto, towards: *with abl.* as far as: -ısh.
åtura, diseased.
åḍhya, *adj.* wealthy; abundant.
-ådı, *adj.* -first; *used as* et cętera: *m.* the beginning.
åp[2], 5. *and* 1. *a.* åpnotı, åpatı; åpa; åptå; åpsyatı; åpat; åpta: *des.* ipsatı: get, obtain.
ips, *desid.* wish.
samåpta[3], *p. p. p.* complete.
åmalaka, *m. n. a plant,* phyllanthus emblıca.
åśu, *adv.* quickly.
aśva[4], *m.* a horse.
aśva-kovıda, *adj.* skilled in horses.
aśvın, (a horseman;) *du.* aśvınau, *two brothers of great beauty, children of the sun.*
ås, 2. *m.* åste, (2 *s.* åsse,) asåṅcakre, åsıtå, åsıṣyate, åsıṣṭa, åsina: sit; dwell.
åsana, *n.* the act of sitting; a seat.
åsya, *n.* the face; the mouth.
ı[5], 1. *a.* ayatı, åyat, ayatu, ayet, ıyåya, eṣit, etum, ıta: *p.* iyate.
2. *a.* etı, eta, etu, ıyåt.
2. *m. w.* adhı, adhite, adhyaıta, adhitåm, adhıyita, adhıȷage, adhyaıṣṭa: go.
atı-, go beyond; excel; transgress; elapse; die.
adhı-, 2. *m.* read, study, call to mind.
anu-, follow; accompany.
abhı-, approach, enter.
ava-, understand; look at, examine.
upa-, go near; enter; take refuge with; obtain.
vı-, perish.
adhyaya, *and* adhyåya, *m.* a lesson, chapter, section.
anvıta, *adj.* endowed with, possessed of.
apåya, *m.* departure; escape; a way of escape.
abhıpråya, *m.* meaning.

apratıma	må	abhıpråya	ı	abhikṣṇa	akṣa
apråptakåla	åp	abhıbhåṣın	bhåṣ	abhyåsa	as
abhıkåma	kam	abhımukha	mukha	amara	mṛı
abhıȷana	ȷan	abhıvådaka	vad	amarṣa	mṛıṣ
abhıȷna	ȷnå	abhıśåpa	śap	amarṣaṇa	,,

[1] εγω; ego; *Go.* ık.
[2] aptus.
[3] *Pal.* samatta.
[4] *Pal.* assa; *Pers.* asp, sıpåh, sıpåhi; *Hind.* asva, asvår; ἵππος; equus.
[5] ειναι; ire.

-aya, *m.* -going.
ayana, *n.* a way, road.
avyaya, *adj.* undying, imperishable.
àyus, *m.* age, duration of life.
àyuṣmat, *adj.* long-lived.
ıta, *past p.* gone.
udaya, *m.* the rising *of a star.*
upàya, *m.* an artifice, a contrivance.
nyàya, *m.* fitness; good conduct.
nyàyya, *adj.* fit.
paràyaṇa, *adj.* adhering to, dependent on.
paryaya, *m.* contrariety, perversity.
pràya, *adj.* like; *n.* sin.
vıparita, *adj.* adverse.
vıparyaya, *m.* reverse of fortune; destruction; enmity.
vyaya, *m.* ruin.
samanvıta, *adj.* =anvıta.
samıtı, *f.* an assembly.
samaya, *m.* a coming together: time, season, opportunity; an agreement, oath.
sahàya, *m.* a companion, helper, follower.
sàhàyya, *n.* companionship, help, alliance.

1

ıtas, *adv.* from hence; from this world.
ıtara, *pron.* an other.
ıtı, *conj.* thus: *used to mark the end of a speech.*
ıdam, *n.* ayam, *m.* ıyam, *f.* this.
ıva[1], *adv.* like, as if: *it follows the thing to which the comparison is made.*
ıha, *adv.* here, hither.
eva, *conj.* indeed.
evam, *adv.* thus.
ın.g, 1. *a.* ın.gatı, ın.gan̄cakàra, ın.gıtà: move one's self.
ın.gıta, *n.* a gesture; a token, mark.
ın.guda, *m.* the name of a plant, the ingua.
ınd, 1. *a.* rule.
ındu, *m.* the moon.
Indra[2], *m. the god of the sky: in comp.* -chief.
Indra-puro-gama, *adj.* preceded by Indra.
ındrıya, *n.* any one of the senses.
ındh, 7. *m.* ınddhe; ınddhàn̄cakre, *or* idhe; ındhıtà; ındhıṣyatı; aındhıṣṭa: *p.* ıdhyate; ıddha: set on fire.
ıddha, *p. p. p.* bright.
ındhana, *n.* fuel; wood.
ıṣ[3], 6. *a.* ıcchatı, wish; seek.
4. *a.* ıṣyatı; ıyeṣa, (*pl.* iṣus;) eṣıtà, *and* eṣṭà; eṣıṣyatı; aıṣit; ıṣıtvà, *and* ıṣṭvà: *p.* ıṣyate; ıṣṭa; ıyeṣa, &c.; ıṣıta): go; lead. *Caus.* send.
anveṣṭrı, *m.* one who seeks.
ıṣu, *m.* an arrow.
preṣya[4], *adj.* that may be sent: *m. f.* a servant.
preṣyatà, *f.* servitude.
ir, 1. *and* 10. *a.* irayatı, iratı: utter; send.
iśa, *m.* a lord; *a name of Śıva.*

amànuṣa	man	aya	ı	araṇya	rı
amıtra	mıd	ayana	"	aràla	"
amrıta	mrı	ayam	"	arı	"
ameya	mà	ayuta	yu	arındama	"

[1] *Pal.* va.
[2] *Pal.* Inda.
[3] *Rus.* iskàt'.
[4] *Pers.* firıṣta.

iśvara[1], *m. id.*

aıśvarya, *n.* lordship, authority, sovereignty.

trı-daś'-eśvaràs, *m. pl.* the thirteen lords, *that is, all the gods except* Brahmà, Śıva, and Vışṇu.

ugra, *adj.* severe, strict, harsh.

uc, 4. *a.* ucyatı ; uvoca ; ucıtà ; ucışyatı ; ucit ; ocıtvà ; ucıta : meet together ; agree.

ucıta, *p. p. p.* fit, worthy, skilful.

oka, *and* okas, *m.* a house.

tath'-ocıta, *adj.* fit for, or deserving this.

dıv'-aukas, *m.* (a sky-dweller,) a god.

ut, *prp. insep.* up, upwards.

anuttama, *adj.* without a superior ; highest, best.

ucca, *adj.* high.

uccaıs, *adv.* aloud.

uttama, *adj. sup.* highest, best.

uttara, *adj. compar.* higher ; northern : *n.* an answer.

uttariya, *n.* an outer garment.

uta, *conj.* or.

udumbara, *m.* ficus glomeràta.

und, 7. *a.* unattı ; undàñcakàra ; undıtà, undışyatı ; *pot.* undyàt ; *prec.* udyàt ; aundit ; unna : make wet.

uda[2], *and* udaka, *n.* water.

udra[3], *m.* an otter.

samudra, *m.* the sea ; the ocean.

samudra-ga, *m.* a river.

upa-[4], *prp. insep.* near.

uparı[5], *prp. w. g.* above, over.

upala, *m.* a stone, rock ; a precious stone.

ubha.

ubhau[6], *dual.* both.

uras[7], *m.* the breast.

ura-ga[8], *m.* a serpent.

urasya, *m.* a son.

uṣ, 1. *a.* oṣatı ; oṣàñcakàra, *and* uvoṣa, (*pl.* ùṣus ;) oṣıtà ; oṣışyatı ; auṣit ; *part. pres.* uṣat, *p. perf.* uvàsa : burn ; annoy, hurt.

uṣṭra[9], *m.* a camel.

uṣṇa, *adj.* hot.

uṣman, *m.* heat.

oṣa, *m.* the act of burning, heat.

oṣadhı, *and* oṣadhi, *f.* any annual plant.

auṣadha, *n.* any medicine.

ùna, less ; one less ; *as,* ùnavıṃśatı = 19.

ùh, 1. *m.* ùhate ; ùhàñcakre ; ùhıtà ; ùhışyate ; auhışṭa : *caus.* ùhayatı : aujıhat : gather ; understand.

ùhıni, *f.* a collection ; an army.

vyùha, *m.* a crowd, multitude.

ṛı, 9. *a.* ṛıṇàtı ; àra, (2 *s.* àrıtha, *pl.* àrus ;) artà, arıtà, *and* arità ; arışyatı ; *prec.* aryàt ; àrat : go.

anṛıta, *adj.* untrue.

arı, an enemy.

arṇava, *m.* an ocean.

àrya, *adj.* noble, worthy.

arışṭa	rış	avadya	vad	avıśan·ka	śan·k
arṇava	ṛı	avaśa	vaś	avıśeṣa	śış
ardha	ṛıdh	avaśya	,,	avıśoka	śuc
avakartana	kṛıt	avastra	vas	avyaya	ı

[1] *Pal.* ıssara.

[2] ὑδωρ ; ùdus, unda ; *Rus.* vodá ; *Go.* vato.

[3] *ενυδρις.*

[4] ὑπο ; sub.

[5] *Pers.* bar ; ὑπερ ; super ; *Go.* ufar.

[6] *αμφω* ; ambo ; *Go.* baı ; *Rus.* óba.

[7] *Hind.* ur.

[8] *Hind.* urag.

[9] *Pers.* ṣutur.

udàra, *adj.* lofty, noble, great, munificent.
ṛita, *adj.* true.
ṛitu[1], *m.* a season of the year.
ṛite, *prp. w. ac.* except.
audàrya, *n.* nobleness, munificence.
dvai-ratha, *n.* a duel in chariots.
ratha[2], *m.* a chariot.
rathin, *adj.* having a chariot.
rath'-opastha, *m.* the seat of a charioteer, *which was below the main body of the car.*
sa-ratha, *m.* one who is with a chariot.
sàrathi, *m.* a charioteer.
sàrathya, *n.* skill in driving; the art of driving.
ṛikṣa[3], *m.* a bear.
ṛikṣavat, *adj.* abounding in bears: *m. the name of a mountain.*
ṛich, 1. *a.* ṛicchati; aràñcakàra: go.
ṛidh, 4. *and* 5. *a.* ṛidhyati, ṛidhnoti; ànardha; ardhità; ardhiṣyati; àrdhit; ardhitvà, *and* ṛiddhvà; ṛiddha: grow; prosper.
ardha, *adj.* half: *n.* a half.
ṛiddha, *p. p. p.* grown; prosperous; rich.
samṛiddha, *adj.* full, prosperous.
sàrdham, *prp. w. inst.* with.
ṛiṣabha, *m.* a bull: *in comp.* chief.
ṛiṣi, *m.* a wise and holy person.
eka[4], *adj.* one.
aneka, *adj.* many.
anekaśas, *adj.* by many; many times.
ekatara[5], *adj.* one out of two, either.
ekatas, *adv.* on one side; in one manner.
ekatra, *adv.* in one place, together.
ekàkin, *adj.* alone, lonely.
ekàdaśa, *adj.* eleventh.
ekàdaśan[6], *num.* eleven.
ekaikaśas, *adv.* separately, singly.

oj
ojas, *n.* brightness, strength.

ka
katara, *adj.* which of the two?
katham, *adv.* how?
kadà, *adv.* when?
kadàcit, *adv.* at some time.
karhi, *adv.* when?
karhicit, *adv.* at any time.
kim[7], *n.* kas, *m.* kà, *f.* what? who?
kaccit, *an interrogative particle.*
kiñcana, *n.* kaścana, *m.* kàcana, *f.* any thing whatever, any one.
kiñcit, *n.* kaścit, *m.* kàcit, *f.* some thing, some one.
kitava, *m.* a gambler; a cheat.
kintu, *conj.* but.
kinnu, *ind.* how much less! what?
kutas, *adv.* whence?
kutra, *adv.* where?
kaitava, *n.* gambling.
kva, *adv.* where?

avyagra	ag	asakṛit	kṛi	asuhṛid	hṛid
aśaknuvat	śak	asita	so	asau	adas
aśeṣa	śiṣ	asukha	khan	asveda	svid
aśoka	śuc	asura	sura	ahan	dah

1 ritus.
2 rota.
3 αρκτος; ursus.
4 *Pers.* yak.
5 ἑκατερος.
6 ἑνδεκα.
7 qui, quis.

kvacıt, *adv.* somewhere.

kvápı, *adv.* any where.

kakṣa, *m.* a gate.

kakṣá, *f.* an inclosure.

kaṭ, 1. *a.* kaṭatı; cakáṭa; kaṭıtá; akaṭit: go; cover; rain; live in distress, or pain.

utkaṭa, *adj.* furious : *m.* an elephant in rut.

kaṭa, *m.* the hip and loins; the temples of an elephant; a mat.

vıkaṭa, *adj.* without a mat *or* covering.

kaṇa, *adj.* small.

kanyá, *and* kanyaká, *f.* a girl, daughter.

kanṭa

kanṭaka, *m. n.* a thorn; an enemy.

kath[1], 10. *a.* kathayatı, acakathat : narrate, tell.

kathá, *f.* a tale.

kadamba, *m.* the name of a plant, nauclea kadamba.

kan, 1. *a.* kanatı; cakána; kanıtá; kanta : shine, see, love.

kanaka, *n.* gold.

kam[2], 10. *m.* kámayate; cakame, kámayáncakre, kámayıtá, kamıtá; kámayıṣyate, kamıṣyate; acikamata, acakamata; kamıtvá, *and* kántvá; kánta : love; wish for.

akáma, *adj.* unwilling.

abhıkáma, *m.* love.

Kandarpa, *m. the god of love,* Káma.

kamala, *n.* a lotus.

kántı, *f.* desire; loveliness.

káma[3], *m.* love; wish; an object of desire: *the god of love.*

káma-ga, *adj.* going at will.

káma-vásın, *adj.* dwelling at will, dwelling where he chooses.

kamp, 1. *m.* kampate; cakampe; kampıtá; kampıṣyate; akampıṣta: tremble, shake.

karuṇa, *adj.* mournful, sad.

karṇ, 10. *a.* split.

karṇıkára, *m.* the name of a plant, pterospermum acerıfolıum.

kal, 1. *m.* kalate; cakale: count; sound. 10. *a.* kálayatı: shake, vibrate: meditate; suppose.

akála, *adj.* untimely, unseasonable.

aprápta-kála, *adj.* not having attained the proper time.

kala, *adj.* gentle, soft, *of the voice.*

kalı, *m.* battle, strife: the demon of strife; the age of strife.

kaluṣa, *adj.* turbid, dark.

kalya, *adj.* prepared, sound: *n.* the dawn; the morrow.

kalyáṇa, *adj.* good; fortunate: *n.* good fortune.

kála, *adj.* black: *m.* blackness; time; death; the god of death.

prápta-kála, *adj.* having attained the proper time.

kavaca, *m. n.* armour, mail.

kaś, 1. *a. m.* kaśatı, -te &c.; kaṣṭa: beat, hurt; sound.

kaṣáya, *adj.* astringent: brown.

ahımsá	han	ákulıta	kul	ágamana	gam
ákára	krı	ákṛtı	krı	ágas	ag
ákáśa	kaś	ákhyána	khyá	ájná	jná
ákula	kul	ágama	gam	átura	tur

---

[1] qvıθan.　　　　[2] amáre.　　　　[3] *Pers.* kám.

kaṣṭa, *p. p. p.* unhappy, sorrowful : *n.* misfortune.
kaśmala, *adj.* dirty: *m.* fainting,
syncope.
kàn·kṣ, 1. *a.* kàn·kṣatı, cakàn·kṣa,
kàn·kṣıtà. desire, wish.
kàn·kṣà, *f.* a desire, wish.
kànana, *n.* a forest.
kàya, *m. n.* a body.
kàś, 1. *and* 4. *m.* kàśate, kàśyate;
cakàśe; kàśıtà; kàśıṣyate;
akàśıṣṭa. shine.
àkàśa, *m.* air.
kàṣṭha, *n.* fuel, wood.
cakṣ, 2. *m.* caṣṭe; cacakṣe: see;
speak. à-, tell.
cakṣus¹, *n.* an eye.
prakàśa², *adj.* bright.
prakàśatà, *f.* brightness ; cele-
brity.
sakàśa, *m.* presence.
kımśuka, *m.* the name of a tree,
butea frondòsa.
kıt, 3. *a.* cıketı; cıketa : perceive,
recognize.
ketu, *m.* a standard, flag.
kıla, *conj.* indeed, certainly.
kuca, *m.* a breast.
kuṅj, *m. n.* an elephant's tusk;
a place abounding with creep-
ing plants.
kuṅjara, *m.* an elephant.
nıkuṅja, *m.* an arbour.
kuṭ
koṭı, *f.* an extremity, a point :
the number ten millions, 10⁷.
kuṇḍ, 1. *a.* be injured : 1. *m.* burn:
10. *a.* keep, guard.
kuṇḍa, *n.* a water-jar ; a well.

kuṇḍala, *n.* a ring; an ear-ring;
a bracelet.
kuṇḍalın, *adj.* having a bracelet.
Kuṇḍına, *n.* the chief city of
the Vıdarbhàḥ.
kutùhala, *n.* pleasure, eagerness.
Kunti, *f.* the wife of king Pàṇḍu.
Kaunteya, *m.* any descendant
of Kunti.
kup³, 4. *a.* kupyatı; cukopa;
kopıtà; kopıṣyatı; akupat :
be angry.
kopa, *m.* anger.
prakopa, *m.* irritation.
kumàra, *m.* a boy, youth.
kaumàra, *n.* youth, *time of life.*
kumbha, *m.* a water-jar; a measure for corn ; a swelling on
an elephant's forehead.
kur, 6. *a.* kuratı : sound.
kurara, *m.* an osprey.
Kuru, *m.* an ancestor of Pàṇḍu.
Kaurava, *m.* any descendant of
Kuru.
kul, 1. *a.* kolatı; cukola: gather.
àkula, *adj.* troubled.
àkulıta, *p. p. p.* troubled, disturbed.
kula, *n.* a family.
kula-ghna, *adj.* family-destroy-
ing.
vyàkula, *adj.* = àkula.
san·kula, *adj.* full ; mixed.
samàkula, *adj. id.*
kuś, 4. *a.* embrace. 1. *and* 10.
shine.
kuśala, *adj.* prosperous, happy ;
skilful: *n.* prosperity, happiness.

àdıtya	dıtı	àpagà	ap	àbharaṇa	bhrı
àdhı	dhyaı	àpad	pad	àbhà	bhà
ànayana	ni	àpıda	pıd	àmaya	am
ànṛısaṃsya	nṛı	àbàdhà	bàdh	àmarṣa	mṛıṣ

¹ *Pal.* cakku; *Pers.* caṣm.   ² *Pal.* pakàsa.   ³ *Pal.* kupatı.

kuśalın, *adj.* *id.*
kośa, *m.* the bud of a flower; a sheath: treasure; gold.
kuṣ, 9. *a.* kuṣṇātı; cukoṣa; koṣıtā, koṣıṣyatı; akoṣit; kuṣıta. draw out.
koṣa, *m.* = kośa.
vıkoṣa, *adj.* without a sheath.
kūj, 1. *a.* sound; caw, coo.
kūṭa, *m.* a peak, summit.
kūrma, *m.* a tortoise.
kṛı[1], 8. *a.* *m.* karotı; kurute; *pot.* kuryāt; kurvita; cakāra, cakre; kartā; karıṣyatı, -te; *prec.* krıyāt, kṛṣiṣṭa; akārṣit, akṛıta; kṛıtvā, *and* kṛıtya: *p.* krıyate; kārıtā; kārıṣyate; akārı, (*pl.* akārıṣata;) kṛıta: make; do. sam-, complete; adorn.
akārya, *adj.* that may not be done.
akurvat, *part.* not doing.
akṛıtvā, not having done.
apakāratā, *f.* an offence.
apakṛıta, *p. p. p.* injured.
asakṛıt, *adv.* not once only, often.
ākāra, *m.* a form, shape.
ākāravat, *adj.* beautiful.
ākṛıtı, *f.* form.
āpta-kārın, *adj.* trusty.
-kara, *adj.* -making, -doing: *m.* a hand; a proboscis.
karın, *adj.* having a hand: *m.* an elephant.
karman[2], *n.* deed.
kartṛı[3], *m.* a maker, doer.
kāra[4], *adj.* -making, -doing: *m.* an effort.
kāraṇa, *n.* a deed, work: cause.
kārın, *adj.* doing.
kārya, *adj.* that may be done: *n.* a business, an affair.
kāryavat, *adj.* busy, attentive.
-kṛıt, *adj.* -making, -doing.
kṛıta, *p. p. p.* made, done.
kṛıte, *prp.* for the sake *of.*
kṛıta-kṛıtya, *adj.* having done what should be done.
kṛıtı, *f.* an act, a work.
kṛıtya, *adj.* that should be done: *n.* a business, duty.
kratu, *m.* a sacrifice.
cıkirṣ, *desid.* wish to do.
duṣkara, *adj.* hard to do.
duṣkṛıta, *n.* an evil deed.
nıkṛıtı, *f.* vileness, wickedness.
prakāra[5], *m.* manner; kind.
prakṛıtı[6], *f.* nature: *pl.* subjects.
pratıkāra, *m.* retaliation.
vıkāra, *m.* a change; disturbance of mind.
saṃskāra, *m.* an ornament, a purpose.
sakṛıt, *adv.* once only.
kṛıt, 6. *a.* kṛıntatı; cakarta; kartıtā; kartıṣyatı, *and* kartsyatı; akartit; kṛıtta: cut, divide.
avakartana, *n.* the act of cutting off.
kartana, *n.* the act of cutting.
kṛıcchra, *adj.* difficult, troublesome: *n.* difficulty, trouble.
kṛıtya, *adj.* annoying.

amātya	amā	āyatana	yat	ārādhana	rādh
āmnāya	man	āyana	ı	ārāva	ru
āmra	am	āyudha	yudh	āroha	ruh
āyata	yam	ārava	ru	ārta	ard

1 *Pers.* kardan; creāre.
2 carmen.
3 creātor.
4 *Pers.* kār.
5 *Pal.* pakāra.
6 *Pal.* pakatı.

kṛıtyakà, *f.* she that annoys.
kṛıtsna, *adj.* all, whole.
kṛıp, 10. *a.* kṛıpayatı: be weak.
kàrpaṇya, *n.* poverty; meanness of spirit.
kṛıpaṇa, *adj.* pitiable, feeble, mean, miserly.
kṛıpà, *f.* pity.
kṛıś[1], 4. *a.* kṛıśyatı, cakarśa, karśıtà, karśıṣyatı, akrıśat, karṣıtvà, *and* krıśıtvà: make thin.
kṛıśa, *adj.* thin, wasted.
kṛıṣ[2], 1. *a. and* 6. *a. m.* karṣatı, kṛıṣatı, -te; cakarṣa, cakṛıṣe; karṣṭà, *and* kraṣṭà; karkṣyatı, -te, *and* krakṣyatı, -te: drag; draw to and fro; tame; annoy. 6. plough.
karṣaṇa, *n.* the act of drawing: *adj.* -vexing.
kṛıṣṇa[3], *adj.* black; dark blue.
kṛıṣṇa-vartman, *m.* (black-path,) fire.
prakṛıṣṭa, *p. p. p.* extended; long.
kṛi[4], 6. *a.* kıratı; cakàra, (*pl.* cakarus;) karıtà, *and* karità; karıṣyatı, *and* kariṣyatı; kiryàt; akàrit: *p.* kiryate; kirṇa[5]: pour out, scatter, sprinkle.
kirṇa, *p. p. p.* scattered, sprinkled.
san·kara, *m.* mixture: a mixed caste.
kṛit, 10. *a.* kirtayatı, acikṛıtat, *and* acıkirtat: praise; recite, name.
kirtı, *f.* praise; fame, glory.
akirtı, *f.* dispraise; dishonour.
akirtı-kara, *adj.* causing dishonour.
klṛıp, 1. *a. m.* kalpate; caklṛıpe; kalpıtà, kalptà; kalpıṣyate, -tı; akalpıṣṭa, aklṛıpta *and* aklṛıpat; klṛıpta, kalpya: suffice, be capable, become.
kalpa[6], *adj.* -like: *m.* a day and night of Brahmà, the duration of each *formation*, being 432 millions of years: a command.
prakalpıta, *p. p. p.* fitted, arranged.
san·kalpa, *m.* counsel, purpose; mind, intelligence.
jàta-san·kalpa, *adj.* having common sense.
keśa, *m.* the hair *of the head.*
keś'-ànta, *m.* a lock of hair.
mukta-keśa, *adj.* with dishevelled hair.
krand, 1. *a.* krandatı; cakranda; krandıtà: cry out sadly, weep. à-, call out to.
kram[7], 1. *and* 4. *a. m.* kràmatı, kramate, kràmyatı; cakràma, cakrame; kramıtà, krantà; kramıṣyatı, kraṃsyate; akramit, akraṃsta; kramıtvà, krantvà, kràntvà: krànta: step, walk. à-, attack.
krama, *m.* a step, series, ròw.
krama-pràpta, *p. p. p.* obtained by succession.

àrya	ṛı	àvàsa	vas	àśirvàda	aś
àlaya	ḷı	àvıla	vıl	àśu	,,
àvarta	vṛıt	àśa	aś	àścarya	car
àvaha	vah	àśıs	,,	àśrama	śram

[1] *Pal.* kısatı.
[2] *Pal.* kassatı; *Pers.* kaṣidan, kıṣtan.
[3] *Pal.* kaṇha; *Rus.* cerno.
[4] *Pal.* kıratı.
[5] *Pal.* kıṇṇa.
[6] *Pal.* kappa.
[7] *Pal.* kamatı.

cakra[1], *m.* a wheel; a quoit used in battle; a district, province; an army.
cakravàka, *m.* the brahmany goose.
paràkrama[2], *m.* power, might.
vıkrama, *m.* a step; power, might.
vıkrànta, *adj.* bold.
kruñc, 1. *a.* kruñcatı: bend.
krauñca, *m.* a heron.
krudh[3], 4. *a.* krudhyatı; cukrodha; kroddhà; krotsyatı; akrudhat; kruddha: be angry.
krodha[4], *m.* anger.
kruś, 1. *a.* krośatı; cukrośa; kroṣṭà; krokṣyatı; akrukṣat: cry out, complain, weep.
anukrośa, *m.* pity.
nıranukrośa, *adj.* pitiless.
klam, 1. *and* 4. *a.* klàmatı, klàmyatı; caklàma; klamıtà; klànta: be weary, languish.
klama[5], *m.* weariness, languor.
klànta, *p. p. p.* wearied.
klıd, 4. *a.* become moist.
akledya, *adj.* that cannot be moistened.
klıś, 4. *m. and* 9. *a.* klıśyate, klıśnàtı; cıkleśa; cıklıśe; kleśıtà, *and* kleṣṭà; kleśıṣyatı, -te, *and* klekṣyatı; akleśit, *and* aklıkṣat, akleśıṣṭa; klıśıtvà, *and* klıṣṭvà; klıśıta *and* klıṣṭa: grieve, annoy, weary.
aklıṣṭa, *adj.* unwearied.
kleśa, *m.* grief, sorrow.

klu, 1. *m.* move one's self.
kliva, *adj.* weak, powerless: *m.* a eunuch.
klaıvya, *n.* weakness; effeminacy.
vıklava, *adj.* agitated.
vaıklavya, *n.* agitation.
kṣaṇ, 8. *a. m.* kṣaṇotı, kṣaṇute; cakṣàṇa, cakṣaṇe; kṣaṇıtà; kṣaṇıṣyatı, -te; akṣaṇit, akṣata; kṣata: strike, hurt, kill.
kṣaṇa, *m.* a period of four minutes, *corresponding to a degree of the equator.*
kṣata, *p. p. p.* struck, killed.
kṣam[6], 1. *m. and* 4. *a.* kṣamate, kṣàmyatı; cakṣame, *and* cakṣàme; kṣamıtà, *and* kṣantà, kṣamıṣyate, -tı, *and* kṣaṃsyate, -tı; akṣamıṣṭa, akṣaṃsta, akṣamat: *p.* kṣamyate, kṣànta: bear with; be patient; excuse.
kṣatra, *and* kṣatrıya, *m.* a man of the military caste.
kṣama, *adj.* bearing, enduring.
kṣamà, *f.* patience: the Earth.
kṣamàvat, *adj.* patient.
kṣal, 10. *a.* kṣàlayatı, acıkṣalat: wash.
prakṣalana, *n.* the act of washing.
kṣı, 1. 5. *and* 9. *a.* kṣayatı, kṣıṇotı, kṣıṇàtı; cıkṣàya; kṣetà; kṣeṣyatı; kṣiyàt; akṣaıṣit; kṣitvà; kṣiya: *p.* kṣiyate; kṣiṇa, *and* kṣıta: strike; kill. 1. *a.* rule.

às		àha	ah	ikṣaṇa	akṣ
àsa	as	àhàra	hrı	idrıśa	drıś
àsana	às	àhıta	dhà	ips	àp
àsya	as	ikṣ	akṣ	uccaya	cı

1 *Pal.* cakka.
2 *Pal.* parakkama.
3 *Pal.* kujjhatı.
4 *Pal.* kodha.
5 *Pal.* kılamatı.
6 *Pal.* khamatı.

akṣaya, *adj.* deathless.
kṣaya, *m.* death, destruction.
-kṣit, *m.* -ruler.
kṣiti, *f.* the earth.
mahi-kṣit, *m.* a ruler of the earth; a king.
kṣip[1], 6. *a. m.* 4. *a.* kṣipati, -te, kṣipyati; cikṣepa, cikṣipe; kṣeptà, kṣepṣyati, -te; akṣaipsit, akṣipta: *p.* kṣipyate, kṣipta: throw.
nikṣepa, *m.* a deposit, stake.
kṣipra, *adj.* quick.
kṣud, 7. *a. m.* kṣuṇatti, kṣunte; cukṣoda, cukṣude; kṣottà; kṣotsyati, -te; akṣudat, akṣautsit, akṣutta; kṣuṇṇa: crush, bruise, pound.
kṣudra, *adj.* small, worthless.
kṣudh, 4. *a.* kṣudhyati, cukṣodha; kṣoddhà; kṣudhitvà, *and* kṣodhitvà; kṣudhita: be hungry.
kṣudh, *and* kṣudhà, *f.* hunger.
kṣema, *adj.* good, happy: *m. n.* happiness.
kṣemin[2], *adj.* happy.
khaḍ, 10. *a.* khàḍayati: split, divide, break, crush.
khaḍga[3], *m.* a rhinoceros; the horn of a rhinoceros: a sword.
khad, 1. *a.* khadati, cakhàda: kill; eat.
khadira, *m.* the sensitive plant.
khan[4], 1. *a. m.* khanati, -te; cakhàna, cakhne: dig.
akhila, *adj.* whole.
asukha, *n.* pain, sorrow.
kha, *m.* the sky, air.
kha-ga, *and* kha-gama, *m.* (skygoer,) a bird.
khila, *adj.* empty.
khe-cara, *m.* (walking in the sky,) a bird.
duḥkha, *adj.* painful, difficult: *n.* pain, difficulty.
duḥkhita, *adj.* pained.
sukha, *adj.* pleasant: *n.* pleasure, ease.
sukhin, *adj.* joyful.
suduḥkha, *adj.* very painful, very difficult.
kharj, 1. *a.* cleanse: annoy.
kharjùra, *m.* a palm tree.
khalu, *conj.* indeed, truly.
khàd, 1. *a.* khàdati; cakhàda; khàdità; khàdiṣyati; akhàdit: eat, devour.
khyà: 2. *a. m.* khyàti; cakhyau, cakhye; khyàtà; khyàsyati, -te; khyàyàt, *and* khyeyàt; khyàsiṣṭa; akhyat, -ta: *p. and impers.* khyàyate, khyàyità, *and* khyàtà; khyàyiṣyate, *and* khyàsyate; akhyàyi: name, call. à-, narrate, tell. pratyà-, refuse. pra-, celebrate, praise. vi-, *id.* sam-, count.
àkhyàna, *n.* a tale.
upàkhyàna, *n.* an episode.
prakhya, *adj.* like.
sakhi, *m.* sakhi, *f.* a friend.
saṅkhya, *n.* battle.
saṅkhyàna, *n.* an enumeration.
gaj[5], 1. *a.* gajati; jagàja: trumpet, *as an elephant.*

utkaṭa	kaṭ	udaya	i	unmatta	mad
utsarga	sṛj	udarka	ark	unmukha	mukh
utsava	su	udàra	ṛi	upacàra	car
utsrastu	sṛj	uddeśa	diś	upadeśa	diś

[1] *Rus.* sivát'.
[2] *Pal.* khema.
[3] *Pal.* khagga.
[4] *Pers.* kandan.
[5] *Pal.* gajjati.

gaja, *m.* an elephant.
gaṇ, 10. *a.* gaṇayatı; ajagaṇat, *and* ajigaṇat: count.
gaṇa, *m.* a number, multitude, crowd, flock.
gad, 1. *a.* gadatı; jagâda; gadıtâ; gadıṣyatı; agâdit, *and* agadit: speak, say.
gandh, *m.* a smell, odour; a sweet smell.
sugandhın, *adj.* having a sweet smell.
saugandhıka, *adj.* *id.* *n.* the white lotus.
gandharva[1], *m.* one of Indra's musicians.
gam[2], 1. *a.* gacchatı; jagâma, (*pl.* jagmus;) gantâ; gamıṣyatı; agamat; *perf. part.* jagmıvas *and* jaganvas; gatvâ, *in comp.* gatya, *and* gamya: gata: go. gâ, 3. *a.* jıgâtı; 1 *pret.* ajıgat; *pot.* jagâyât; 3 *pret.* agat: go.
aga, *and* agama, *m.* (that goes not,) a tree; a mountain.
adhıgamana, *n.* finding, obtaining.
anuga, *adj.* following.
abhıgamana, *n.* arrival.
âgama, *adj.* -going to: *m.* the act of going to, or coming.
âgamana, *n.* the act of coming.
-ga, *adj.* -going.
gata, *past p.* gone.
gatı, *f.* gait, manner of going.
gamana, *n.* the act of going.
gâtra, *n.* a limb; a body.
durga, *adj.* hard to reach *or* pass.
naga, *m.* (that goes not,) a tree; a mountain.
nagara, *n.* nagari, *f.* a city.
nâga, *m.* a serpent: an elephant.
san·ga, *and* san·gama, *m.* a meeting, an assembly.
san·gatı, *f.* coming together.
san·gatyâ, by chance.
san·gama, *m.* union.
sadâ-gatı, *m.* (always going,) the wind.
samâgama, *m.* a coming together.
sv-âgata, *adj.* welcome.
gambhira, *adj.* deep; deep *in sound*, deep sounding.
garut, *m.* a wing.
garutmat, *adj.* winged: a bird.
gah, *and* gâh, 10. *a.* be thick, impassable, *as a forest.*
gahana, *adj.* thick, impassable: *n.* a forest.
gâḍha, *p. p. p.* thick, hairy; close.
gâḍham, *adv.* greatly, very.
gâdha, *adj.* fordable, shallow.
agâdha, *adj.* not fordable, deep.
gırı[3], *m.* a mountain.
guṇa[4], *m.* a quality: a good quality, virtue: a cord.
guṇavat, *adj.* having good qualities, virtuous.
guṇṭh, 10. *a.* guṇṭhayatı: cover.
gup, 1. *and* 10. *a. m.* gopâyatı; jugopa, *and* gopayâñcakâra; goptâ, gopıtâ, gopâyıtâ; gop-

upapanna	pad	upâkhyâna	khyâ	ekâgra	ag
upama	mâ	upâya	ı	etat	ta
upavana	vana	ûḍha	vah	etâvat	,,
upastha	sthâ	ûrdhvan	vṛdh	aıkâgrya	ag

[1] *Pal.* gandhabba.
[2] *Pal.* gacchatı, *and* gametı; *Go.* gaggan, qıman.
[3] *opos*; *Rus.* gorá.
[4] *Pers.* gûnah.

syati, gopiṣyati, gopàyiṣyati; agaupsit, agopit, agopàyit: guard.
goptṛi, *m.* a protector.
guru[1], *adj.* heavy; honoured: *m. and f.* a teacher, guide.
gaurava, *n.* honour, dignity.
gulma, *m.* a shrub, bush: a clump of grass.
guh, 1. *a. m.* gùhati, -te; jugùha, jugùhe; gùhità, *and* goḍhà; gùhiṣyati, -te, ghokṣati, -te; agùhit, aghukṣat, agùhiṣṭa, agùḍha, aghukṣata; gùhitvà, gùḍhvà; *p.* guhyate; agùhi; gùḍha: cover; conceal.
guhà, *f.* a cave.
gùḍha, *p. p. p.* hidden.
gṛi[2], girati, *and* gilati, gṛiṇàti; jagàra *and* jagàla; garità *and* galità, garìtà *and* galìtà; gariṣyati *and* galiṣyati, garìṣyati, *and* galìṣyati; giryàt; agàrit *and* agàlit: *p.* giryate; girṇa: *des.* jigariṣyati *and* jigaliṣyati. 6. *a.* swallow. 9. *a.* sound.
gir[3], *f.* the voice.
gai, 1. *a.* gàyati; jagau; gàtà; gàsyati; geyàt; agàsit: *p.* gìyate; agàyi; gìta: sing.
gàthà, *f.* a song.
go[4], *m.* a bull: *f.* a cow; the earth.
grabh[5], *an old form of* grah.
garbha[6], *m.* the womb; the calyx of a flower: an embryo.
gras, 1. *m.* grasate; jagrase; grasità; grasiṣyate; agrasiṣṭa; grasitvà, *and* grastvà; grasta: devour.
grah, 9. *a. m.* gṛihṇàti, gṛihṇìte; jagràha; grahìtà; grahìṣyati, -te; gṛihyàt, grahìṣìṣṭa; agrahìt, agrahìṣṭa; grahìtum; gṛihìtvà: *p.* gṛihyate; jagṛihe; grahìtà *and* gràhità; grahìṣyate, *and* gràhiṣyate; grahìṣìṣṭa, *and* gràhiṣiṣṭa; agràhi; gṛihìta: take, seize, grasp.
gṛiha, *m.* a house: *pl.* a wife.
geha, *m. id.*
graha, *m.* a planet.
grahaṇa, *n.* the act of seizing.
gràma[7], *m.* a village; a multitude.
gràmin, *m.* a villager.
gràmya, *adj.* domestic, tame.
gràha, *m.* the act of seizing; a serpent; any large water animal.
san-grahana, *n.* the act of enclosing, guiding, or driving.
san-gràma, *m.* a battle.
ghur, 6. *a.* ghurati: frighten: utter a noise; *either* to frighten, or in fear.
ghora, *adj.* terrible.
ghuṣ, 1. *a.* ghoṣati; jughoṣa; ghoṣità; ghoṣiṣyati; aghoṣit, *and* aghuṣat: make a noise, proclaim.
ghoṣa, *m.* a noise, sound: a shepherd's station.
nirghoṣa, *m.* a noise.

kartana	kṛit	kirti	kṛi & kṛit	gatacetas	cit
kàmaduh	duh			garbha	grabh
kàṣàya	kaṣ	kṛitàñjali	añj	gir	gṛi
kirṇa	kṛi	kṛitàtman	ah	ghna	han

[1] gravis.
[2] gula; *Rus.* górlo.
[3] γηρυς; *Rus.* golos'.
[4] *Pers.* gàv. γη.
[5] *Pers.* giriftan; *Go.* greipan.
[6] *Pal.* gabbha.
[7] *Pal.* gàma.

ghrâ[1], 1. *a.* jıghratı: smell.
  vyâghra, *m.* a tiger.
  nara-vyâghra, *m.* a tiger of men, *chief of men in bravery.*
-ca, *an enclitic conjunction,* and.
catur[2], *num.* four.
cand, 1. *a.* candatı; cacanda; candıtâ: shine; gladden.
  canda, *m.* the moon.
  candana, *m. n.* sandal wood.
  candra, *m.* the moon.
  candramas, *m. id.*
cam, 1. *and* 5. *a.* camatı, cacâma, camıtâ, acamit: eat.
  câmikara, *n.* gold.
car, 1. *a.* caratı; cacâra; carıtâ; carıṣyatı; acârit: walk.
  âścarya, *adj.* wonderful: *n.* a wonder, marvel.
  upacâra, *m.* service; an act.
  caraṇa, *n.* the act of walking; an act.
  carıta, *n.* conduct.
  carya, *f.* the act of walking; service; performance, office.
  câra, *m.* the act of walking.
  câritra, *n.* way of acting: good conduct.
  câru, *adj.* fair, beautiful, pleasing.
  parıcaryâ, *f.* service, dependence, veneration, worship.
  parıcâra, *adj.* attentive, diligent.
  parıcâraka, *m.* a servant.
  parıcârıkâ, *f. id.*
  vıcâra, *m.* vıcâraṇa, *n.* deliberation, hesitation.
  sañcâra, *m.* a passage, entrance, door-way.
cal, 1. *a.* calatı; cacâla; calıtâ; calıṣyatı; acâlit. *sometimes m.* totter, shake, tremble.
  acala, *adj.* immovable: *m.* a mountain.
  cala, *adj.* moving, tottering, trembling.
cah, 1. *and* 10. *a.* crush, injure; deceive.
  cıhna, *n.* a spot, stain, mark: a banner, standard.
cı[3], 5. *a. m.* cınotı, cınute; cıkâya *and* cıcâya, cıkye, *and* cıcye; cetâ; ceṣyatı, -te; ciyât, ceṣıṣṭa; acaıṣit, aceṣṭa; *p.* ciyate; câyıtâ; câyıṣyate; câyıṣiṣṭa; acâyı, acâyıṣata; ceya, *and* cetavya; cıta: gather; seek.
  acıra, *adj.* short.
  uccaya, *m.* a heap.
  caya, *m.* a collection, multitude, heap.
  cıra[4], *adj.* long, *of time.*
  na-cırât, *adv.* in no long time.
  nıścaya, *m.* a determination, decree: truth, certainty.
  mâ-cıram, *adv.* soon.
-cıt, *an enclitic particle that makes interrogatives become indefinite.*
cıt, 1. *a.* cetatı; cıceta; cetıtâ; cetıṣyatı; acetit; cetıtvâ *and* cıtıtvâ; cıtta; *and* cınt, 10. *a.* cıntayatı: think, perceive.
  acıntya, *adj.* that is unthought, inconceivable.
  aceta, *adj.* having no thought, void of intelligence, unconscious.

cakra	kram	cıkirṣ	kṛı	jıhmaga	hâ
cakravaka	„	jâtasan-kalpa	klṛıp	tathâvıdha	dhâ
cakṣ	kâś	jıhirṣ	hṛı	tadanantara	ant
câturvarṇya	vṛı	jıhma	hâ	taru	tṛımh

[1] fragrâre.
[2] *Pers.* cıhâr; quatuor; *Go.* fidvor; *Wel.* pedwar; *Rus.* cetüre.
[3] *Pers.* cidan.
[4] *Wel.* hır.

acetana, *adj.* thoughtless.

anucıntayat, *part.* thinking of.

gata-cetas, *adj.* deprived of understanding.

cıtta, *n.* thought : the mind.

cıtra, *adj.* various; of various colours.

cıntà, *f.* thought, meditation.

cıntà-para, *adj.* thoughtful.

cetas, *n.* the mind.

vıcıtra, *adj.* much varied, very various.

cud, 10. *a.* codayatı; acùcudat : urge, impel; command.

cet, *conj.* if.

Cedı, *m. the name of a country.*

cest, 1. *m.* palpitate; roll; struggle.

cyu¹, 1. *m.* cyavate; cucyuve; cyotà; cyosyate; acyosta: fall; perish.

acyuta, *adj.* unfallen; firm; lofty.

cyuta, *p. p. p.* fallen.

chad, 10. *and* 1. *a. m.* chàdayatı, -te, chadatı, -te; chàdıta *and* channa : cover.

chada, *m.* a leaf; a wing.

chadman, *n.* concealment; wearing another's form.

chadmın, *adj.* clothed in another's form.

chanda, *n.* a desire, wish.

chàyà², *f.* a shadow.

parıcchada, *m.* a retinue.

pracchàdana, *n.* the act of covering : an upper garment.

chıd³, 7. *a. m.* chınattı, chınte; cıccheda, cıcchıde; chettà,

chetsyatı, -te; acchıdat, *and* acchaıtsit, *and* acchıtta : *p.* chıdyate; acchedı; chınna : cut, cleave, split.

achedya, *adj.* that cannot be divided.

chedya, *adj.* that may be divided.

jat, 1. *a.* heap up.

jatà, *f.* the matted hair *of Śıva, and of ascetics.*

jatıla, *adj.* having matted hair.

jan⁴, 3. *a.* jajantı; jajàna : beget; bring forth : 4. *m.* jàyate; jajne; janısyate; ajanısta, *and* ajanı; jàta : be born.

aja, *adj.* unborn.

apraja, *adj.* childless.

abhıjana, *m.* a family.

-ja, *adj.* -born.

jana, *m.* a man, person.

janani, *f.* a mother.

janapada, *n.* land; the country.

janman, *n.* birth.

janm'-àntara, *n.* an other birth.

janıtrı⁵, *m.* a father.

janıtri⁶, *f.* a mother.

jàta⁷, *p. p. p.* born.

jàta-rùpa, *n.* gold.

jàtı, *f.* birth; a family.

jàtu, *ind.* ever. na j', never.

jànapada, *m.* a countryman, rustic.

dvı-ja, *adj.* twice-born, applied to birds, and Bràhmans, also to men of the second and third classes.

nırjana, *adj.* unpeopled.

praja⁸, *f.* progeny : *pl.* subjects.

tu	ta		traılokya	lok		dari		dri
tejas	tıj		danta	ad		darśana		drıś
trıdıva	dıv		dantın	,,		darśın		,,
trıdıveśvara	,,		dara	dri		dàruna		dri

¹ *Pers.* ṣudan.

² σκια; *Pers.* sàyah; *Rus.* ṣyen'.

³ σχιζειν; scındere.

⁴ γενος; genus; *Go.* kunı; *Pers.* zan; *Wel.* cenaw.

⁵ genıtor.

⁶ genıtrıx.

⁷ nàtus; *Pers.* zàdah.

⁸ prògenıès.

prajà-kàma, *adj.* desirous of progeny.
vijana, *adj.* unpeopled.
jambu, *m.* the rose-apple, eugenia jambolàna.
Jambudvipa, *m.* India.
jal, 1. *and* 10. *a.* cover.
jala[1], *adj.* cold; stupid: *n.* coldness; cold; water.
jala-da, *m.* a cloud.
jàla, *n.* a net; a multitude.
jànu[2], *n.* a knee.
ji, 1. *a. m.* jayati, -te, jigàya, jigye, jetà, jeṣyati, -te, jiyàt, jiṣiṣṭa, ajaiṣit, ajeṣṭa: *p.* jiyate, jàyità, jàyiṣyate, jàyiṣiṣṭa, ajàyi, ajàyiṣata: conquer.
aparàjita, *adj.* unconquered.
jaya, *m.* victory; *name of* Arjuna: *adj.* -conquering.
jita, *p. p. p.* conquered.
paràjaya, *m.* defeat.
paràjita, *p. p. p.* = jita.
vijaya, *m.* victory.
jimùta, *m.* a cloud.
jiv[3], 1. *a.* jivati, jijiva, jività, jiviṣyati, ajivit: live.
jiva, *adj.* alive: *m.* life.
jivana, *n.* jivikà, *f. and* jivita, *n.* life.
ju, 1. *a. m.* javati: go; go quickly.
java, *m.* haste, quickness, speed.
javana, *n. and* jùti, *f. id.*
juṣ, 1. *and* 10. *a.* examine: delight. 6. love, desire; inhabit.
jṛ, 1, 4, 9, 10, *a.* grow old, decay; be digested.
jarà, *f.* old age.
jnà[4], 9. *a. m.* jànàti, jànite; jajnau, jajne; jnàtà; jnàsyati, -te; jnàyàt, jneyàt; jnàsiṣṭa; ajnàsit, ajnàsta: *p.* jnàyate; jajne; jnàtà, *and* jnàyità; jnàsyate, *and* jnàyiṣyate; jnàsiṣṭa, *and* jnàyiṣiṣṭa; ajnàyi, ajnàsata, *and* ajnàyiṣata; jnàta; jneya. *caus.* jnàpayati. *des.* jijnàsate: know. anu-, allow. prati-, assent, promise.
ajnàta, *adj.* unknown.
ajnàta-vàsa, *adj.* whose dwelling was not known.
anabhijna, *adj.* unskilful.
abhijna, *adj.* skilful.
àjnà, *f.* a command.
-jna, *adj.* -knowing.
jnàti, *m.* a kinsman.
jnàna, *n.* knowledge, intellect.
nàman[5], *n.* a name.
pràjna, *adj.* wise.
vijna, *adj. id.*
sañjnà, *f.* consciousness; mind; thought.
jvar, 1. *a.* jvarati; jajvàra; jvarità; jvariṣyati; ajvàrit; jùrṇa: be sick.
jvara, *m.* sickness; grief; trouble.
vi-jvara, *adj.* free from grief.
jval, 1. *a.* jvalati; jajvàla; jvalità; jvaliṣyati; ajvàlit: burn, shine. pra-, begin to burn.
jhaṣ, 1. *a. m.* take; cover.
jhaṣa, *m.* a fish.
jhilli, *f.* a cricket.

dàsi	dàsa	duḥkhita	khan	duṣkara	kṛ
digvàsas	diś	duḥsaha	sah	deya	dà
divaukas	uc	durdharṣa	dhṛṣ	deva	div
duḥkha	khan	durbuddhi	budh	dvipa	pà

[1] gelù.
[2] *Pers.* zànù; γονυ; genù; *Go.* kniu.
[3] ζαειν; vivere; *Pers.* zistan.
[4] *Rus.* znat'; *Pers.* ṣinàxtan; γνωναι; nòvisse; *Go.* kunnan.
[5] *Pers.* nàm; *Rus.* imyà, -meni; ονομα; nòmen; *Go.* namo.

jhillikā, *f.* *id.*
jhṛi, 4. *a.* jhiryati: grow old.
nirjhara, *m.* a water-fall.
ta
etat, eṣa, eṣā, *pron.* thát.
etāvat, *adj.* such: *n. adv.* so much, so.
tat, sas *and* sa, sā: it, he, she; thát.
tat, (*after* yat,) *conj.* therefore.
tatas, from thát; after thát.
tattva, *n.* truth, the exact thing.
tattva-jna, *adj.* knowing the truth.
tatra, there.
tathā, thus.
tadā, then.
tāvat, *adj.* so great, so much: *n. adv.* now.
tu, *conj.* also, indeed, too; but.
taḍ, 10. *a.* strike, kill.
taḍāga, *n.* a fish-pond, lake.
tan[1], 8. *a. m.* tanoti; tanute; tatāna, tene; tanitā, taniṣyati, -te; atānit, *and* atanit, atata, *and* ataniṣṭa; tanitvā, *and* tatvā: *p.* tanyate, *and* tāyate; tata: stretch, spread.
ātata, *adj.* continued, spread.
ātatāyin, *adj.* going in all directions, marauding.
tata, *p. p. p.* stretched; continued.
tanaya, *m.* tanayā, *f.* a child; son, daughter.
tanu[2], *adj.* thin, slender: *f. n.* the body.
tanus[3], *n. and* tanū, *f.* the body.
tanū-ruha, *m. n.* the hair of the body.
satata, *adj.* continual: *n. adv.* continually.
tandrā, *f.* weariness; sloth.
atandrita, *adj.* unwearied.
tap[4], 1. *a. m.* tapati, -te; tatāpa, tepe; taptā, tapsyati, -te; atāpsit: *p.* tapyate, atapta: *caus.* tāpayati, -te; atitapat, -ta: burn; be hot; torture, pain; be grieved. *Pass.* endure pain, *as a religious exercise.*
-tapa, *adj.* -vexing.
tapas, *n.* heat; the hot season: torture of body, penance; devotion, piety.
tapasvin[5], *adj.* pious; addicted to penance.
tapo-dhana, *adj.* rich in piety *or* penance.
tapo-vana, *n.* a penance-grove.
tapo-vṛiddha, *adj.* grown old in penance.
tāpasa, *m.* an ascetic.
tam[6], 4. *a.* tāmyati; tatāma, tamitā: *p.* 3. *pret.* atami: waste away, be grieved.
tamas, *n.* darkness.
tamisra, *n.* *id.*
tāmra[7], *n.* copper: *adj.* copper-coloured; dark.
timira, *n.* darkness.
vitimira, *adj.* bright.
tamb, 1. *a.* move.

dvipad	pad	nagara	gam	nāman	jnā
dvipa	ap	nanu	nu	niḥśabda	śabda
dvairatha	ṛi	nabhas	bhā	niḥśvāsa	śvas
naga	gam	nāga	gam	niḥsaṃśaya	śi

[1] τείνειν; tendere, tenēre.
[2] tenuis; *Rus.* ton'ko.
[3] *Pers.* tan.
[4] ταφεῖν; tepēre; *Pers.* tāftan; *Rus.* topit'.
[5] *Pal.* tapassin.
[6] *Rus.* temnotá.
[7] *Pal.* tamba.

nıtamba, *m.* the side of a cliff: a hill.
tark[1], 10. *a.* tarkayatı; tarkayâmâsa; tarkayıtâ: consider, think, suppose.
tala, *n.* the ground; the sole *of the foot;* the palm *of the hand;* the surface.
tâla, *m.* the palm *of the hand:* the fan-palm tree.
taskara, *m.* a thief.
tıȷ, 10. *a.* teȷayatı: sharpen. *desid. m.* tıtıkṣate: endure.
tıgma, *adj.* hot, burning; sharp; passionate: *n.* heat.
tıgm'-âṃśu, *adj.* having hot rays: *m.* the sun.
tikṣṇa[2], *adj.* sharp, hot.
teȷas, *n.* brightness, fire; power; dignity, fame.
tıthı, *m.* a day of the moon.
tınduka, *m.* the name of a tree, dıospyros glûtınôsa.
tiv, 1. *a.* tivatı; tıtiva; tivıtâ: become fat, be fat.
tivra, *adj.* great, violent.
tul[3], 10. *and* 1. *a.* tolayatı; atutulat: tolatı: lift up.
atula, *adj.* unequalled.
tulayatı, *denom.* weighs.
tulâ, *f.* a balance.
tulya, *adj.* equal.
tulyatâ, *f.* equality.
tuṣ, 4. *a.* tuṣyatı; tutoṣa; toṣṭâ; tokṣyatı; atuṣat: *caus.* toṣayatı, atûtuṣat: be pleased, be glad.
tuṣṭı, *f.* pleasure, gladness.
tûr, 4. *m.* = tvar.
tûrṇa, *p. p. p.* swift.
toraṇa, *n.* a gate; the ornamental arch of a gateway.
tûṣṇim, *adj.* silently.
tṛṃh, 1. *a.* grow.
taru[4], *m.* a tree.
tṛṇa, *n.* grass.
tṛp[5], 4, 5, *and* 6. *a.* tṛpyatı, tṛpnotı, tṛpatı; tatarpa; tarpıtâ, tarptâ, *and* traptâ; tarpıṣyatı, tarpsyatı, *and* trapsyatı; atṛpat, *and* atarpit, atârpsit, atrâpsit; tṛpta: be satisfied, pleased: satisfy, please.
tṛṣ[6], 4. *a.* tṛṣyatı; tatarṣa; tarṣıtâ; tṛṣıtvâ, *and* tarṣıtvâ; tṛṣıta: thirst.
tṛṣ[7], *and* tṛṣâ, *f.* thirst.
tṛi[8], 1. *a.* taratı; tatâra, (*pl.* terus;) tarıtâ *and* taritâ; tarıṣyatı, *and* tariṣyatı: tiryât; atârit; tarıtum *and* taritum; tirṇa: *caus.* târayatı: go over, cross; escape; save, preserve; finish, conquer.
ava-, go down. ut- go up. vı-, give, grant; conquer.
kâ-tara, *adj.* weak, timid.
taras, *n.* speed, swiftness.
sa-kâ-tara, *adj.* silly.
toya, *n.* water.
tyaȷ, 1. *a.* tyaȷatı; tatyâȷa; tyaktâ; tyakṣyatı; atyâkṣit: leave; give up; give.
tyâga[9], *m.* the act of leaving

nıkṛtı	kṛı	nıdhana	dhan	nımıtta	mâ
nıkṣepa	kṣıp	nıdhı	dhâ	nımeṣa	mıṣ
nıtamba	tamba	nıpuṇa	puṇ	nıyoga	yuȷ
nıdrâ	draı	nıbha	bhâ	nırghoṣa	ghuṣ

1 *Pal.* takkatı.
2 *Pers.* tiz.
3 tollere.
4 δρυς; *Go.* triu; *Rus.* dérevo.
5 *Pal.* tappatı; τερπειν.
6 *Pal.* tasatı.
7 *Go.* thaurstei.
8 -trâre.
9 *Pal.* câga.

or giving; liberality.
parityága, *m.* the act of forsaking.
tras[1], 1 *and* 4. *a.* trasyati, *and* tarsati; tatrása, (*pl.* tatrasus, *and* tresus;) trasitá, trasiṣyati; atrásit *and* atrasit; trasta: *caus.* trásayati; atitrasat: tremble with fear; fear.
vitrásita, *p. p. p.* frightened away.
tri[2], *num.* three.
trai, 1. *m.* tráyate; tatre; trátá; trásyate; atrásta; tráṇa *and* tráta: save, deliver.
tvac, 6. *a.* tvacati; tatváca; tvacitá: cover.
tvac[3], *f.* the skin; the bark *of a tree.*
tvam[4], *pron.* thou.
tvat, *pron.* from thee: *used as the root in compounds.*
tvadíya, *adj.* thy.
tvar, 1. *m.* tvarate; tatvare; tvaritá; túrṇa, *and* tvarita: *caus.* tvarayati; atatvarat: make haste.
tura-, *in comp.* swift.
tvará, *f.* haste, speed.
daṃś[5], 1. *a.* daśati; dadaṃśa; daṃṣṭá; daṅkṣyati; daśyát; adáṅkṣit: *p.* daśyate; daṣṭa: bite.
daṃṣṭrá, *f.* a tusk.
daṃṣṭrin, *adj.* tusked, having tusks.
dakṣa[6], *adj.* apt, fit, skilful; upright, honourable.
dakṣiṇa,[7] *adj.* right, *not left;* southern; civil, polite.
dakṣiṇá, *f.* the south: a price or reward *to a priest or tutor.*
dákṣya, *n.* skill, cleverness.
daṇḍ, 10. *a.* daṇḍayati: punish.
daṇḍa, *m.* a rod, staff, sceptre: punishment.
daṇḍa-dháraṇa, *n.* punishment.
daṇḍin, *adj.* having a staff: *m.* a mace-bearer, door-keeper.
daṇḍya, *adj* that should be punished; guilty.
Danu, *f. a wife of Kasyapa, and the mother of the Asurs.*
Dánava, *m. any one of the Asurs.*
dam[8], 4. dámyati; damitvá, *and* dántvá; damita, *and* dánta: tame, subdue.
dama, *m.* restraint, self-restraint.
day, 1. *m.* dayate; dayáñcakre; dayitá; dayita: pity, love; guard; give.
dayá, *f.* pity.
dayita, *p. p. p.* beloved.
daśan[9], *num.* ten.
daśama, *adj.* tenth.
dah[10], 1. *a.* dahati, 4. *a.* dahyati; dadáha; dagdhá; dhakṣyati;

nirjana	jan	nirviśeṣa	śiṣ	niveṣa	viś
nirjhara	jhri	nirvriti	vri	niveṣana	,,
nirmala	mal	nivárana	,,	niśá	śi
nirmálya	,,	nivása	vas	niśákara	,,

[1] τρεσαι; *Pers.* tarsidan; *Rus.* tryasti.
[2] τρια, tria; *Wel. and Rus.* tri; *Pers.* sih.
[3] *Pal.* taca.
[4] *Pers.* tú; συ; tú.
[5] δακνειν; δακρυ; lacryma; *Go.* tagr.
[6] δεξιος; dexter.
[7] *Pal.* dakkhiṇa.
[8] *Pal.* damati; δαμαειν; domáre.
[9] *Pal.* dasa; *Rus.* desyat'; *Pers.* dah; δεκα; decem; *Go.* taihun.
[10] δαιειν.

adhàkṣit; dagdha: inflame, burn, destroy: *pass.* be annoyed. 4. *a.* be on fire.
adàhya, *adj.* incombustible.
ahan, *n.* day.
ekàhnà, *adv.* in one day.
dava, *and* dàva, *m.* heat, fire; a conflagration.
dà[1], 3. *a. m.* dadàti, (dattas, dadati;) datte; dadate; *pot.* dadyàt, dadita; *imper.* dehi, datsva; 1 *pret.* 3 *pl.* adus, adadata; dadau, dade, *and* dadade, dadadàte, dadadire, dàtà; dàsyati, -te; *prec.* deyàt, dàsiṣṭa; adàt, adita, adiṣata; datva, -dàya; *part. pres. act.* dadat, dadati: *p.* diyate; dade; dàyita, dàyiṣyate; dàyiṣiṣṭa, adàyi, (*pl.* adàyiṣata,) datta: *caus.* dàpayati, adidapat: *des.* ditsati, -te: give. à-, *m.* take.
-da, *adj.* -giving.
datta, *p. p. p.* given.
dàtṛi[2], *m.* a giver.
dàna[3], *n.* a gift.
deya, *adj.* that may be given.
vyàtta, *adj.* open.
dàra, *m. in pl.* a wife.
dàraka, *m.* a child.
sa-dàra, *adj.* together with his wife.
dàsa, *m.* dàsi, *f.* a servant.
dàsatva, *and* dàsya, *n.* servitude.
Diti, *and* Aditi, *wives of Kasyapa.*
Àditya, *m.* any son of Aditi: the sun.
Daitya, *m.* any son of Diti.
div, 4. *a.* divyati; dideva; devità; deviṣyati; adevit; devitvà *and* dyùtvà; dyùta: shine: play, jest; play at dice, gamble.
tridiva, *n.* the heaven of Indra.
div, *f.* diva, *n.* the sky, heaven.
divà[4], *adv.* by day.
divà-niśa, *n.* a day and night.
divà-ràtra, *n. id.*
divya, *adj.* heavenly.
deva[5], *adj.* shining: *m.* a god; a king.
devatà, *f.* a goddess: divinity.
devatva, *n.* divinity.
devana, *n.* play, gaming.
deva-pati, *m.* the lord of the gods.
devi, *f.* a goddess; a queen.
daiva, *n.* fate, destiny.
dyùta, *m. n.* play; gambling.
dyùti, *f.* brilliancy, beauty.
vidyut, *f.* lightning.
diś[6], 6. *a. m.* diśati, -te; dideśa, didiśe; deṣṭà; dekṣyati, -te; adikṣat, -ta: *p.* diṣyate; diṣṭa[7]: show; tell; command. à-, teach; command. upa-, teach, warn. nir-, desire; show. vi-nir-, desire; show. sam-, show, teach; give.
uddeśa, *m.* a description; a country.
upadeśa, *m.* instruction; advice.

niścaya	ci	naipuṇya	puṇ	nyàyya	i
niṣùdana	sùd	nyagrodha	añc	nyàsa	as
nisvana	svan	nyabhra	ap	para	pṛi
naipuṇa	puṇ	nyàya	i	parantapa	,,

[1] *Pers.* dàdan; δοῦναι; dare; *Rus.* dat' *and* davát'.
[2] dator.
[3] dònum.
[4] diès.
[5] deus.
[6] δεῖξαι, dicàre, dicere; *Go.* teihan.
[7] *Pal.* diṭṭha.

dig-vâsas, *adj.* (having the sky for his clothing,) naked.
diś, *f.* a direction, quarter; a space, part; a quarter of the sky; the sky.
diṣṭi, *f.* pleasure, happiness.
deśa, *m.* a country; a part; an ordinance.
vidiś, *f.* an intermediate direction *or* point of the compass.
dih, 2. *a. m.* degdhi, digdhe; dideha, didihe; degdhâ; dhekṣyati, -te; adhikṣat, -ta, adigdha: anoint, daub, pollute.
deha, *m. n.* the body.
sandeha, *m.* doubt.
di, 4. *m.* diyate; didiye; dâtâ; dâsyate; adâsta; dina: decay, waste away.
dina, *p. p. p.* decayed, poor, timid.
adina, *adj.* fearless.
dip, 4. *m.* dipyate; didipa; dipitâ; dipiṣyate; adipi, *and* adipiṣṭa; dipta[1]: burn, be on fire; shine.
dundubhi, *m.* a drum.
dul, 10. *a.* throw.
dola, *m.* dolâ, *f.* a swing.
duṣ, 4. *a.* duṣyati; dudoṣa; doṣṭâ; dokṣyati; aduṣat, *and* adukṣat; duṣṭa: sin; be stained by guilt.
doṣa, *m.* sin.
dus-[2], *part. insep.* badly, ill, evil.
duh[3], 2. *a. m.* dogdhi, dugdhe; dudoha, duduhe; dogdhâ; dhokṣyati, -te; adhukṣat, -ta, *and* adugdha: *p.* duhyate, adohi: milk; press out; obtain.
kâma-duh, *f.* Indra's cow that yields every wish.
duhitṛ[4], *f.* (the milker *of the domestic animals,*) a daughter.
dûta, *m.* dûti, *f.* a messenger.
dautya, *n.* the office of a messenger; a message.
dûra, *adj.* distant.
dṛś[5], *a.* paśyati; dadarśa (dadarśitha, *and* dadraṣṭha;) draṣṭâ; drakṣyati; adarśat, *and* adrâkṣit, draṣṭum; *perf. part.* dadṛśvas, *and* dadṛśivas: *p.* dṛśyate; dadṛśe; darśitâ, *and* draṣṭâ; darśiṣyate *and* drakṣyate, darśiṣiṣṭa, *and* drakṣiṣṭa; adarśi, adarśiṣata, *and* adrakṣata; dṛṣṭa: see. prati-, look back.
idṛś, *adj.* of this kind.
tâdṛś, *adj.* of that kind.
darśana[6], *n.* the act of seeing; sight; purpose; a mirror: a kind, sort.
darśin, *adj.* seeing.
dṛś, *adj.* seeing: *f.* the sight.
dṛśya, *adj.* that can *or* should be seen; beautiful.
dṛṣṭi, *f.* the sight.
sadṛś[7], *and* sadṛśa, *adj.* of the same kind; like.
su-sadṛśa, *adj.* very like.
dṛh, 1. *a.* darhati, dadarha, dar-

parasparatas	pṛi	parâc	ac	paricâra	car
parâ	,,	parâyaṇa	i	parichada	chad
parâkrama	kram	parigha	han	pariniṣṭhâ	sthâ
parân-mukha	ac	paricarya	car	paridhâna	dhâ

[1] *Pal.* ditta.
[2] δυς-; *Pers.* duṣ.
[3] *Rus.* doit'.
[4] *Rus.* doc', -eri; *Pers.* duxtar; θυγατηρ; *Go.* dauhtar.
[5] δερκεσθαι.
[6] *Pal.* dassana.
[7] *Pal.* sadis.

hıtà; darhıta, *and* dṛıḍha: grow.
dirgha[1], *adj.* long, *in space* or *time.*
dṛıḍha, *p. p. p.* grown; strong.
druma[2], *n.* a tree.
dṛi[3], 9. *a.* dṛıṇàtı; dadàra, (*pl.* dadarus, *and* dadrus;) darıtà *and* daritá; darıṣyatı *and* dariṣyatı; adàrit: *p.* diryate, dirṇa: split, break, tear.
dara, *m. n.* dari, *f.* a cavern.
dàruṇa, *adj.* frightful.
sudàruṇa, *adj.* very frightful.
dev, 1. *m.* devate; dıdeve; devıtà: lament. parı-, *id.*
do, 4. *a.* cut asunder.
dàman, *n. and f. also* dàmani, a cord.
sudàman, *m.* a cloud.
saudàmını, *f.* lightning.
dru[4], 1. *a.* dravatı; dudràva, (dudruma, dudrotha;) drotà; droṣyatı; adudruvat: run.
dravya, *and* dravıṇa, *n.* wealth.
druta, *adj.* quick.
druh, 4. *a. m.* injure.
droha, *m.* injury.
draı, 1. *a.* sleep.
nıdrà, *f.* sleep.
dvàr[5], *f.* dvàra, *n.* a door, gate.
dvàra-stha, *m.* a door-keeper.
dvı[6], *num.* two.
dvà-para, *adj.* (after two;) the third age of the world.
dvıtiya[7], *adj.* second.
dvıdhà, *adv.* twofold; twice.
vı-, *an insep. prefix, denoting either* variety *or* separation.
vıṃśa, *adj.* twentieth.
vıṃśatı[8], *f. num.* twenty.
vınà, *prp. w. ac. or inst.* without, except.
dvıṣ, 2. *a. m.* dveṣṭı, dvıṣṭe; 1 *pret.* advet, (*pl.* advıṣus, *and* advıṣan;) advıṣṭa; dıdveṣa, dıdvıṣe; dveṣṭà; dvekṣyatı, -te; advıkṣat, -ta; dvıṣṭa: hate.
dveṣaṇa, *n.* hatred.
vıdveṣaṇa, *n. id.*
dhan, 1. *a.* dhanatı: sound. dhan, 3. *a.* dadhantı: bear fruit.
dhana, *n.* wealth.
dhanın, *adj.* wealthy.
dhanus, *n.* a bòw.
dhanvın, *m.* a bòwman.
nıdhana, *m.* death. *See* han.
dhava, *m.* a husband; a kind of tree, grıslea tomentòsa.
dhà[9], 3. *a. m.* dadhàtı, (dhattas, dadhatı,) dhatte, (dadhate,); *pot.* dadhyàt, dadhita, *imper.* dhehı, dhatsva; 1 *pret.* adadhus, adadhata; dadhau, dadhe; dhàtà; dhàsyatı, -te; *prec.* dheyàt, dhàsiṣṭa; adhàt, adhıta, adhıṣata; hıtvà, -dhàya, *part. act.* dadhat: *p.* dhiyate; dadhe; dhàyıtà: dhàyısyate; dhàyıṣiṣṭa; adhàyı, adhàyıṣata; hıta: place; give: *m.* take, hold. antar-, *m.* place between: *pass.* dis-

parıdhvaṃsa	dhvaṃs	parıhàsa	has	paryaya	ı
parıvatsara	vatsa	parikṣa	akṣ	parvata	pṛi
parıvartın	vṛıt	parivàra	vṛı	palvala	plu
parıṣad	sad	parokṣa	akṣ	pavana	pù

[1] *Pal.* digha; δολιχος; *Rus.* dolgo.
[2] *Pal.* ḍuma.
[3] *Pal.* daratı; *Pers.* daridan; *Rus.* drat'; *Go.* taıran.
[4] δραναι.
[5] *Pers.* dar; θυρα; *Go.* daur; *Rus.* dver'.
[6] *Pers.* dù; δυο; duo; *Wel.* dau; *Go.* tvaı; *Rus.* dva.
[7] *Pal.* dutıya; *Rus.* vtoro.
[8] *Pers.* bist; εικοσι; vigınti.
[9] θειναι, -dere.

appear. abhı-, set before, narrate. â-, apply, give. samâ-, apply, attend. vı-, arrange.
âhıta, *adj.* attentive, diligent.
tathâ-vıdha, *adj.* of that kind.
-dhâ, *forms adverbs of arrangement; as* dvı-dhâ, in two ways.
dhâtu, *m.* a mineral; metal: the root *of a verb.*
dhâtṛı, *m.* the arranger, creator.
dhâtri, *f.* a nurse.
nıdhı, *m.* a treasury.
parıdhâna, *n.* an inner garment.
vıdha, *m.* vıdhâ, *f.* a kind, sort: nature, character.
vıdhâna, *n.* a rule, manner.
vıdhı, *m.* rule; fate.
vıdhıvat, *adv.* according to rule.
vıvıdha, *adj.* various.
sannıdhı, *f.* presence.
samâhıta, *adj.* attentive, diligent.
susamâhıta, *adj.* very attentive.
hıta, *p. p. p.* placed; good: *n.* happiness.
dhâv[1], 1. *a. m.* dhâvatı, -te; dadhâva, -ve; dhâvıtâ; dhâvıṣyatı, -te; adhâvit, adhâvıṣṭa; dhâvıtvâ *and* dhautvâ: *caus.* dhâvayatı; adidhavat: run; wash.
dhâvana, *n.* the act of washing.
dhû, 5. *and* 9. *a. m. and* 6. *a.* dhûnotı, dhunâtı, dhuvatı, dhûnute, dhunite; dudhâva, dudhuve; dhavıtâ, *and* dhotâ; dhavıṣyatı, -te, *and* dhoṣyatı, -te; adhâvit, adhuvit; adhavıṣṭa, adhoṣṭa: *p.* dhûyate; dhûta, *and* dhûna: shake.
dhûma[2], *m.* smoke.
dhṛı, 1. *a. m.* dharatı, -te; dadhâra, dadhre; dhartâ; dharıṣyatı, -te; adhârṣit, adhṛıta: *p.* dhṛıyate, adhṛıta; dhṛıta: hold; keep back; support, nourish; place: *pass.* be, live.
-dhara[3], *adj.* -holding.
dharaṇi, *and* dharâ, *f.* the earth.
dharma[4], *m.* justice, duty, fitness: *the god Yama.*
dharma-jna, *and* dharma-vıd, *adj.* knowing what is fit, wise in duty.
dharmya, *adj.* lawful.
dhâraṇa, *n.* the act of holding or carrying.
dhira, *adj.* firm; sensible, sedate.
dhṛıtı[5], *f.* dhaırya, *n.* firmness, constancy.
dhaırya, *n.* firmness, strength.
dhṛıṣ[6], 5. *a.* dhṛıṣṇotı; dadharṣa; dharṣıtâ; dharṣıṣyatı; adharṣit; dhṛıṣṭa: dare, be bold. 10 *and* 1. *a.* dharṣayatı, *and* dharṣatı: conquer; oppress.
atı-dur-dharṣa, *adj.* very hard to conquer.
dur-dharṣa, *adj.* hard to conquer.

paśyatı	dṛıś	pârthıva	prath	paurṇamâsa	mâs
pâra	pṛi	pâvaka	pû	prakâra	kṛı
pâraga	,,	pina	pyaı	prakâśa	kâś
pârıṣada	sad	pûrṇamâsa	mâs	prakṛıtı	kṛı

1 *Pers.* davidan; θεειν.
2 fûmus.
3 *Pal.* ḍaratı.
4 *Pal.* dhamma.
5 *Pal.* dhıtı.
6 θαρσειν; *Go.* gadaursan; *Rus.* derznut'.

dharṣa, *m.* pride, arrogance.
dhmâ, 1. *a.* dhamati; dadhmau; dhmâtâ; dhmâsyati; dhmâyât, *and* dhmeyât; adhmâsit: *p.* dhmâyate; adhmâyi; dhmâta: blow.
dhyai, 1. *a.* dhyâyati; dadhyau; dhyâtâ; dhyâsyati; dhyâyât, *and* dhyeyât; adhyâsit; dhyâta: think; meditate.
âdhi, *m.* thought, anxiety.
dhi, *f.* thought, mind, intellect.
dhimat, *adj.* having intellect, wise.
dhyâna, *n.* meditation, thought.
dhyâna-para, *adj.* full of thought.
sandhyâ, *f.* meditation; prayer at sunrise and sunset: the twilight.
dhru, 1 *and* 6. *a.* dhravati, dhruvati; dudhrâva; dhrotâ, *and* dhruvitâ; dhroṣyati, *and* dhruviṣyati; adhrauṣit, *and* adhruvit: be fixed, firm.
dhruva[1], *adj.* fixed, firm, certain.
dhvaṃs, 1. *m.* dhvaṃsate; dadhvaṃse; dhvaṃsitâ; dhvaṃsiṣyate; adhvaṃsiṣṭa, *and* adhvasta: *p.* dhvasyate, dhvasta: fall; go.
dhvaṃsa, *m.* the act of falling; ruin.
paridhvaṃsa, *m. id.* the act of wandering.
dhvaj, 1. *a.* go; move one's self.
dhvaja, *m.* a standard, banner.

na[2], *adv.* not; *used both separately, and as a prefix.*
nakta.
naktam[3], *adv.* by night.
nakṣatra, *n.* a star; a constellation.
naj, 1. *a.* be ashamed.
nagna[4], *p. p. p.* ashamed; naked.
nad, 1. *a.* nadati; nanâda; anadit, *and* anâdit; nadiṣyati; naditum: sound, make a noise. pra, make a great noise.
nada, *m.* nadi, *f.* a river.
nâda, *m.* a sound.
nâdin, *adj.* sounding.
nand, 1. *a.* nandati; nananda; anandit; nandiṣyati; nanditum: rejoice, be glad.
nanda, *m.* nandi, *f.* happiness.
-nandana, *adj.* -delighting, causing happiness: *m.* a son. *f.* a daughter.
nandin, *adj.* happy.
nam, 1. *a.m.* namati, -te; nanâma; naṃsyati; anaṃsit, -sata: nantum; natvâ; namya, *and* natya: *p.* namyate, nata: bend, bow; bow one's self; bow with reverence to, *w. dat. g. or ac. of person.*
pra-, *id.* salute by bowing.
namas, *indec.* the act of bowing; salutation.
namas-kâra, *m. id.*
naraka, *m. n.* hell.
nala, *m.* a reed.
navan[5], *num.* nine.

prakopa	kup	praṇayin	ni	pratima	mâ
prakṣâlana	kṣal	pratipad	pad	prativacas	vac
prakhya	khyâ	pratipâṇa	paṇ	prativâkya	,,
praṇaya	ni	pratibhaya	bhi	pratyakṣa	akṣ

[1] *Pal.* dhuva.
[2] nè.
[3] νυκτος; noctù; *Go.* nahts.
[4] *Pal.* nagga; *Rus.* nago; *Go.* naqaths.
[5] *Pal.* nava; *Pers.* nuh; εννεα; novem; *Wel.* naw; *Go.* niun.

navama, *adj.* ninth.
naś[1], 4. *a.* naśyati; nanāśa; anaśat; naśiṣyati, *and* nakṣyati; naśitum, *and* naṣṭum; naṣṭa; naṣṭvā, *and* naṃṣṭvā: perish, die.
anāśin, *adj.* imperishable.
naṣṭa, *p. p. p.* lost.
naṣṭa-sañjna, *adj.* having lost his understanding.
nāśa, *m.* death, destruction.
nāśana, *n. id.*
nah, 4. *a. m.* nahyati, -te; nanāha, nehe; anātsit, anaddha; natsyati, -te; naddhum; naddha: bind, fasten together.
naddha[2], *p. p. p.* bound.
nānā-, various-.
ni-, *prp. insep.* down.
nitya[3], *adj.* continual: *n. adv.* continually.
nityaśas, *adv.* continually.
nica, *adj.* low.
nind, 1. *a.* nindati; nininda; ninditum: blame, despise.
Niṣadha, *name of a people in India.*
Naiṣadha, *adj.* belonging to the Niṣadhāḥ.
nis-, *prp. insep.* out; without.
ni, 1. *a. m.* nayati, -te; anayat, -ta; nayatu, -tām; nayet, -ta; ninaya, ninye; anaiṣit, aneṣṭa; netum: *p.* niyate; anāyi, nita: lead; bring; spend *time: m.* instruct. pra-, bring forward; offer; favour, cherish.
anātha, *and* anāthavat, *adj.* having no protector.
ānayana, *n.* the act of bringing.
naya, *m.* the act of leading, or guiding.
nayana, *n.* guidance; an eye: *f.* the pupil of an eye.
nātha, *m.* a protector, master, lord.
nāthavat, *adj.* having a protector.
nirnāthatā, *f.* unprotectedness.
netra[4], *n.* an eye.
praṇaya, *m.* affection; esteem.
praṇayin, *adj.* loving, affectionate.
vinaya, *m.* submissiveness, modesty.
vinita, *adj.* submissive.
senā, *f.* an army.
nu, *a particle usually denoting doubt, and sometimes being interrogative.*
nanu, *an interrogative with a negation,* nonne?
nūnam, *adv.* surely.
nṛi[5], *and* nara, *m.* a man.
anṛi-śaṃsa, *adj.* harmless to men, harmless.
ānṛiśaṃsya, *n.* harmlessness.
nara-vara, *m.* best of men.
nāri, *f.* a woman.
nṛi-pa, *and* nṛi-pati, *m.* a lord of men, a king.
nṛi-śaṃsa, *adj.* injurious to men, mischievous.
paṃś, *and* paṃs, 10. *a.* destroy.
pāṃśu, *m.* dust.
pakṣa[6], *m.* a side: *n.* a wing.
pakṣin, *adj.* winged: *m.* a bird.
pakṣman, *n.* hair; an eye-lash.

pratyac	ac	prabhu	bhū	pramathin	math
prathama	pri	prabhṛiti	bhṛi	pramukha	mukha
prabhā	bhā	pramada	mad	pralāpa	lap
prabhāva	bhū	pramāṇa	mā	pralāpin	,,

1 νεκρος, νεκυς, necāre.
2 nodus.
3 *Pal.* nicca.
4 *Pal.* nitta.
5 ανηρ.
6 *Pal.* pakkha.

pan-ka, *m. n.* mud.
pan-ka-ja, *m.* a lotus.
pañcan[1], *num.* five.
pañcama, *adj.* fifth.
paṭ, 1. *a.* paṭati; papâṭa; paṭitâ: go. 10. *a.* paṭayati: surround; clothe. pâṭayati: cleave, split.
paṭa, *m.* cloth; a garment.
paṇ, 1. *m.* paṇate; peṇe; paṇitâ; paṇiṣyate; apaṇiṣṭa: play *at a game*; make a bargain.
paṇa[2], *m.* a game; a price; a stake.
pâṇa, *m.* a game.
pâṇi, *m.* a hand.
pratipâṇa, *m.* a counter-stake *in a game.*
baṇij, *m.* a merchant.
paṇḍ, 1. *m.* go. 10. *a.* collect.
paṇḍâ, *f.* wisdom.
paṇḍita, *adj.* learned.
pâṇḍu, *adj.* pale.
pat[3], 1. *a.* patati; papâta; patitâ; patiṣyati; apaptat; patita: fall; fly. ut-, rise up; fly up.
nipâtin, *adj.* causing to fall down.
patatra, pattra[4], *and* patra, *n.* a wing; a leaf.
patatrin, *adj.* winged: a bird.
patâkâ, *f.* a standard, banner.
pâtaka, *n.* sin; crime.
śata-patra, *n.* (hundred-leaved,) the lotus.
path, 1. *a.* pathati, papâtha, apathit: go.
-patha[5], *m.* a way; country.
pathin, *m.* a way.
pad, 4. *m.* padyate; pede; pattâ; patsyate; apâdi; *p.p.p.* panna: go. ut-, arise, come into being. upa-, go near. prati-, come back, get.
âpad, *f.* a calamity.
upapanna, *p.p.p.* endowed *with.*
dvi-pad, *m.* (a biped,) a man.
pad[6], *m.* a foot.
pada, *m.* a foot; step; section; place; country.
padâti, *m.* a foot-soldier.
pan-na-ga, *m.* (not going with feet,) a serpent.
pâda, *m.* a foot; the root of a tree.
pâda-pa, *m.* (drinking at foot,) a tree.
pratipad, *f.* the first *or* fifteenth day of the moon.
sampad, *f.* completeness; happiness, good fortune.
padma, *m. n.* a lotus: the number 10^{10}.
padmini, *f.* a lake full of lotuses.
pari-[7], *prp. insep.* around; very.
parṇa, *n.* a leaf.
pallava, *m. n.* a bud, shoot.
paś, 10. *a.* pâśayati: bind.
paśu[8], *m.* a domesticated animal; cattle.
pâśa, *m.* a cord.
pâśava, *adj.* belonging to cattle.
paśca[9], *used only in abl.* paścât,

praśâkhikâ	śâkh	prasan-ga	sañj	prasravaṇa	sru
pravara	vṛi	prasanna	sad	prâk	ac
pravâda	vad	prasâda	,,	prâc	,,
praśriya	śri	prasûta	su	prâñjali	añj

[1] *Pers.* panj; *Wel.* pump; *Rus.* pyast'; πεντε; quinque; *Go.* fimf.
[2] pignus.
[3] *Pers.* uftâdan; πιπτειν; *Rus.* pádat'.
[4] *Pal.* patta; *Pers.* par; πτερον; *Rus.* peró.
[5] *Rus.* put'.
[6] *Pers.* pâ; ποδες; pêdes; *Go.* fotus.
[7] περι.
[8] πωυ; pecus; *Go.* faihu.
[9] *Pers.* pas; *Pal.* pecca.

adv. behind, back; afterwards; westward.
paścima, *adj. sup.* hindmost; last; western.
apaścima, *adj.* last of all.
pâ, 2. *a.* pâti; papau; pâtâ; pâsyati; pâyât; apâsit: *p.* pâyate; apâyi; pâta: defend, guard: *causat. and* 10. *a.* pâlayati.
pâ[1], 1. *a.* pivati; papau; pâta; pâsyati; peyât; apât; pitvâ: *p.* piyate, apâyi, pita: drink.
adhipa, *m.* chief guardian, ruler; king.
adhipati, *m. id.*
âdhipatya, *n.* sovereignty.
dvi-pa, *m.* (twice-drinking,) an elephant.
nṛi-pa, *and* nṛi-pati, *m.* (lord of men,) a king.
-pa, *adj.* -guarding, -drinking.
pati[2], *m.* a lord, husband.
patitva, *n.* the rank of husband.
patni[3], *f.* a lady, wife.
payas[4], *m.* drink; water; milk.
payo-dhara, *m.* (drink-holder,) a cloud; a breast.
pâna, *n.* drink.
pâniya, *n.* water.
pâla, *m.* a guardian, ruler, king.
pâlana, *n.* guardianship, protection.
pitâ-maha, *m.* a grandfather.
pitṛi[5], *m.* a father: *dual,* parents: *pl.* ancestors.
pipâsâ, *f.* (a wish to drink,) thirst.
bhûmi-pa, *m.* (earth-guarding,) a king.
sa-patna, *adj.* (having the same husband,) rival.
pâpa, *adj.* sinful: *n.* sin.
pârśva, *m. n.* a side *of the body.*
piplu, *m.* a mark, spot, mole.
piśâca, *m.* piśâci, *f.* a malevolent demon.
piḍ, 10. *a.* piḍayati; apipiḍat, *and* apipiḍat. press; oppress; annoy. abhi-, annoy.
âpiḍa, *m.* a chaplet, wreath.
piḍâ, *f.* pressure; torture.
puṃs[6], *m.* a man; a male.
pun-nâga, *m.* a male elephant; a lotus; a certain tree, rottlêria tinctória.
puṇ, 6. *a.* puṇati: act honourably; be good.
nipuṇa, *adj.* fit, skilful.
naipuṇa, *and* naipuṇya, *n.* fitness; skill.
puṇya[7], *adj.* pure, just, good, fair: *n.* virtue.
puṇyavat, *adj.* virtuous.
puṇy'-âhan, *m.* a holy day.
puṇy'-âha-vâcana, *n.* a summons to a holy day.
Puṇya-śloka, *m.* (pure-verse,) *an epithet of Nala.*
putra[8], *m.* a son.
putraka, *m. id.*
putrikâ, *f.* a daughter.
putrin, *adj.* having children.

prâṇa	an	prâya	i	baṇij	paṇ
prâṇayâtra	,,	prâsâda	sad	bâhu	vah
prâptakâla	âp	preṣya	iṣ	bhûyas	baṃh
prâjna	jnâ	preṣyatâ	,,	mat	ah

[1] πιειν; bibere; *Rus.* pit'.
[2] ποσις.
[3] ποτνια.
[4] *Rus.* pivo.
[5] *Pers.* pidar; πατηρ; pater; *Go.* *pl.* fadrein.
[6] homo; *Go.* guma.
[7] *Pal.* puñña.
[8] *Pal.* putta; *Pers.* pisar.

pautra, *m.* a grandson.
punar, *adv.* again.
pur, 6. *a.* precede.
puras, *adv.* before, in front.
purà, *adv.* formerly; in old time.
puràṇa, *adj.* ancient.
puràtana, *adj. id.*
purogama, *adj.* going before.
pùrva[1], *adj.* former; old; eastern.
pùrvatas, *adv.* eastward.
pul, 1 *and* 6. *a.* polatı; pulatı; pupola; polıtà: be or become great. 10. *a.* polayatı; apùpulat: heap together; be high or great.
pula, *adj.* great: *m.* the rising of the hair, *from emotion.*
vıpula, *adj.* large.
puṣ, 1, 9, 10. *a.* poṣatı, puṣṇàtı, poṣayatı, puṣyatı; pupoṣa; poṣıtà, poṣṭà; poṣıṣyatı, pokṣyatı; apoṣit, apuṣat: nourish; 4. *a.* nourish; enjoy.
puṣkala, *adj.* plenteous.
puṣṭa, *p. p. p.* nourished, fed.
puṣpa[2], *n.* a flower.
puṣpa-bhan-ga, *m.* a festoon of flowers.
puṣpa-vṛıṣṭı, *f.* a shower of flowers.
pù, 9. *a. m.* 1. *m.* punàtı, punite, pavate; pupàvà, pupuve; pavıtà; pavıṣyatı, -te; apàvit, apavıṣṭa; pùtvà, *and* pavıtvà: *p.* pùyate; pùta, *and* pavıta: purify.
pavana, *m.* wind.
pàvaka, *m.* fire.
pùȷ, 10. *a.* pùȷayatı, apùpuȷat: honour; worship.
pùȷà, *f.* honour, worship, respect.
pṛi, (pùr, pàr,) 3 *and* 9. *a.* pıpartı, pṛıṇàtı; papàra, (*pl.* paparus, *and* paprus;) parıtà, *and* parità; parıṣyatı, *and* pariṣyatı; pùryàt; apàrit: *p. and refl.* pùryate; apùrı, *and* apùrıṣṭa; pùrta, pùrıta *and* pùrṇa: fill.
antaḥ-pura, *n.* (inner-city) a palace; the apartments for females.
apara, *adj.* other.
apare-dyus, *adv.* on the morrow.
para, *adj.* other; more distant: an enemy; chief: -ful.
paran-tapa, *adj.* that annoys the enemy.
para-puraṅ-ȷaya, *m.* a conqueror of the city of the enemy.
parama, *adj.* farthest, highest, best.
para-vira-han, *m.* a slayer of a hero of the enemy.
paras-para, *adj.* each other.
paras-paratas, *adv.* from each other.
parasva, *n.* what belongs to another.
parà-, *insep. partic.* far; behind.
parvata, *m.* a mountain.
pàra[3], *m.* the farther side.
pàra-ga, *adj.* going to the farther side; reading through.
pura[4], *n.* puri, *f.* a city.
puru, *adj.* much; many: *m. a king so named.*

maraṇa	mṛı	mahànasa	an	màs	mà
martya	,,	mahàbàhu	vah	màsa	,,
mardana	mṛıd	mahàbhuȷa	bhuȷ	mùrtı	mṛı
marṣa	mṛıṣ	màcıram	cı	mùrtımat	,,

[1] *Pal.* pubba.
[2] *Pal.* puppha.
[3] *Pers.* pàr.
[4] πολις.

puruṣa[1], *m.* a man, person; the mind, soul.
pùrṇa[2], *p. p. p.* full.
paura, *and* paurajana, *m.* a citizen.
paurajànapada, *m. pl.* country people.
pra-[3], *prp. insep.* forward.
pratı, *prp. insep. and sep. w. acc.* towards; opposite; against; again.
prathama, *adj.* first.
pṛıṣ, 1. *a.* sprinkle.
pṛıṣṭa, *n.* back.
pṛıṣṭatas, *adv.* behind.
pyaı, 1. *m.* pyàyate; papye, *and* pıpye; pyàtà, *and* pyàyıtà; pyàsyate, *and* pyàyıṣyate; apyàsta, *and* apyàyıṣṭa, apyàyı; *part.* pyàna, *and* pina: grow; become fat.
pina[4], *adj.* fat, plump.
prach[5], 6. *a.* pṛıcchatı; papraccha; praṣṭà; prakṣyatı; apràkṣit; pṛıṣṭvà; pṛıṣṭa: ask, inquire. parı-, ask particularly.
prath[6], 1. *m.* prathate; paprathe; prathıtà: be stretched out; be increased; be praised.
pàrthıva, *adj.* earthly: *m.* (lord of the land,) a king.
pṛıthıvi, *f.* the earth.
pṛıthu[7], *adj.* large, wide, broad.
protha, *m. n.* the nose *of an animal.*
pri[8], 9. *and* 1. *a. m.* priṇàtı, priṇite, prayatı, -te; pıpràya, pıprıye; pretà; preṣyatı, -te; apraıṣit, apreṣṭa: love.
prıya[9], *adj.* beloved; pleasing; loving.
pritı, *f.* love, pleasure.
vıprıya, *adj.* displeasing.
plakṣa, *m.* the holy fig-tree, ficus rèlıgıòsa.
plu[10], 1. *m.* plavate; pupluve; plotà; ploṣyate; aploṣṭa, *pl.* aploḍhvam: swim; go by ship.
palvala, *n.* a pool.
phal, 1. *a.* phalatı; paphàla, (*pl.* phelus;) phalıtà; phalıṣyatı; aphàlit; phalıta: bear fruit.
phala, *n.* fruit.
phalavat, *adj.* fruitful.
sa-phala, *adj. id.*
baṃh, bah, vaṃh, *and* vah, *m.* baṃhate; babaṃhe; baṃhıtà: grow.
bahu, *adj.* much.
bahutıtha, *adj. ordinal,* many-eth, *of time.*
bahudhà, *adv.* in many ways.
bahula, *adj.* much.
bahu-vıdha, *adj.* of many kinds.
bhùyas, *adj. comp.* more.
bhùyıṣṭha, *adj. sup.* most.
bandh, 9. *a.* badhnàtı; babandha; banddhà; bhantsyatı; abhàntsit: *p.* badhyate; baddha; abadhı: bind.
pratıbandha, *n.* a hindrance.

meya	mà	yathàrham	arh	vayam	ah
mnà	man	ratha	ṛı	vàdh	vṛı
yacchatı	yam	rathın	,,	vàra	,,
yata	,,	rathopastha	,,	vàraṇa	,,

[1] *Pal.* purısa.
[2] *Pers.* pur; πλεος; plènus; *Rus.* polno.
[3] *Pal.* pa-.
[4] πιων.
[5] *Pal.* pucchatı; *Pers.* pursidan; *Rus.* prosit'; poscere.
[6] *Pal.* puthatı.
[7] πλατυς.
[8] φιλεειν; *Go.* frıjon.
[9] *Pal.* pıya; φιλος.
[10] πλεειν; *Rus.* plüt'.

prabandha, *m.* perseverance, continuance.
bandha[1], *m.* a bond.
bandhana, *n.* the act of binding; a bond.
bandhu, *m.* a relative, friend.
bandhu-varga, *m.* the whole body of *his* relatives.
sa-bandhin, *m.* a kinsman.
bala[2], *n.* strength; an army: a *demon killed by Indra.*
balavat, *adj.* strong.
Bala-Vṛitra-han, *m.* the slayer of Bala and Vṛitra.
balin, *adj.* strong.
bála, *adj.* young: a young person.
bálaka, *m.* a boy.
bála-bháva, *m.* childhood, youth.
bálya, *n. id.*
bádh, *and* vádh, 1. *m.* bádhate; babádhe; bádhitá; bádhiṣyate; abádhiṣṭa: force; strike, kill; annoy.
ábádhá, *f.* annoyance, vexation.
badhya, *adj.* worthy of death.
bádhá, *f.* hindrance.
budh[3], 1. *a. m.* 4. *m.* bodhati, -te; budhyate; bubodha; bubudhe; bodhitá, *and* boddhá; bodhiṣyati, -te, *and* bhotṣyate; abudhat, abodhit, abuddha; buddha: know; perceive; think. 4. awake, become conscious. ni-, attend.
dur-buddhi, *adj.* having a foolish mind; evil-minded.
buddhi, *f.* the mind, understanding; a purpose, plan.
budha, *adj.* wise.
vibudha, *m.* (very wise,) a god.
su-dur-buddhi, *adj.* having a very foolish mind.
brahman, *m.* the god Brahmá: a brahman.
brahmaṇya, *adj.* pious.
brahmarṣi, *m.* a divine saint.
bráhmaṇya, *m.* a brahman.
brú, 2. *a. m.* braviti, brúte; abravit: say. prati-, answer.
bhakṣ, 1. *a. m.* 10. *a.* eat.
bhakṣya, *adj.* eatable: *n.* food.
bhikṣ, 1. *m.* beg.
bhikṣá, *f.* alms.
bhikṣu, *m.* a beggar.
bhaikṣya, *n.* mendicity.
bhaj, 1. *a. m.* bhajati, -te; babhája, bheje; bhaktá; bhakṣyati, -te; abhákṣit, abhakta; bhakta: cherish, love; obtain, have.
bhañj[4], 7. *a.* bhanakti; babhañja; bhan·ktá; bhan·kṣyati; abhan·kṣit; bhan·ktvá, *and* bhaktvá: *p.* bhajyate; abháji; bhagna: break.
bhakti[5], *f.* attachment, love.
bhaga, *m.* a share; good fortune.
bhagavat, *adj.* holy; divine.
bhan·ga, *m.* breaking, crushing.
bhága = bhaga.
bhága-dheya, *m.* an heir: *n.* fate, lot.
bhágin, *adj.* one who shares; a co-heir: *m.* a brother: *f.* a sister.

vári	vṛi	vikára	kṛi	vicára	car
vi	dvi	vikoṣa	kuṣ	vicáraṇa	"
viṃsa	"	vikrama	kram	vicitra	ci
vikaṭa	kaṭ	vighnan	han	vijana	jan

[1] *Pers.* band; *Go.* bindan.
[2] valère.
[3] *Pal.* bujjhati; πιθεσθαι; *Rus.* budit'.
[4] ῥηξαι; frangere; *Go.* brikan.
[5] *Pal.* bhatti.

bhágya, *n.* fate, lot; good fortune.
su-bhaga, *adj.* happy, fortunate.
saubhágya, *n.* happiness; good fortune.
bhand, 1. *m.* bhandate: be happy, prosperous.
bhadra[1], *adj.* happy, prosperous, excellent: *n.* happiness, prosperity.
bhá[2], 2. *a.* bhátı; babhau; bhátá; bhásyatı; bháyát; abhásit: *p. impers.* bháyate: shine.
bhás, 1. *m. a. id.*
ábhá, *f.* brightness; likeness.
na-bhas[3], *n.* (not-shining, a cloud;) the sky.
-nıbha, *adj.* like.
prabhá, *f.* brightness.
-bha, *adj.* -shining.
bhávın, *adj.* bright; beautiful; excellent.
vıbhá, *f.* brightness.
vıbhávasu, *m.* the sun: fire.
vıbhásu, *m.* fire.
san-nıbha, *adj.* like.
sabhá, *f.* an assembly; a house; a cottage.
bháṣ[4], 1. *m.* bháṣate[5]; babháṣe; bháṣıtá: speak. abhı-, *and* á-, speak to. pra-, speak. pratı-, answer.
abhıbháṣın, *adj.* speaking to.
bháṣın, *adj.* speaking.
su-bháṣıta, *adj.* speaking well.
bhıṣaȷ, *m.* a physician.
bheṣaȷa, *n.* a medicine.
bhi[6], 3. *a.* bıbhetı, (*du.* bıbhitas, *and* bıbhıtas;) bıbháya, *and* bıbhayáñcakára; bhetá; bheṣyatı; abhaıṣit: *p.* bhiyate; bhita: fear.
pratıbhaya, *adj.* frightful.
bhaya[7], *n.* fear.
bhaya-kartṛı, *m.* one that causes fear.
bhayan-kara, *adj. id.*
bhay'-á-bádha, *adj.* not disturbed by fear.
bhay'-árta, *adj.* afflicted by fear.
bhita, *p. p. p.* afraid.
bhima, *adj.* formidable: *name of a king.*
bhima-parákrama, *adj.* having formidable power.
bhiru, *adj.* timid.
Bhaıma, *adj.* belonging to Bhima: *f.* the daughter of Bhima.
vıbhitaka, *m.* *the name of a plant,* belerıca termınálıa.
bhuȷ[8], 6. *a.* 7. *a. m.* bhuȷatı, bhunaktı, bhun-kte; bubhoȷa, bubhuȷe; bhoktá; bhokṣyatı, -te; abhaukṣit, abhukta; bhugna, *curved.* bhukta, *eaten.* bend, curve. 7. *a. m.* enjoy, eat.
bhuȷa, *m.* the arm; an elephant's trunk.
bhuȷa-ga, *and* bhuȷan-gama, *m.* a serpent.
bhuȷıṣya, *m.* a servant.

vıȷna	ȷná	vıdveṣaṇa	dvıṣ	vıdhıvat	dhá
vıtımıra	tam	vıdha	dhá	vınaya	ni
vıdıś	dıś	vıdhána	,,	vıná	dvı
vıdyut	dıv	vıdhı	,,	vıparyaya	ı

[1] *Pal.* bhadda.
[2] φαειν.
[3] núbés; *Rus.* nebo; *Wel.* nef.
[4] φηναι.
[5] *Pal.* bhásatı.
[6] φοβεισθαι.
[7] φοβος.
[8] *Pers.* bázú; *Go.* bıugan.

bhoga, *m.* enjoyment; food: a serpent.
bhogavat, *adj.* full of serpents: *f.* the world of serpents.
bhojana, *n.* the act of eating; food.
bhojaniya, *adj.* that may be eaten: *n.* food.
mahâ-bhuja, *adj.* great-armed.
bhû[1], 1. *a.* bhavati; babhûva, (*pl.* babhûvus;) bhavitâ; bhavishyati; bhûyât; abhût, (*pl.* abhûvan;) bhûta: be. anu-, be present at. pra-, be over, be powerful.
adbhuta, *adj.* (*for* atibhûta,) preternatural; wonderful.
prabhâva[2], *m.* superiority, power.
prabhu[3], *m.* a superior, chief.
prabhûta, *adj.* abundant.
bhava, *m.* being, origin.
bhavat, (1) *part. pres.* (*nom. m.* bhavan,) being. (2) *adj.* (*nom. m.* bhavân,) thou, a *word of respect, used with the third person of verbs.*
bhavana, *n.* a house, palace.
bhâva, *m.* being; a state, nature; the mind.
bhuvana, *n.* the world.
bhû, *f.* the earth.
bhûta, *past p.* having been: *n.* a being.
bhû-tala, *n.* the surface of the earth.
bhûmi[4], *f.* the earth; a place.
bhûmi-pa, *m.* a king.
bhûmi-ṣṭha, *adj.* standing on the ground.
vibhu, *m.* = prabhu.
vibhûti, *f.* superiority, power, majesty.
bhûri, *in comp.* much.
bhûṣ[5], 1 *and* 10. bhûṣati; bhûṣayati; bubhûṣa; bhûṣitâ: adorn.
bhûṣana, *n.* an ornament.
bhṛi[6], 1. *and* 3. *a. m.* bharati, -te, bibharti, bibhṛite; babhâra, (*du.* babhriva,) *and* bibharâñcakâra, babhre, *and* bibharâñcakre; bhartâ; bhariṣyati, -te; bhriyât, bhṛiṣiṣṭa; abhârṣit, abhṛita: *p.* bhriyate, bhṛita: bear, bring, support, feed, maintain. â-, wear. ni-, hide.
âbharaṇa, *n.* an ornament.
prabhṛiti, *adv. following the abl.* after, forward *in time.*
bharaṇa, *n.* support.
bhartṛi[7], *m.* (he that supports,) a husband; lord.
bhârya, *adj.* that must be supported: *f.* a wife.
-bhṛit, *adj.* -carrying.
bhṛiti, *f.* wages.
sa-bhârya, *adj.* with *his* wife.
sambhâra, *m.* wealth.
bhṛiśa, *adj.* much.
bho, *and* bhos, *inter.* ho! *used in a respectful address.*
bhraṃś, 4. *a. and* 1. *m.* bhraśyati,

vipula	pul	vibhâ	bhâ	vibhu	bhû
vipina	vep	vibhâvasu	,,	vibhûti	,,
vipriya	pri	vibhita	bhi	vibhrânta	bhram
vibudha	budh	vibhitaka	,,	vimâna	mâ

[1] *Pers.* bûdan; φυναι; fuisse; *Wel.* bod.
[2] *Pal.* pabhâva.
[3] πρεσβυς.
[4] *Pers.* bum.
[5] *Pal.* bhusati.
[6] *Pers.* burdan; φερειν; ferre; *Go.* bairan.
[7] bhatta.

bhraṃśate; babhraṃśa, -śe; bhraṃśitā; bhraṃśiṣyati, -te; abhraśat, abhraṃśiṣṭa; bhraṃśitvā, *and* bhraṣṭvā; bhraṣṭa, *fallen*: fall.
bhrami[1], 1. *and* 4. *a.* bhramati, bhramyati, *and* bhrāmyati; babhrāma, (*pl.* babhramus, *and* bhremus;) bhramitā; bhramiṣyati; abhramit; bhramitvā, *and* bhrāntvā; bhrānta: wander.
vibhrānta, *p. p. p.* confused, disturbed.
sambhrānta, *id.*
bhrāj, 1. *m.* bhrājate; babhrāje, *and* bhreje; bhrājitā; bhrājiṣyate; abhrājiṣṭa: shine.
bhrātṛi[2], *m.* a brother.
bhrū[3], *f.* the brow.
subhru, *adj.* having beautiful brows.
maṃh, 1. *m.* grow.
maṅg, 1. *a.* go; move one's self.
maṅgala, *adj.* happy; healthful: *n.* good fortune.
mah, 1. *a.* honour, worship.
magha, *m.* happiness.
Maghavat, *m.* Indra.
mahat, *adj.* great: *in comp.* mahā-.
mahiṣa, *m.* a buffalo.
mahiṣī, *f.* a she buffalo; a queen.
mahī, *f.* the earth.
mahī-kṣit, *adj.* earth-ruling.
mahī-dhara, *adj.* earth-holding: *m.* a mountain.
mahī-pāla, *adj.* earth-guarding.
mahī-bhṛit, *adj.* earth-bearing.
mah-endra, *m.* a great chief.
majj[4], 6. *a.* majjati: mamajja, (2. *s.* mamajjitha, *and* mamaṅktha;) maṅktā; maṅkṣyati; amāṅkṣit; maṅktvā *and* maktvā: *p. p. p.* magna: sink, be drowned.
magna, *p. p. p.* sunk.
maṇi, *m. f.* a jewel.
Maṇi-bhadra, *m.* (happy in jewels,) the god of riches.
maṇḍ, 1. *m.* maṇḍate: clothe; distribute. 1 *and* 10. *a.* maṇḍati; mamaṇḍa; maṇḍitā; maṇḍita: maṇḍayati, amamaṇḍat: adorn.
maṇḍa[5], *m.* an ornament.
maṇḍana, *n. id.*
maṇḍala, *m. n.* a circle; a circuit.
math, *and* manth, 1 *and* 9. *a.* mathati; mamātha; amathit: manthati, *and* mathnāti; mamantha; manthitā; manthiṣyati; amanthit; mathitvā, *and* manthitvā: *p.* mathyate; mathita: shake, disturb.
pramāthin, *adj.* disturbing.
mad, 4. *a.* mādyati; mamāda; maditā; matta; madya: be intoxicated; be glad.
unmatta, *adj.* mad.
unmatta-darśana, *adj.* looking like one mad.
pramatta, *adj.* inobservant, careless.

vimocana	muc	vilāpa	lap	viśaṅka	śaṅk
virajas	rañj	vivarṇa	vṛi	viśārada	śal
virahita	rah	vivardhana	vṛidh	viśāla	,,
virūpa	ruh	vividha	dhā	viśiṣṭa	śiṣ

[1] *Pal.* bhamati.
[2] *Pers.* birādir; φρατηρ; frāter; *Go.* broθar; *Wel.* brawd; *Rus.* brat".
[3] *Pers.* abrū; οφρυς; *Rus.* brov".
[4] mergi.
[5] mundus.

pramada, *adj.* mad; drunk: *m.* joy, delight; *f.* a beautiful woman.
matta, *p.p.p.* maddened, drunk.
mada, *m.* the juice that flows from the elephant's temples.
madhu[1], *adj.* sweet, pleasing: *n.* sweetness; honey; sugar: any spirituous liquor.
madhura, *adj.* sweet, pleasing.
matan-ga, *m.* an elephant.
madhya[2], *adj.* middle: *m. n.* the waist.
madhyama, *adj. id.*
su-madhyama, *adj.* having a fine waist.
man, 4 *and* 8. *m.* manyate[3], manute; mene; manıtà, *and* mantà; manışyate *and* mansyate; amata, *and* amansta, *and* amanışṭa; mata: think; value, honour.
anumata, *p. p. p.* having been agreed on.
amànuṣa, *adj.* not human.
àmnàya, *m.* the Vedas.
bahu-mata, *adj.* much esteemed.
mata, *p.p.p.* thought, imagined; approved.
matı[4], *f.* thought, purpose; understanding.
manas[5], *n.* the mind.
Manu, *m. the father and lawgiver of mankind.*
manu-ȷa, *adj.* (Manu-born,) human.
manuṣya, *m.* a man.
mano-ȷava, *adj.* swift as thought.
Mano-hara, *and* Mano-hàrın, *m.* (the mind-seizer,) *the god of love*, Kàma.
mantra[6], *n.* advice, counsel; a mystical verse; a religious formula.
mantr, 10. *m.* consult. à-, address, salute. nı-, call, invite.
mantrın, *m.* a counsellor.
Man-matha, *m.* (the mind disturber,) Kàma.
manyu, *m.* anger, sorrow.
manyumat, *adj.* angry, sorrowful.
màna, *n.* honour.
màna-da, *m.* a giver of honour.
mànasa, *n.* = manas.
mànuṣa, *adj.* human.
mànuṣya, *n.* human nature.
munı, *m.* one given up to meditation, a hermit.
mauna, *n.* silence.
vımanas, *adj.* insane.
sam-mata, *n.* consent.
mnà[7], 1. *a.* manatı; mamnau; mnàtà; mnàsyatı; mnàyàt, *and* mneyàt; amnàsit: mnàyate; mnàta: commemorate, praise, meditate.
mand, 1. *m.* mandate; mamande; mandıtà: rejoice; be praised; sleep.
manda, *adj.* slow, foolish; small: *n. adv.* little.
manda-bhàgya, *n.* misfortune.
manda-bhàȷ, *adj.* unfortunate.
marut, *m.* wind: the god of winds.
màruta, *m.* air, wind.

vıśeṣa	śıṣ	vıṣamastha	mà	vısmıta	smı
vıśoka	śuc	vısarȷana	sṛıȷ	vita	ı, vye
vıśrabdha	śrambh	vıstara	stṛi	vega	vıȷ
vıṣama	mà	vısmaya	smı	veda	vıd

[1] *μεθυ*, *Rus.* med"; *Eng.* mead.
[2] *Pal.* maȷȷha; *μεσος*; medıus; *Go.* mıdȷa.
[3] *Pal.* mannatı.
[4] *μητις.*
[5] *μενος*; mens.
[6] *Pal.* manta.
[7] *μνησαι*; memınısse.

mala, *m. n.* any bodily excretion; filth: sin: *f.* rust.
nirmala, *adj.* (free from filth,) pure, clean.
nirmâlya, *n.* purity, cleanness, clearness.
malina, *adj.* defiled, filthy.
mâ, *adv.* not; *used in prohibitions either with the imperative or 3rd pret.*
mâ, 2. *a.* 3 *and* 4. *m.* mâti, mimite, (*pl.* mimate,) mâyate; mamau, mame; mâtâ; mâsyati, -te; meyât; mâsiṣṭa; amâsit, amâsta; mitvâ: *p.* miyate; amâyi; mita: measure; give. nir-, make, cause.
atimâtra, *adj.* beyond measure.
anupama, *adj.* unlike.
apratima, *adj.* unequalled.
ameya, *adj.* that cannot be measured.
upama, *adj.* like.
nimitta, *n.* a cause; mark, omen: —for the sake of.
pûrṇa-mâsa, *m.* the full moon.
paurṇamâsa, *adj.* belonging to the full moon.
pratima, *adj.* equal.
pramâṇa[1], *n.* measure, authority.
prameya, *adj.* that can be measured.
mâtula, *m.* a maternal uncle.
mâtṛi[2], *f.* a mother.
mâtṛivat, *adj.* like a mother.
mâtra[3], *n.* measure; the whole: —only.
mâtraka, *m.* a measure.
mâs[4], *m.* the moon; a month.
mâsa, *m.* a month.
meya, *adj.* that can be measured.
vimâna, *n.* a vehicle.
viṣama, *adj.* unequal; uneven; rugged; difficult.
viṣama-stha, *adj.* (standing in an uneven place,) distressed.
vaiṣamya, *n.* inequality; injustice; difficulty.
sama, *adj.* equal; level; whole; fair, just.
mâṃsa[5], *n.* flesh.
mârg, 1 *and* 10. *a.* mârgati, mârgayati: seek.
mṛig, 4. *a. and* 10. *m.* mṛigyati, mṛigayate: *id.*
mârga, *m.* a search; a road.
mârgaṇa, *n.* the act of searching.
mṛiga, *m.* search; any animal; a deer.
mṛigayâ, *f.* the chase, hunting.
mṛiga-jîvana, *m.* (who lives by hunting,) a hunter.
mṛigi, *f.* a deer; a woman.
mâla, *m.* a man: *f.* a garland: *n.* a field.
mâlya, *n.* a garland; a string of beads.
mithuna, *n.* a pair of animals, one of each sex.
mithyâ, *adv.* falsely; in vain.
mid, *and* mind, 1. *m.* 4. *a.* medate, medyati; mimide, mimeda; meditâ; mediṣyate;

vep	vep	veśman	viś	vyakta	añj
velâ	vil	vairûpyatâ	ruh	vyagra	ag
veś	viś	vaiśasa	śas	vyabhra	ap
veśana	„	vaiṣamya	mâ	vyaya	i

[1] *Pal.* pamâna; *Pers.* farmân.
[2] *Pers.* mâdar; μητηρ; mâter.
[3] μετρον.
[4] μην; mensis.
[5] *Rus.* myaso.

amediṣṭa, amidat; miditvá, meditvá: *p.* midyate, minna: be slippery; cherish, love.
amitra, *adj.* unfriendly, hostile.
mitra, *adj.* friendly: *n.* a friend.
medás, *n.* marrow.
medini, *f.* the earth.
miṣ, 1. *a.* meṣati; mimeṣa; meṣitá; meṣitvá, miṣitvá *and* miṣṭvá; miṣṭa: sprinkle; pour out.
6. *a.* miṣati; mimeṣa, meṣitá; meṣiṣyati; ameṣit: resist. ni-, close the eyes.
nimeṣa, *m.* a wink; winking: a moment.
mih[1], 1. *a.* mehati; mimeha; meḍhá; mekṣyati; amikṣat: pour out; make water.
mútra, *n.* urine.
megha, *m.* a cloud.
mukha, *n.* a mouth; face; a beginning: *m.* the beak *of a bird: adj.* first, chief.
adhomukha, *adj.* with downcast face.
abhimukha, *adj.* in front of; near: present.
unmukha, *adj.* with upturned face.
pramukha, *adj.* first, chief.
pramukhe, *adv.* in front.
mukhya, *adj.* chief.
mukhyaśas, *adv.* chiefly.
muc, 6. *a. m.* muñcati, -te; mumoca, mumuce; moktá; mokṣyati, -te; amucat, amukta; *p.* mucyate: let go; free; neglect; throw; pour out.
mocana, *n.* the act of setting free.
vimocana, *n. id.*
mud, 1. *m.* modate[2]; mumude; moditá; modiṣyate; amodiṣṭa; mudita: rejoice.
mud, *f.* joy, pleasure; a wife.
muṣ[3], 9. *a.* muṣṇáti; mumoṣa; moṣitá; moṣiṣyati; amoṣit: steal.
muṣṭi[4], *f.* a fist.
muh, 4. *a.* muhyati; mumoha; mohitá, mogdhá, *and* moḍhá; mohiṣyati, *and* mokṣyati; amuhat; mohitvá, muhitvá, mugdhvá, *and* múḍhvá; mugdha, *and* múḍha: be troubled in mind.
muhúrta, *m. n.* a thirtieth part of twenty-four hours.
muhus, *adj.* again *and again.*
múḍha, *p. p. p.* troubled, foolish.
múrdhan[5], *m.* a head; the chief place.
múla, *n.* a root; the origin.
mṛi[6], 6. *m.* mriyate; mamára; martá; mariṣyate; mṛiṣiṣṭa; amṛita; mṛita: die. 9. *a.* mṛiṇáti; mamára; amárit: kill.
amara, *adj.* undying.
amáravat, *adj.* like an immortal.
amṛita, *n.* nectar, ambrosia.
maraṇa, *n.* death.
martya, *adj.* mortal, human.

vyavasáya	so	vyúḍha	vah	śaraṇya	śṛi
vyasana	as	vyúḍhoraska	„	śarad	śṛi
vyághra	ghrá	vyúha	úh	śarira	śri
vyátta	dá	vyoman	div	śva	śvan

[1] mingere.
[2] *Pal.* modati.
[3] μυς; mús.
[4] *Pal.* muṭṭhi.
[5] *Pal.* muddha.
[6] *Pers.* murdan; mori; *Wel.* marw; *Rus.* merét'.

mùrti, *f.* matter, form, figure: a body.
mùrtimat, *adj.* embodied.
mṛta[1], *past p.* dead.
mṛtyu[2], *m.* death.
mṛj[3], 1. *a.* màrjati; mamàrja, (*pl.* mamarjus), *and* 2. *a.* màrṣṭi, (*pl.* mṛjanti;) mamàrja, (*pl.* mamṛjus;) màrjità, *and* màrṣṭa; màrjiṣyati, *and* màrkṣyati; amàrjit, *and* amàrkṣit; marjitvà, *and* mṛṣṭvà: *p.* mṛjyate; mṛṣṭa; màrgya, *and* mṛjya. rub; smooth; soothe; sweep; cleanse by wiping, polish; adorn. pra-, soothe, cleanse, polish.
mṛṇ, 6. *a.* mṛṇati; mamarṇa. strike, hurt.
mṛṇàla, *m.* *n.* mṛṇàli, *f.* a fibre of the stalk of a lotus.
mṛd[4], 9. *a.* mṛdnàti; mamarda; mardità; mardiṣyati; amardit; mṛditvà; mṛdita. rub, crush.
mardana, *n.* the act of rubbing or crushing; destruction.
mṛd, *and* mṛdà, *f.* earth, mould, dust.
mṛdu[5], *adj.* tender, soft; slew.
mṛdu-pùrva, *adj.* beginning with soft words.
mṛdh, 1. *a.* *m.* be soft: kill.
mṛdha, *n.* war.
mṛś, 6. *a.* mṛśati; mamarśa; marṣṭà, *and* mraṣṭà; markṣyati, *and* mrakṣyati; amàrkṣit *and* amràkṣit. touch; consider. vi-, soothe; consider.
mṛṣ, 4 *and* 1. *a.* *m.* mṛṣyati, -te, *and* marṣati, -te; mamarṣa, mamṛṣe; marṣità; marṣiṣyati, -te; amarṣit, amarṣiṣṭa; marṣitvà, mṛṣitvà, *and* mṛṣṭvà; marṣita, *and* mṛṣṭa. 10. *a.* *m.* marṣayati, -te; amimṛṣat, -ta, *and* amamarṣat, -ta: endure.
amarṣa, *m.* impatience, anger.
amarṣaṇa, *adj.* impatient, angry.
àmarṣa, *m.* -amarṣa.
marṣa, *m.* endurance, patience.
màriṣa, *m.* a venerable person, dramatic manager.
medha, *m.* a sacrifice.
medhas, *n.* *and* medhà, *f.* mind, intellect.
mlecch, 1. *and* 10. *a.* mlecchati, mlecchayati; mimleccha; mlecchità: speak a foreign tongue.
mleccha, *m.* a foreigner.
mlai, 1. *a.* mlàyati; mamlau; mlàtà; mlàsyati; mlàyàt, *and* mleyàt; amlàsit; mlàna: wither, fade.
mlàna, *past p.* withered, faded.
ya
yat[6], *n.* yas, *m.* yà, *f.* who, which. yat, *conj.* because.
yatas, *adv.* whence. yatra, *adv.* where. yathà, *adv.* as, so that. yadà, *adv.* when.
yathà-tatham, *adv.* truly.
yathàvat, *adv.* fitly.
yathà-śraddham, *adv.* faithfully.

śasya	śaṃs	śitàṃśu	śyat	sakàtara	tri
śiras	śri	śṛṅ-ga	śri	sakàśa	kàś
śita	śyat	saṃrabdha	rabh	sakṛt	kṛ
śitala	„	saṃskàra	kṛ	sakhi	khyà

[1] *Pal.* mata; mortuus; *Pers.* mard.
[2] *Pal.* maccu; mors.
[3] *Pal.* majjati.
[4] *Pal.* maddati.
[5] *Pal.* mudu.
[6] ὅς.

yadı, *conj.* if.
yad-ṛıcchayȧ, *adv.* spontaneously.
yadyapı, *conj.* even if.
yȧvat, *conj.* as long as, until.
yaȷ, 1. *a. m.* yaȷatı, -te; ıyȧȷa, iȷe; yaṣṭȧ; yakṣyatı, -te; ıȷyȧt, yakṣiṣṭa; ayȧkṣit, ayaṣṭa: *p.* ıȷyate; 1 *pret.* aıȷyate; ıṣṭa: sacrifice.
yakṣ, 10. *m.* honour, worship.
yakṣa, *m.* *an attendant on* Kuvera, *the god of riches.*
yaȷña, *m.* a sacrifice.
yaṣṭṛı, *m.* a sacrificer.
yat, 1. *m.* yatate; yete; yatıtȧ; yatıṣyate; ayatıṣṭa; *part.* yatta: make an effort, labour.
ȧyatana, *n.* a dwelling; an altar.
yatna, *m.* an effort.
yam, 1. *a.* yacchatı; yayȧma; yantȧ; yaṃsyatı; ayaṃsit; *part.* yata: rule, restrain. ȧ-, stretch. ut-, raise.
ȧyata, *adj.* long.
udyata, *p. p. p.* prepared, eager.
nıyata, *p. p. p.* fixed, certain.
prayata, *p. p. p.* dutiful, self-restrained.
yata, *p. p. p.* ruled, restrained.
yantṛı, *m.* a charioteer.
yama, *m.* restraint; punishment: Yama, *the god of punishment and justice.*
Yayȧtı, *m.* *name of an ancient king.*
yaśas, *n.* brightness; glory.
atıyaśas, *adj.* very bright, beautiful, or glorious.
yaśasvın, *adj.* bright, beautiful, or glorious.
yȧ, 2. yȧtı; ayȧt, (*pl.* ayȧn *or* ayus;) yayau; yȧtȧ; yȧsyatı; yȧyȧt; ayȧsit; yȧt, yȧn: go.
prayȧṇa, *n.* act *or* way of going; departure, *from life:* the crupper *of a horse.*
yȧtrȧ, *f.* a journey; food.
yȧna, *n.* the act of going; a walk; a chariot.
yȧc, 1. *a. m.* yȧcatı, -te; yayȧca, -ce; yȧcıtȧ: ask, request.
yu, 2 *and* 9. *a. m.* yautı, yunȧtı, yunite; yuyȧva, yuyuve; yavıtȧ, yavıṣyatı, -te; ayȧvit, ayavıṣṭa: *p.* yu̇yate; *f.* yȧvıtȧ, yavıṣyate; *prec.* yȧvıṣiṣṭa; *aor.* ayȧvı: join.
ayuta, *n. num.* ten thousand, 10^4.
yuvan[1], *adj.* young.
yuva-rȧȷa, *m.* the young king; *i. e.* the heir-apparent.
yu̇tha, *n.* a flock, herd.
yu̇thaśas, *adv.* in herds.
yoṣıt, *f.* a woman.
yauvana, *n.* youth, *time of life.*
yuȷ, 7. *a. m.* yunaktı, yuṅkte; yuyoȷa, yuyuȷe; yoktȧ; yokṣyatı, -te; ayuȷat *and* ayaukṣit, ayukta: *p.* yuȷyate, yukta: join. ȧ-, yoke *horses.* nı-, bind; enjoin; place.
nıyoga, *m.* injunction, order; appointment; effort.
prayoȷana, *n.* object, occasion, business.
yuga[2], *m.* a yoke: *n.* a pair; an age.

sakhi	khyȧ	san·ga	saṅȷ &	san·grȧma	grah
san·kalpa	klṛıp		gam	sat	as
san·kula	kul	san·gama	gam	satata	tan
san·khyȧna	khyȧ	san·grahaṇa	grah	satkara	as

[1] *Pers.* ȷavȧn; *Rus.* yuno; ȷuvenıs; *Go.* ȷuggs.
[2] ζυγον; ȷugum; *Go.* ȷuk.

yoga, *m.* a junction, meeting; devotion; fitness: employment.
yojana, *n.* the act of joining; a measure of length, (a stage,) varying from 4½ to 9 miles.
viyoga, *m.* separation.
yudh, 4. *m.* yudhyate; yuyudhe; yoddhà; yotsyate; ayuddha: fight.
àyudha, *m.* a weapon.
yuddha, *n.* war; a battle.
yuddha-dyùta, *n.* the game of war.
yudh, *f.* war; a battle.
yoddhṛ[1], *m.* a warrior.
yodhin, *m. id.*
raṃh, 1. *a* raṃhati; raraṃha; raṃhità: run, haste.
raṃhas, *n.* speed, swiftness.
rakṣ, 1. *a.* rakṣati[2]; rarakṣa: rakṣità; rakṣiṣyati; arakṣit: guard, defend, rule.
rakṣaṇa, *n.* rakṣà, *f.* the act of guarding or ruling.
Rakṣas, *n.* Ràkṣasa, *m. a demon hostile to man.*
rakṣitṛ, *m.* a guardian, ruler.
ran·ga, *m.* an inclosure, place of meeting.
rañj, 1 *and* 4. *a. m.* rajati, -te, rajyati, -te; rarañja, -je; ran·ktà; ran·ksyati, -te; rajyàt; ran·kṣiṣṭa; aran·kṣit, aran·kta; ran·ktvà, *and* raktvà: *p.* rajyate; arañji, *and* aràñji; rakta: *caus.* rañjayati: dye, colour; be attached, devoted. anu-, be attached.
anurakta, *p. p. p.* attached.
anuràga, *m.* attachment.
rakta, *p. p. p.* coloured; red.
rajani, *f.* the night.
rajas, *n.* dust; any violent feeling.
rajju, *m.* a cord, rope.
ràga, *m.* love, attachment; eagerness.
virajas, *adj.* free from dust.
raṇ, 1. *a.* raṇati; raràṇa; raṇità: sound.
ràṇa, *m. n.* war; a battle.
rabh, 1. *m.* rabhate; rebhe; rabdhà; rapsyate; arabdha: *p.* rabhyate; arambhi: desire. à-, begin.
saṃrabda, *p. p. p.* excited, furious.
su-rabhi, *adj.* of good odour: *f.* the cow Kàmaduh.
ram, 1. *a. m.* ramati, -te; reme; rantà; raṃsyate; araṃsta; rata, -ramya, -ratya: rejoice, delight one's self.
rata, *p. p. p.* delighted.
rati, *f.* delight, pleasure.
ratna, *n.* a jewel; a pearl.
ramaṇiya, *and* ramya, *adj.* delightful.
ràtri, *f.* night. *In comp.* ràtra.
rasa, *m.* taste.
rah, 1. *and* 10. *a.* rahati; raràha; rahità: *and* rahayati; ararahat, *and* arirahat: forsake, leave.
rahas, *n.* a place of retirement: *adv.* secretly.
virahita, *p. p. p.* forsaken.
ràj[3], 1. *a. m.* ràjati, -te; raràja, (*pl.* raràjus, *and* rejus,) ra-

sattama	as	sadà	sa	sandeha	dih
sattva	,,	sadàra	dàra	sannidhi	dhà
satya	,,	sadṛś	dṛś	sannibha	bhà
satyavàdin	,,	sadṛśa	,,	sandhyà	dhyai

[1] *Hind.* jodhi. [2] *Pal.* rakkhati. [3] regere.

râȷe, *and* reȷe; râȷıtâ, shine, rule.
râȷan[1], *m.* a king. *In comp.* -râȷa, *and* -râȷ.
râȷa-sûya, *n.* a sacrifice made by a victorious king.
râȷni[2], *f.* a queen.
râȷya[3], *n.* a kingdom.
râṣṭra, *m. n.* a kingdom, country.
râdh, 5. *a.* râdhnotı; rarâdha; râddhâ; arâtsit: *caus.* râdhayatı; ariradhat: complete, finish. apa-, injure. â-, *caus.* propitiate.
aparâdha, *adj.* injuring: *n.* an injury, offence.
ârâdhana, *n.* worship; the act of pleasing.
râś, 1. *m.* sound.
râśı, *m.* a heap.
râhu, *m.* the ascending node of the moon, *a demon with a serpent's tail, supposed to devour the sun and moon in an eclipse.*
rıpu, *m.* an enemy.
ru, 2. *a.* rautı *and* ravitı; rurâva; ravıtâ; ravıṣyatı; arâvit: sound, murmur, shout, howl.
ârava, *and* ârâva, *m.* a shout, noise.
rava[4], *m.* any noise.
ravı, *m.* the sun.
ruru, *m.* a kind of deer.
ruc[5], 1. *m.* rocate; ruruce; rocıtâ; rocıṣyate; arucata, *and* arocıṣṭa; rucıtvâ, *and* rocıtvâ; rucıta: shine; please, *w. dat.* vi-, shine.
raṣmı, *m.* a ray of light; a rein.
rucıra, *adv.* bright, beautiful.
rud[6], 2. *a.* rodıtı; *imp.* rudıhı; ruroda; rodıtâ; rodıṣyatı; 1 *pret.* arodit *and* arodat, (*pl.* arudan,) 3 *pret.* arodit, (*pl.* arodıṣus,) *and* arudat; rudıtvâ: weep. pra-, burst into tears.
Rudra, *n. a name of* Śıva; *one of a certain class of demons.*
raudra, *adj.* belonging to Śıva: terrible, frightful.
rudh[7], 7. *a. m.* ruṇaddhı, runddhe; rurodha, rurudhe; roddhâ; rotsyatı, -te; arudhat, *and* arautsit, aruddha: *p.* rudhyate; arodhı; *refl.* aruddha; ruddha: block up, hinder. anu-, 4. *m.* rudhyate: love. sam-, block up, restrain.
ruṣ, 1. *and* 4. *a.* hurt; kill. 4. *and* 10. *a.* be angry.
ruṣ, *f.* anger.
roṣa, *ib.*
ruh[8], 1. *a.* rohatı; ruroha; roḍhâ; rokṣyatı; arukṣat; ruḍha: *des.* rurukṣatı. *int.* roruhyate: *caus.* rohayatı, *and* ropayatı; arûruhat, *and* arûrupat: spring forth, be born, grow. â-, ascend, mount *a vehicle. Caus.* ropı, *and* rohı.

sannyâsa	as	sabhârya	bhṛı	samanvıta	ı
sapatna	pâ	sama	mâ	samaya	,,
saphala	phal	samakṣam	akṣ	samartha	arth
sabhâ	bhâ	samanuvrata	vṛı	samardha	ṛıdh

[1] rex.
[2] régina.
[3] regnum.
[4] *Rus.* rev''.
[5] *Pers.* rûz, rûṣan.
[6] *Pal.* rudatı; *Rus.* rûdât'.
[7] *Pal.* rundhatı.
[8] *Rus.* rodit'.

anurûpa, *adj.* conformable, suitable.
abhirûpa, *adj.* beautiful.
âroha, *m.* height; waist, figure.
rûpa, *n.* form; beauty.
rûpavat, *adj.* beautiful.
Rohiṇi, *f.* *a constellation, a wife of the moon.*
virûpa, *adj.* deformed, ugly.
vairûpyatâ, *f.* deformity, ugliness.
sva-rûpin, *adj.* having his proper form.

lakṣ[1], 10. *a. m.* lakṣayati, -te; alalakṣat, -ta: see, perceive.
lakṣaṇa[2], *n.* a mark.
lakṣmi[3], *f.* happiness, good fortune: the wife of Viṣṇu.

laghu[4], *adj.* light, nimble.
lâghava, *n.* lightness; contempt.

laj, 6. *m.* lajate; leje; lajitâ; *also* lajjate; lalajje; lajjitâ; lajjiṣyate; alajjiṣṭa; lajjita, *and* lagna: be ashamed, blush. vi-, *id.*
lajjâ, *f.* bashfulness, modesty.
lajjâvat, *adj.* bashful, modest.
vilajja, *adj.* immodest.

lañj, 10. *a.* shine.

lap[5], 1. *a.* lapati; lalâpa; lapitâ: *caus.* lâpayati: alilapat: *des.* lilâpiṣati: speak; lament. vi-, lament.
pralâpa, *m.* lamentation.
pralâpin, *adj.* lamenting.
vilâpa, *m.* lamentation.

labh[6], 1. *m.* labhate; lebhe; labdhâ; lapsyate; alabdha: *p.* labhyate; alambhi: *caus.* lambhayati; alalambhat: *des.* lipsate: get, upa-, get, find; perceive. pra-, deceive.
lâbha, *m.* the act of getting; gain.

lamb[7], 1. *m. n.* lambate; lalambe; lambitâ; lambiṣyate; alambiṣṭa: slip, fall down. â-, lean.

lalâṭa, *n.* the forehead.

las, 1. *a.* lasati; lalâsa; lasitâ: embrace; shine.
lâlasa, *adj.* desiring.

likh, 6. *a.* likhati; lilekha; lekhitâ; lekhiṣyati; alekhit; lekhitvâ *and* likhitvâ: write, paint.
lekhâ, *f.* a line, *drawn or painted.*

lin·g, 1. *a.* lin·gati: go. â-, embrace.
lin·ga, *n.* a mark, emblem, symbol.

lip[8], 6. *a. m.* limpati, -te; lilepa, lilipe; leptâ; lepsyati, -te; alipat, -ta, *and* alipta: anoint, daub, pollute.

li, 9. *a. and* 4. *m.* linâti, liyate; lilâya, *and* lalau, lilye; letâ *and* lâtâ; leṣyati, *and* lâsyati, lasyate; alaiṣit *and* alâsit; aleṣṭa *and* alâsta; litvâ, -lâya *and* -liya; lina: join to one's self, get. 4. *m.* join one's

samâkula	kul	samipa	ap	sampad	pad
samâgama	gam	samudra	und	sambhâra	bhṛi
samâpta	âp	samudraga	,,	sambhrânta	bhram
samâhita	dhâ	samṛiddha	ṛidh	samyak	añc

1 *Pal.* lakkhati.
2 *Pal.* lakkhana.
3 *Pal.* Lakkhi.
4 *Pal.* lahu; *Rus.* legók'; ἐλαχυς; levis.
5 loqui.
6 λαβειν; *Rus.* lovit'.
7 lâbi.
8 *Pal.* limpati; ἀλειφειν; λιπαινειν; *Rus.* lipok".

self to, adhere. à-, languish, faint.
  àlaya, *m.* a dwelling, home.
lubh[1], 4. *a.* lubhyati; lulobha; lobhità *and* lobdhà; lobhiṣyati; alubhat; lubdha; lobhitvà, lubhitvà *and* lubdhvà; *caus.* lobhayati; alùlubhat: *des.* lulubhiṣyati, *and* lulobhiṣyati: desire.
  lubdhaka, *m.* a hunter.
  lobha, *m.* desire.
lok, 1. *m.* lokate; luloke; lokità: see.
  trai-lokya, *n.* the three worlds.
  loka, *m.* the world: *pl.* mankind; people.
  loka-pàla, *m.* a guardian of the world.
loc, 1. *m.* locate; luloce; locità: see.
  locana, *n.* an eye.
lodhra, *m.* *the name of a tree,* symplocos racèmòsa.
loṣṭa, *and* loṣṭu, *m.* a clod of earth.
vaṃśa, *m.* a reed; a family, race.
  vaṃśa-bhojya, *adj.* (to be enjoyed by the family,) heritable.
vaka, *m.* a crane.
vakula, *m.* *the name of a plant,* mimusops elengi.
vakṣ[2], 1. *a.* grow.
  vakṣas, *n.* a breast.
vac, 1 *and* 2. *a.* vacati, vakti; uvàca, (*pl.* ùcus;) vaktà; vakṣyati; avocat: *p.* ucyate, ukta: say. pra-, narrate. prati, answer.
  prativacas, *n.* an answer; echo.
  prativàkya, *adj.* that may be answered: *n.* an answer.
  vaktra, *n.* a mouth; a face.
  vacana, *n.* a speech; a word.
  vacas, *and* vàkya, *n.* *id.*
  vàgmin, *adj.* eloquent.
  vàc[3], *f.* the voice; a speech.
  vàcya, *adj.* that may be spoken.
vaj, 1. *a.* go. 10. *a.* adorn.
  vàjin, *m.* a horse.
vata, *inter.* oh! alas!
vatsa[4], *m.* a calf: a year: *n.* a breast. *m. f.* *a title of affection addressed to* children *and* pupils.
  parivatsara, *m.* a year.
  vatsara, *m.* a year.
  vatsala[5], *adj.* affectionate, fond: *n.* affection; fondness.
vad[6], 1. *a. m.* vadati, -te; uvàda, ùde; vadità; vadiṣyati, -te; avàdit, avadiṣṭa, uditvà, *and* udya: *p.* udyate; udita: speak. abhi-, salute.
  anavadya, *adj.* blameless, faultless.
  abhivàdaka, *m.* one who salutes.
  avadya, *adj.* that must not be spoken; low, worthless; faulty.
  pravàda, *m.* a rumour, common saying.

saratha	ṛi	sarjana	sṛij	sàkṣivat	akṣ
saras	sṛi	sahàya	i	sàgara	sàgara
sarit	”	sàkṣàt	akṣ	sàgaraṃgama	”
sarga	sṛij	sàkṣin	”	sàgnika	an-g

[1] lubère; *Go.* liuban; *Rus.* liùbit'.
[2] αυξειν; auxisse; *Go.* vahsjan.
[3] *Pers.* àvàz; vox.
[4] *Pers.* bacah.
[5] vitulus.
[6] *Rus.* vyetovat'.

vadana, *n.* the mouth, face.
vadari, *f.* the jujube tree.
vadya, *adj.* that may be spoken or mentioned.
vâda, *m.* talk; a sound.
vâdın, *adj.* speaking.
vana, *n.* a forest, grove.
upavana, *n.* a grove, park.
vanya, *adj.* belonging to a forest, wild.
vand, 1. *m.* vandate; vavande; vandıtâ. salute, *by inclining the body;* praise, celebrate.
vap, 1. *a. m.* vapatı, -te; uvâpa, ûpe; vaptâ; vapsyatı, -te; avâpsit, avapta: *p.* upyate; upta. throw, scatter, sow; weave.
vapus, *n.* the body.
vâpi, *f.* a lake.
vıpra, *m.* a brahman.
vam¹, 1. *a.* vamatı; vavâma, (*pl.* vavamus;) vamıtâ; vamısyatı; avamit. vomit.
vay, 1. *m.* vayate; veye; vayıtâ. go.
vayas², *n.* age; youth.
varâha, *m.* a boar.
varc, 1. *m.* varcate; vavarce; varcıtâ. shine.
varcas, *n.* brightness; glory; beauty.
varcasvın, *adj.* bright; glorious; beautiful.
su-varcas, *adj.* very bright, glorious, or beautiful.
val, 1. *m.* cover; adhere to.
valka, *n.* bark.

valkala, *m. n.* bark: a *hermit's* dress made of bark.
vaś, 2. *a.* vaṣṭı, (*du.* uṣṭas, *pl.* uśantı;) vaṣṭu, (2. s. uddhı;) uvâśa; vâśıtâ; vaśıṣyatı; avaśit, *and* avâśit. wish.
avaśa, *adj.* not under *another's* will, independent.
avaśya, *adj.* not under *one's own* will, inevitable: *n. adv.* necessarily.
vaśa, *m. n.* a wish: *n.* authority.
vaśa-vartın, *adj.* obedient.
vaśya, *adj. id.*
vas, 1. *a.* 2. *m.* vasatı, vaste; uvâsa, (*pl.* ûṣus;) vastâ; vatsyatı; avâtsit; vastum; uṣıtvâ, ûṣıvas; uṣıta: *p.* uṣyate. dwell.: 2. *m.* put on one's garment.
avastra, *adj.* without clothes.
avastratâ, *f.* nakedness.
âvâsa, *m.* an abode, house.
ekavasana, *adj.* having only one robe.
ekavastratâ, *f.* the state of having only one robe.
nıvâsa, *m.* the act of dwelling.
paryuṣıta, *p. p. p.* worn; old; stale.
vasana, *n.* the act of dwelling or wearing.
vasu, *n.* wealth: *m.* one of eight deified elements.
vasu-dhâ, *and* vasun-dharâ, *f.* (wealth-holder *or* bearer,) the earth.
vastu, *n.* a thing.
vastra³, *n.* a garment, cloth.

sâmarthya	arth	sârathı	rı	sârthavâha	arth
sâya	so	sârathya	„	sârdham	rıdh
sâyâhana	„	sârtha	arth	sâhâyya	ı
sâra	srı	sârthaka	„	sıta	sı, so

---

¹ ἐμεειν; vomere.   ² αιων; ævum.   ³ vestire, vestıs.

vása, *m.* an abode, house.
vásas, *n.* clothes; cloth.
-vásin, *adj.* -dwelling; -wearing, -clad.
váso-yuga, *n.* a pair of garments.
vivastra = avastra.
vivastratá = avastratá.
vivása, *adj.* unclothed: *m.* banishment.
vivásas, *adj.* unclothed.

vah[1], 1. *a.* m. vahati, -te; uváha, (2 *s.* uvahitha *and* uvoḍha,) úhe; voḍhá; vakṣyati, -te; uhyát, vakṣiṣṭa; avákṣit, (avoḍham, avákṣus,) avoḍha; voḍhum: *p.* uhyate; úḍha. carry; marry *a wife.*
ávaha, *adj.* bringing.
úḍha, *p. p. p.* carried.
báhu, *m.* the arm.
vaha, *and* váha, *m.* a carriage.
vahis, *prp. and adv.* outside.
váḍham, *adv.* well! *in assent.*
váhaka, *m.* a horseman, carrier, porter.
váhana[2], *n.* a vehicle.
váhin, *adj.* carrying.
váhya, *adj.* outward.
váhyatas, *adv.* on the outside.
viváha, *m.* marriage.
vyúḍha, *adj.* broad.
vyúḍh'-oraska, *adj.* having a broad breast *or* chest.

vá[3], *conj.* or.

vá[4], 2. *a.* váti; vavau; vátá; vásyati; avásit: *prt.* ván, váta. blow.
váta[5], *m.* váyu, *m.* air, wind.
váta-java, *adj.* swift as the wind.

váñch, 1. *a.* váñchati; vaváñcha; váñchitá. wish.

váma, *adj.* the left: pleasing.

váś, *and* vás, 1 *and* 4. *m.* cry out, shout, howl.

váṣpa, *m.* a tear.

vi-, *prefix, signifying separation or change,* dis-.
viná, *prp.* without, *c. w. instrumental.*

vij, 7. *a.* vinakti; viveja; vijitá; vijiṣyati; avijit; vijitvá; vigna. *also* 1. *m. and* 6 *a.* tremble, fear.
nir-ud-vigna, *p. p. p.* undisturbed.
vega, *m.* an impulse; speed.
vegatas, *adj.* violently, speedily.

vid[6], 2. *a.* vetti, *and* vedá; vettu, (2 *s.* veda *and* viddhi,) 1 *pret.* 3 *pl.* avidus, 2 *s.* aved *and* aves; viveda; veditá; vediṣyati, *and* vetsyati; avedit; viditvá; vidita: *p.* vidyate, avedi. know. *caus.* vedayati; avividat. make known. ni-, tell.
-vid, *and* -vida, *adj.* -knowing.
vidyá[7], *f.* knowledge.
vidvas, *adj.* wise, learned.

sindhu	syandh	suduḥkha	khan	subháṣita	bháṣ
sukha	khan	sudurbuddhi	budh	subhru	bhru
sukhin	„	subáhu	vah	sumadhyama	madhya
sugandhin	gandh	subhaga	bhaj		

[1] *οχος*, vehere.
[2] vehiculum; *Ger.* wagen.
[3] ve.
[4] *αειν*; *Rus.* vyeyat'; *Go.* vaian.
[5] *Pers.* bád; ventus; *Rus.* vyetr."
[6] *ιδειν, ειδεναι*; vidére; *Rus.* vyedat'; *Go.* vitan; *Ger.* wissen.
[7] *Pal.* vijjá.

veda, *m.* (knowledge,) *one of the four sacred books.*
veda-vıd, *adj.* knowing the vedas.
ved-àn·ga, *m.* a book subordinate to the vedas.
vınd, 6. *a. m.* vındatı, -te; vıveda, vıvıde; vedıtà; vedıṣyatı, -te; avıdat, avıdata; *part. perf. ac.* vıvıdıvas, *and* vıvıdvas: *p. or* 4. *m.* vıdyate; vıvıde; vettà; vetsyate; avıtta; vıtta: find, get. *pass. or* vıd, 4. *m.* be found, be.
vıtta, *p. p. p.* found, gained: *n.* wealth; *any* thing.
vıttavat, *adj.* wealthy.
Vıdarbha, *m. pl. a people living in Berar.*
Vaıdarbha, *m.* Vaıdarbhi, *f.* belonging to Vıdarbha.
vıpra, *m.* a brahman.
vıl, 6. *a.* vılatı: cover, hide.
àvıla, *adj.* foul.
vıla, *n.* a hole, cave: *m.* a reed, cane.
vılva, *m. the name of a tree,* æglė marmelos.
velà, *f.* a limit; shore, bank *of a river;* time.
vıś[1], 6. *a.* vıśatı; vıveṣa; veṣṭà; vekṣyatı; avıkṣat; *perf. part. ac.* vıvıśvas *and* vıvıśıvas, *p. p. p.* vıṣṭa: enter; go to. upa-, sit down.
nıveśa, *m.* an entrance.
nıveśana, *n.* a house, city.
vıś, *m.* a man of the third (or mercantile and agricultural class *or* tribe.
veśa, *m.* an entrance, house; dress.
veśana, *n.* the act of entering; a house.
veśman, *n.* a house.
Vıśravas, *m. the father of Kuvera.*
Vaıśravaṇa, *m.* Kuvera.
vıṣa, *m. n.* poison.
vıha, the air, sky.
vıha-ga, vıhan·-ga, *and* vıhan·-gama, *m.* a bird.
vıhàyas, *m. n.* the sky.
vi, 2. *a.* vetı, (vitàm, vıyantı;) vıvàya; vetà; veṣyatı; avaıṣit: *p.* viyate, vita: go; go to; get: conceive, bear; love; throw.
vye, 1. *a. m.* vyayatı, -te; vıvyàya, (2. *s.* vıvyıtha,) vıvye; vyàtà; vyàsyatı, -te; *prec.* viyàt, vyasiṣṭa; avyàsit, avyàsta. *p. p. p.* vita: cover.
vita, *p. p. p. of* vi *or* vye.
veṇu, *m.* a bamboo.
vetana, *n.* wages; livelihood.
vetas, *n.* vetasi, *f.* the ratan.
vetra, *m.* a reed: *n.* a stick.
vṛı, 5, 9, 1. *a. m.* vṛıṇotı, vṛıṇute, vṛıṇàtı, vṛıṇite, varatı, -te; vavàra, (*du.* vavrıva, *and* vavarıva, *pl.* vavrus, *and* vavarus,) vavre, *and* vavare; varıtà, *and* varità; varıṣyatı, -te, *and* variṣyatı, -te; *prec.* vrıyàt, *and* vùryàt; varıṣiṣṭa, vùrṣiṣṭa; avàrit, avarıṣṭa; avṛıta, avùrṣṭa: *p.* vrıyate;

surabhı	rabh	susvara	svar	sauharda	hṛıd
suvarcasa	varc	suhṛıd	hṛıd	sauhṛıda	,,
suvarṇa	vṛı	saugandhıka	gandh	snuṣa	su
susamàhıta	dhà	saubhàgya	bhaȷ	svayaṃvara	vṛı

[1] ἱκεσθαι, οικος; vicus; *Go.* veıhs.

avárı; vṛita *and* vûṛṇà. 5.
a.m. cover; surround: choose.
9. *a. m.* choose. 10. *a. m.*
repel, hinder.
var, 10. *a. m.* choose.
anuvrata, *adj.* devoted to.
câtur-varṇya, *n.* the four tribes,
taken collectively.
nara-vira, *m.* a heroic man.
nırvṛıta, *p.p. p.* freed; happy.
nırvṛıtı, *f.* pleasure; boldness.
nıvâraṇa, *n.* the act of hinder-
ing.
parivâra, *m.* a retinue, family.
pravara, *adj.* excellent; best.
vara, *m.* a choice; a boon ; a
husband: *adj.* choice, best.
varuṇa, *n.* the god of the waters.
varṇa¹, *m.* a colour; class, tribe:
a quality.
varṇ, 10. *a.* describe.
vara-varṇın, *adj.* having choice
qualities.
vâra, *m.* a multitude, heap.
vâraṇa, *n.* a defence; an ob-
stacle: *m.* an elephant.
vârı, *n.* water.
vıvara, *m.* expansion.
vıvarṇa, *adj.* colourless.
vira², *m.* a defender, hero.
vira-han, *m.* a slayer of heroes.
virya³, *n.* heroism, bravery.
viryavat, *adj.* heroic, brave.
vṛıta, *p. p. p.* surrounded;
chosen.
vrata, *m. n.* a vow: -vrata, *adj.*
devoted.

sam-anuvrata, *adj.* wholly devoted to-.
su-varṇa, *adj.* of a good colour
or tribe: *n.* gold.
svayaṃ-vara, *m.* self-choice, free
choice of a husband.
vṛıj, 1. *a.* 2. *m.* 7. *a.* 10. *a.* varjatı,
vṛıkte, vṛıṇaktı, varjayatı;
vavarja,vavṛıje; varjıtâ; var-
jısyatı, -te; avarjit, avarjıṣṭa:
p. vṛıjyate; vṛıkta : repel;
leave.
varga⁴, *m.* a class, order, multitude.
vṛıt⁵, 1. *m. a.* vartate; vavṛıte;
vartıtâ; vartıṣyate, *and* vartsyatı; avartıṣṭa, *and* avṛı-
tata; vartıtvà, *and* vṛıttvà ;
vṛıtya; vṛıtta⁶: turn him-
self; dwell; be; act; become.
nı-, come back.
pra-, go forwards. sam-pra-, go
towards, become, be.
anuvartın, *adj.* following.
anuvrata, *adj.* devoted.
âvarta, *n.* a whirlpool; a curl,
lock *of hair.*
parıvartın, *adj.* revolving, re-
turning.
vartın, *adj.* turning, being.
vartman, *n.* a road, path.
vṛıttânta, *m.* tidings.
vrata, *m. n.* a vow; piety.
vṛıdh⁷, 1. *a. m.* vardhate; vavṛı-
dhe; vardhıtâ; vardhıṣyate,
and vartsyatı; avardhıṣṭa,
and avṛıdhat; vardhıtvà, *and*

svarûpın	ruh	svastı	as	svâmın	sva
svalaṃkṛıta	al	svastha	sthâ	svaıra	,,
svalpa	,,	svâgata	gam	hıta	dhâ
svasıta	so	svâdu	ad		

¹ *Pal.* vaṇṇa.
² ἥρως; vir.
³ *Pal.* vırıya.
⁴ *Pal.* vagga.

⁵ vertere, versâri.
⁶ *Pal.* vutta.
⁷ *Pal.* vudhatı.

vṛiddhvà; vṛiddha, vṛidhya: grow, increase.
ùrddhva, *adj.* above; high.
vardhana, *n.* increase.
vivardhana, *m.* an increaser.
vṛiddha, *p. p. p.* grown; old.
vṛiṣ, 1. *a.* varṣati; vavarṣa; varṣità; varṣiṣyati; avarṣit; varṣitvà, *and* vṛiṣṭvà; vṛiṣṭa: rain.
varṣa[1], *m. n.* rain; a year.
vṛiṣa, *m.* a bull.
vṛiṣa-bha, *m. id.* *In comp.* excellent, best.
vṛiṣṭi[2], *f.* a shower.
vṛih, 1. *a.* varhati; vavarha; varhità: grow.
vṛikṣa[3], *m.* a tree.
vṛihat, *adj.* great.
vep, 1. *m.* vepate; vivepe; vepità: tremble.
vipina, *n.* a forest.
vepathu, *m.* trembling.
vai, *conj.* indeed, but.
vyath, 1. *m. a.* be agitated.
vyadh, 4. *a.* vidhyati; vivyàdha; vyaddhà; vyatsyati, *and* bhyatsyati; vidhyàt; avyàtsit, *and* abhyàtsit: *p.* vidhyate; viddha: strike, wound.
vyàdha, *m.* a hunter.
vyàla, *adj.* cruel, vicious: *m.* a serpent.
vraj, 1. *a.* vrajati; vavràja; vrajità; vrajiṣyati; avràjit: go, walk. anu-, follow.
vriḍ, 4. *a.* vriḍyati; vivriḍa; vriḍità; vriḍiṣyati; avriḍit; vriḍita: feel ashamed, be bashful.
śaṃs, 1. *a. m.* śaṃsati; śaśaṃsa; śaṃsità; śaṃsiṣyati; aśaṃsit; śasyàt; śasitvà, *and* śastvà; śasta: *caus.* śaṃsayati; aśaśaṃsat; śaṃsita: tell, praise, desire,
śasya, *n.* grain, fruit.
śak[4], 5. *a. and* 4. *a. m.* śaknoti, śakyati, -te; śaśàka, śeke; śakta; śakṣyati, -te; aśakat, -ta; śakta: *p. and impers. p.* śakyate, *part.* śakita, śakya: *caus.* śàkayati; aśiśakat: *des.* śikṣati, -te: be able; endure, bear. *Desid.* learn. *The passive of* śak *transfers its passive signification to the infin. of a verb following it.*
aśaknuvat, *adj.* unable.
śakuna, *m. either,* the Indian vulture, *or* the kite: any bird.
śaknuvan, *p. pres.* able.
śakti[5], *f.* power.
śakya, *adj.* possible.
Śakra, *m.* Indra.
Śaci, *f.* the wife of Indra.
śan·k, 1. *m.* śan·kate; śaśan·ke; śan·kità: suspect, doubt. pari-, *id.*
aviśan·ka, *adj.* free from doubt.
viśan·ka, *f.* suspicion, doubt.
śan·kà, *f. id.*
śata[6], *n.* 100.
śata-kratu, *adj.* (having a hundred sacrifices), Indra.
śata-patra, *n.* a lotus.
śad, 1 *and* 6. *m. in the conj. tenses and a. in the others.* śiyate; śaśàda; śattà; śatsyati; asadat. *des.* śiśatsati: *int.* śàśadyate; śàśatti: *caus.* śàtayati: fall; perish.
śatru[7], *m.* an enemy.
śatru-ghna, *m.* a slayer of enemies.
śana, *pl. ins.* śanais, slowly.
śanaka, *pl. ins.* śanakais, *id.*
śap, 1. 4. *a. m.* śapati, -te, śapya-

[1] *Pal.* vassa.
[2] *Pal.* vuṭṭhi.
[3] *Pal.* rukkha.
[4] *Pal.* sakati.
[5] *Pal.* satthi.
[6] *Pal.* sata; *Pers.* śad; ἑκατον; centum; *Rus.* sto.
[7] *Pal.* sattu.

tı, -te; śaśâpa, śepe; śaptâ; śapsyatı, -te; aśâpsit, aśapta; *caus.* śâpayatı; aśiśapat: curse; swear.

abhıśâpa, *m.* a curse.

śâpa, *m. id.*

śabda, *m.* a sound, noise.

nıhśabda, *adj.* noiseless.

śam, 4. *a.* śamyatı; śaśâma; śamıtâ; śamısyatı; aśamat; śamıtvâ, *and* śântvâ; śânta: *p. impers.* śamyate; aśamı: *intrans.* become still, motionless; cease; become quiet, composed. *trans.* quiet; purify; repel, kill. nı-, perceive, *by sight or hearing.*

śama, *m.* quietness, *pec.* of mind, composure.

śânta, *p. p. p.* quiet, composed.

śântı, *f.* a settlement of differences; tranquillity.

śal, 1. *m.* śalatı, -te; śaśâla; śele; śalıtâ: go; move one's self, spread: 1. *a.* run. 10. *m.* praise.

vıśârada, *adj.* skilful.

vıśâla, *adj.* great.

śâla, *m. name of a tree,* shôrea rôbusta: *name of a fish,* a gilt-head, ophıocephalus.

śâlâ, *f.* a house; a stable.

śava, *m. n.* a carcase, dead body.

śâva, *adj.* dead: *m.* a young animal.

śaś, 1. *a.* śaśatı; śaśâśa (*du.* śaśaśatus;) śaśıtâ: leap.

śaśa, *m.* a hare.

śaśın, *m.* the moon.

śaśvat, *adv.* always.

śâśvata, *adj.* everlasting.

śas, 1. *a.* śasatı; śaśâsa, (*pl.* śasasus;) śasıtâ; śasıtvâ, *and* śastvâ; śasta: strike, kill.

vı-, cut to pieces, kill.

vaıśasa, *n.* slaughter.

nrıśamsa, *adj.* hurtful to man.

praśasta, *adj.* happy.

śasta, *adj.* blessed, happy: *n.* happiness.

śastra, *n.* a weapon; an arrow.

śastra-pânı, *adj.* weapon-handed.

śâkh, 1. *a.* embrace, fill.

praśâkhıkâ, *f.* a small branch.

śâkhâ[1], *f.* a branch.

śâkhâ-mrıga, *m.* a monkey.

śâlmalı, *m. f. and* -lı, *f.* the silk cotton tree, bombax heptaphyllum.

śâs, 2. *a.* śâstı, (*du.* śıştas, *pl.* śâsatı;) *imp.* śâstu, śâdhı; *pot.* śıṣyât; 1 *pret.* aśât; śaśâsa; śâsıtâ; śâsıṣyatı; aśıṣat; śâsıtvâ, *and* śıṣṭvâ; śıṣṭa, śıṣya: rule, command; punish; teach. anu-, *id.* â-, tell; command; bless.

anuśâsana, *n.* a word, saying.

śâsana, *n.* a command, precept.

śâstra, *n.* a command: a book of precepts.

śıṣya, *m.* a pupil.

śı, 5. *a. m.* śınotı, śınute; śıśâya, śıśye; śetâ; śeṣyatı, -te; aśaıṣıt; aśeṣṭa; śıtvâ: śıta: *caus.* śâyayatı, aśıśayat: sharpen.

vıśıta, *p. p. p.* sharpened.

śıkhara, *m. n.* a peak.

śıkhâ, *f.* the top: the crest *of a bird;* a flame.

śıkhın, *adj.* crested: *m.* a peacock; fire.

śın-gh, 1. *a.* smell.

śıghra, *adj.* swift.

śıl, 6. *a.* glean.

śılâ, *f.* a stone, rock.

śaıla, *adj.* stony, rocky: *m.* a mountain.

śılpa, *n.* an art, a handicraft.

śıva, *adj.* happy: the god Śıva.

śıṣ, 7. śınaṣṭı; *imp.* śınḍhı; śı-

. [1] *Rus.* suk".

śeṣa; śeṣṭā; śekṣyatı; aśıṣat: *p*. śıṣyate; śıṣṭa; leave: *pass.* be left, remain. vı-, excel; distinguish.

avıśeṣa, *adj.* without a remainder, entire: *n. adv.* wholly.

aśeṣa, *adj.* endless.

nırvıśeṣa, *adj.* without a difference; the same.

vıśıṣṭa, *p. p. p.* distinguished, excellent.

vıśeṣa, *m.* a difference, distinction. vıśeṣena, *adv.* especially.

vıśeṣatas, *adv.* = vıśeṣeṇa.

śeṣa, *adj.* remaining: *m.* the rest.

śi, 2. *m.* śete, (*du.* śayāte, *pl.* śerate;) *imper.* śetāṃ, śayātāṃ, śeratām: *pot.* śayita; 1 *pret.* aśeta, aśayātāṃ, aśerata; śıśye; śayıtā; śayıṣyate; aśayıṣṭa; śayıta: lie down; sleep. sam-, be doubtful.

nıḥsaṃśaya, *adj.* without doubt.

nıśā, *f.* night.

nıśā-kara, *m.* the moon.

-śaya, *adj.* -lying, -dwelling.

śayana, *n.* the act of lying down; a bed.

śayyā, *f.* the act of lying down *or* sleeping.

saṃśaya, *m.* doubt.

śila[1], *m. n.* nature; quality, character; *pec.* good character.

śilavat, *adj.* having a good character.

śuc, 1. *a. and* 4. *a. m.* śocatı, śucyatı, -te; śuśoca, śuśuce; śocıtā; śocıṣyatı, -te; aśocit, aśucat, aśocit, aṣocıṣṭa; śocıtvā, *and* śucıtvā; śukta: *caus.* śocayatı; aśūśucat: be pure; shine: 1. *a.* grieve, mourn. anu-, mourn after.

avıśoka, *adj.* not free from sorrow.

aśoka, *adj.* free from sorrow: *m. the name of a tree,* jonésıa asôka.

vıśoka, *adj.* free from sorrow.

śucı, *adj.* pure, white: *m.* the planet Venus, *and* its guardian.

śoka, *m.* grief, sorrow.

śoka-ja, *adj.* sorrow-born.

śauca, *n.* purity; purification.

śudh, 4. *a.* śudhyatı; śuśodha; śoddhā; śotsyatı; aśudhat; śuddha: *caus.* śodhayatı; aśūśudhat: become pure.

śuddha, *p. p. p.* purified, pure.

śubh, 1. *m. and* 6. *a.* śobhate, śubhatı; śuśobha, śuśubhe; śobhıtā; śobhıṣyatı, -te; aśubhat, aśobhıṣṭa: *caus.* śobhayatı; aśūśubhat. shine, upa-, adorn.

śubha[2], *adj.* bright; beautiful; fortunate.

śubhra, *adj.* bright, splendid.

śobhana, *adj.* beautiful.

śuṣ[3], 4. *a.* śuṣyatı; śuśoṣa; śoṣṭā, śokṣyatı; aśuṣat: become dry; languish, wither.

śuṣka[4], *adj.* dry.

śuṣka-srota, *adj.* having its stream dried up.

śūnya, *adj.* empty.

śūra, *m.* a hero.

śṛi, 9. *a.* śṛınātı; śaśāra, (*pl.* śaśarus *and* śaśrus;) śarıtā, *and* śaritā; śarıṣyatı, *and* śariṣyatı; *pre.* śiryāt; aśārit: *p.* śiryate; śirṇa: hurt, break.

śara, *m.* an arrow: *n.* water.

śarad, *f.* autumn; a year.

śarira, *n.* the body.

śārada, *adj.* autumnal.

śārdūla, *m.* a tiger.

---

1 *Rus.* sila.
2 *Pers.* xūb.
3 *Pers.* xūṣidan.
4 *Pers.* xuṣk; *Rus.* suxo.

śirṇa, *p. p. p.* broken.
śyâla, *m.* a wife's brother.
śyai, 1. *m.* go; become congealed.
śita, *adj.* cold.
śitâṃśu, *adj.* having cold rays: *m.* the moon.
śyâma, *adj.* black.
śrat[1], *indec.* faith.
śraddha, *adj.* believing.
śraddhâ[2], *f.* belief.
śram[3], 4. *a.* śrâmyati; śaśrâma; śramitâ; śrânta: undergo penance; be wearied; be distressed. vi-, rest from suffering or toil.
âśrama[4], *m.* a hermitage.
śrama, *m.* fatigue, toil.
śrânta, *p. p. p.* weary.
śrambh, 1. *m.* śrambhate; śaśrambhe; śrambhitâ; śrambhitvâ, *and* śrabdhvâ: neglect. vi-, be confident.
viśrabdha, *p. p. p.* confident, bold.
śri, 1. *a. m.* śrayati, -te; śiśrâya, śiśriye; śrayitâ; śrayiṣyati, -te; aśiśriyat, -ta; *perf. part.* śiśrivas: *p.* śriyate; aśrâyi; śrita: enter; obtain; take refuge. adhi-, *and* â-, flee to. ut-, raise.
pratiśraya, *m.* a house, dwelling.
śaraṇa, *n.* a house, refuge, protection.
śaraṇya, *adj.* that affords protection.
śiras, *n.* a head.
śirṣa, *n. id.*
śṛṅga, *n.* a horn; mountain-peak.

śri, *f.* good fortune; beauty, grace: the wife of Viṣṇu.
śrimat, *adj.* fortunate.
śreyas, *adj. comp.* better: *n.* good fortune, happiness.
śreṣtha, *adj. sup.* best.
śru[5], 5. *a.* śṛṇoti; śuśrâva, śuśruve; śrotâ; śroṣyati; aśrauṣit: *part. perf.* śuśruvas: *p.* śrûyate; aśrâvi: *caus.* śrâvayati; aśiśravat: *des.* śiśrâvayiṣyati: hear. prati-, promise. vi-, *pass.* be famous. sam-, hear, obey; promise.
śroṇi[6], *f.* the hip and loins.
ślakṣṇa, *adj.* soft, gentle, sweet.
śloka, *m.* a line *of poetry*, a verse.
Puṇyaśloka, *m. an epithet of* Nala.
śvan[7], *m.* a dog.
śvâ-pada, *m.* (dog-footed,) any beast of prey.
śvaśura[8], *m.* a father-in-law.
śvaśrû[9], *f.* a mother-in-law.
śvas, *adv.* to-morrow.
śvas, 2. *a.* śvasiti; *impf.* aśvasit *and* aśvasat; *pot.* śvaset; śaśvâsa; śvasitâ; śvasiṣyati; *caus.* śvâsayati; aśiśvasat: breathe, live. *caus.* refresh. â-, breathe; take courage; sigh. *caus.* encourage, console. ni- *and* nis-, sigh. vinis-, sigh deeply.
niḥśvâśa, *m.* breath; a sigh.
śvâsa, *m.* breath.
ṣaṣ[10], *num.* six.
pariṣoḍaśa, sixteen.
ṣaṣṭha, *adj.* sixth.
ṣoḍaśa, *adj.* sixteenth.
sa-, *prp. insep.* with.

---

1 crêdere.
2 *Pal.* saddhâ.
3 *Pal.* samati.
4 *Pal.* assama.
5 *Pal.* suyati; *Pers.* ṣanidan; κλυ-, κλυτος; cliens, inclytus; *Go.* hlisan; *Rus.* slûṣat'; *Wel.* clywed.
6 clûnis.
7 κυων; canis; *Go.* hunds.
8 ἑκυρος; socer; *Go.* svaihra.
9 ἑκυρα; socrûs; *Go.* svaihro.
10 *Pers.* ṣaṣ; ἑξ; sex; *Go.* saihs; *Pal.* cha; *Wel.* chwech; *Rus.* ṣest'.

sadà, *adv.* always.
san·gaṭa, *adj.* narrow; crowded: *n.* a strait; difficulty.
sañj, 1. *a.* sajatı; sasañja; san·ktà; san·kṣyatı; *prec.* sajyàt: asàn·kṣit: *p.* sajyate; sakta: adhere.
prasan·ga, *m.* attachment.
san·ga, *m.* *id.* *See also* gam.
sad[1], 1 *and* 6. *a.* sidatı, sasàda; sattà; satsyatı; asadat; *perf. part.* sedıvas; sanna: *caus.* sàdayatı; asiṣadat: sit; dwell: sink *with sorrow;* perish.
ava-, sink down; waste away.
à-, sit; go to; find; attack.
nı-, sit down. pra-, be inclined towards, favour.
apasada, *m.* a low mean person.
parıṣad, *f.* an assembly, multitude.
pàrıṣada, *m.* an attendant.
prasanna[2], *p. p. p.* propitious.
prasàda, *m.* favour, kindness.
pràsàda, *m.* a palace.
saptan[3], *num.* seven.
saptama, *adj.* seventh.
sam-[4], *prp. insep.* with, wholly.
sarva[5], *adj.* all.
sarvatas, *adv.* on all sides, from all directions.
sarvathà, *adv.* every way, in every manner.
sarvadà, *adv.* at all times.
sarvaśas, *adv.* wholly.
sal, 1. *a.* go.
salıla, *n.* water.
sàla, *m.* *the name of a tree,* shòrea ròbusta.
sah, 1. *m.* sahate; sehe; sahıtà, *and* soḍhà; sahıṣyate; asahıṣṭa; sahıtum, *and* soḍhum; soḍha, sahya: endure, bear with; support; resist; conquer; be able.
utsàha, *m.* an effort.
duḥsaha, *adj.* hard to bear.
-saha, *adj.* -enduring.
saha, *prp. w. inst.* with.
saha-ja, *adj.* inborn, innate.
sahas, *n.* power, strength.
sahasà, *adv.* immediately, quickly.
sahıta, *adj.* joined with, associated.
sahasra[6], *num.* a thousand.
sàgara, *m.* the sea, ocean.
sàgaran-gama, *m.* a river.
sàdh, 5. *a.* sàdhnotı, sàdhyatı; sasàdha; sàddhà; sàtsyatı; asàtsit: finish, complete. 4. *a.* be finished.
sàdhu, *adj.* good.
sàntu (*or* śàntu), *w. a.* console.
sı, 5, *and* 9. *a. m.* sınotı, sınute, sınàtı, sınite; sıṣàya, sıṣye; setà; seṣyatı, -te; asaıṣit, aseṣṭa; sıta: bind.
asıta, *adj.* black.
sıta, *adj.* white.
sv-asıta, *adj.* very black.
sıṃha, *m.* a lion.
sıc, 6. *a. m.* sıñcatı, -te; sıṣeca; sektà; sekṣyatı, -te; asıkat, -ta *and* asıkta; sıkta: sprinkle.
sıdh, 4. *a.* sıdhyatı; sıṣedha; seddhà; setsyatı; asıdhat; sedhıtvà, sıdhıtvà, *and* sıddhvà; sıddha: be finished, prosper, succeed.
su-[7], *adv. insep.* well; very.
su, *and* sù, 1. *and* 2. *a.* savatı, *and* sautı; suṣàva; sotà; soṣyatı; asauṣit *and* asàvit. 2.

---

1 ἕδος; sedere; *Go.* sıtan; *Rus.* syest'.
2 *Pal.* pasanna.
3 *Pers.* haft; *Pal.* satta; ἑπτα; septem; *Go.* sıbun; *Rus.* sedm'.
4 *Pers.* ham; συν; con-.
5 *Pal.* sabba; *Hind.* sab; *Pers.* har.
6 *Pers.* hazàr.
7 εὐ.

and 4. *m.* sûte, sûyate; suṣûve; sotâ, *and* savitâ; sosyate *and* saviṣyate; asoṣṭa, asaviṣṭa: *p.* sûyate; sâvitâ; sâviṣyate; asâvi, (*pl.* asâviṣata;) suta, sûta, *and* sûna: bring forth *a child*, beget.

utsava, *m.* a feast.

utsuka, *adj.* eager, desirous.

prasûta, *p. p. p.* born.

savitṛ, *m.* the sun.

suta, *p. p. p.* born; a child.

sûta, *m.* a charioteer.

sûtatva, *n.* the office of charioteer.

sûna, *p. p. p.* born.

sûnu[1], *m.* a son.

strî[2], (*for* sutrî,) *f.* a female; a woman.

snuṣâ[3], *f.* a son's wife.

sundara, *adj.* beautiful.

sur, 6. *a.* surati; susora; soritâ; asorit: shine; rule.

asura, *m.* a demon, *hostile to the gods.*

sura, *m.* a god.

sûrya[4], *m.* the sun.

sûryodaya, *m.* sun-rise.

svar, *indec.* heaven.

svarga, *m.* the heaven of Indra.

sûc, 10. *a.* sûcayati: prove; declare, show.

sûcita, *p. p. p.* revealed.

sûd, 1. *m.* sûdate; suṣûde; sûditâ: *caus. and* 10. *a.* sûdayati, asûṣudat: strike, kill.

niṣûdana, *m.* killer.

-sûdana, *m. id.*

sṛ, 1. *a. and* 3. sarati, sisarti; sasâra, (*du.* sasriva;) sartâ; sariṣyati; *prec.* sriyât; asârṣit, *and* asarat: go; go to; flow.

saras, *n.* a lake.

sarit, *f.* a river.

sâra, *n.* water: *m.* marrow, strength.

sṛj[5], 6. *a. and* 4. *m.* sṛjati, sṛjyate; sasarja, (2 *s.* sasarjitha *and* sasraṣṭha,) sasṛje; sraṣṭâ; srakṣyati; asrâkṣit: *p.* sṛjyate; asarji; sṛṣṭa: leave, quit; be left; let go; create.

utsarga, *m.* the act of forsaking; a gift.

utsraṣṭu-kâma, *adj.* wishing to let loose.

visarjana, *n.* the act of leaving.

sarga[6], *m.* a rest, pause: creation; nature.

sarjana, *n.* the act of leaving.

sraj, *f.* a garland.

sṛp[7], 1. *a.* sarpati; sasarpa; sarptâ, *and* sraptâ; sarpsyati, *and* srapsyati; asṛpat; sṛpta: creep; go.

sev, 1. *a. m.* sevati, -te; siṣeve; sevitâ; seviṣyate; aseviṣṭa: inhabit, dwell. ni-, *id.*

sairandhrî, *f.* a free woman living by her work.

so, 4. *a.* syati, sasau; sâtâ; sâsyati; seyât; asât, *and* asâsit: *p.* siyate; sita: end; destroy. ava-, determine. vyava-, *id.*

vyavasâya, *m.* determination, purpose; labour, effort.

sita, *adj.* ended; white.

asita, *adj.* black.

soma, *m.* the moon; the moon-plant, asclepias acida; the juice of the moon-plant.

soma-pa, *m.* one who drinks the soma juice; a sacrificer.

saumya, *adj.* beautiful.

---

1 *Go.* sunus; *Rus.* sün".
2 *Hind.* istrî.
3 nurus.
4 *Pal.* sûra; *Pers.* xûr.
5 *Pal.* sajjati.
6 *Pal.* sagga.
7 *Pal.* sappati; ἕρπειν; serpere.

skandha, *m.* a shoulder.
stambh, 5 *and* 9. *a.* stambhnoti, stambhnáti; astambhit, *and* astambhat; stambhitvá, *and* stabdhvá; stabdha: support, prop. vi-, prop; hinder.
stabdha, *p. p. p.* stiff; immovable; obstinate.
stambha, *m.* a pillar, column.
stim, *and* stím, 4. *a.* stimyati, stímyati; tiṣṭema, tiṣṭima; stimita: be moist, wet.
stṛi[1], *and* stṝi, 5 *and* 9. *a. m.* stṛinoti, -ṇute, stṛiṇáti, -ṇíte; tastára, tastare; startá, staritá, staritá; stariṣyati, -te, *and* stariṣyati, -te; *prec.* staryát, stiryát, stṛiṣiṣṭa, stariṣiṣṭa, stirṣiṣṭa; astárṣit, astárít, astṛita, astariṣṭa, astariṣṭa, astirṣṭa; stṛita, stírṇa: strow; cover; spread over.
vistara[2], *m.* expansion, fulness: a long tale.
sthá[3], 1. *a. m.* tiṣṭhati, -te; tasthau, tasthe; sthátá, sthásyati, -te; stheyát, sthásiṣṭa; asthát, asthita, asthiṣata: *p. impers.* sthiyate; stháyitá; stháyiṣyate, stháyiṣiṣṭa; astháyi, astháyiṣata; sthita: *caus.* sthápayati, -e; atiṣṭhipat: stand; continue: *caus.* place. ava-, descend, depart. á-, mount; go to; set about. upa-, stand near, wait upon. pra-, go forward, set out. prati-, be occupied in.
adhiṣṭhána, *n.* rule, authority; a kingdom, city.
upastha, *m.* the hip.
pariniṣṭhá, *f.* a house, dwelling.
pratiṣṭha, *adj.* famous: *f.* fame.
-stha, *adj.* -standing, -being.
sthavira[4], *adj.* firm; old.
sthána[5], *n.* the act of standing; a place.
stháṇu, *adj.* firm.
sthávara, *adj.* firm: *m.* a mountain.
sthiti[6], *f.* the act of standing: firmness, constancy.
sva-stha, *adj.* in health.
snih, 4. *a.* snihyati; siṣṇeha; snehitá, snegdhá, *and* sneḍhá; snehiṣyati, *and* snekṣyati; asnihat; snehitvá, snihitvá, snigdhvá, *and* sniḍhvá; snigdha, *and* sniḍha: love.
snigdha, *p. p. p.* beloved, pleasing: fat, oily.
sneha, *m.* love: fat, oil.
spaś, 1. *a. m.* spaśati, -te; paspáśa, paspaśe; spaśitá, spaśiṣyati, -te; aspáśit, aspaśiṣṭa; spaṣṭa. restrain: join.
vispaṣṭa, *p. p. p.* clear, distinct.
spṛiś, 6. *a.* spṛiśati; pasparśa; spraṣṭá, *and* sparṣṭá; sprakṣyati *and* sparkṣyati; *prec.* spṛiśyát; asprákṣit, aspárkṣit, aspṛikṣat: spṛiṣṭa: touch: sprinkle.
sparśa, *m.* touch.
-spṛiś, *and* -spṛiśa, *adj.* -touching.
spháy, 1. *m.* spháyate; paspháye; sphayitá; sphita: *caus.* sphávayati; apisphavat: grow; become fat.
sphita, *p. p. p.* swollen, turbid.
sma, *an expletive; which, however, sometimes gives a past sense to the present tense.*
smi, 1. *m.* smayate; siṣmiye;

---

[1] *Rus.* streti; στορνυναι; struere; *Go.* straujan.
[2] *Pers.* bistar.
[3] *Pers.* istádan; στηναι; stáre; *Go.* standan; *Rus.* stat'.
[4] *Rus.* star".
[5] *Pal.* thána.
[6] *Pal.* thiti.

smetâ; smeṣyate; asmeṣṭa; smıta: smile. vı-, wonder.
vısmaya, *m.* wonder, astonishment.
vısmıta, *past p.* astonished.
smaya[1], *m.* a smile; wonder.
smıta, *n.* laughter; a smile.
smıta-pûrva, *adj.* beginning with a smile.
smṛı[2], 1. *a.* smaratı; sasmâra, (*pl.* sasmarus;) smartâ; smarıṣyatı; asmârṣit: *p.* smaryate; *prec.* smṛıṣiṣṭa, *and* smarıṣiṣṭa: remember.
syand, 1. *m.* syandate; sasyande; syandıtâ *and* syantâ; syandıṣyate, syantsyate, *and* -tı; asyandıṣṭa, asyanta; asyandat; syandıtum, *and* syantum; syandıtvâ, *and* syantvâ; syanna: flow; pour out; run to and fro.
sındhu, *m.* a river: the Indus: Sındh.
syandana, *m.* a chariot: *the name of a tree,* dalbergıa ougeinensıs.
sraṃs, 1. *m.* fall, slip.
sru, 1. *a.* sravatı; susrâva, (*du.* susruva;) srotâ; sroṣyatı; asusruvat: *caus.* srâvayatı; asusravat, *and* asısravat. flow.
prasravaṇa, *n.* a flood, stream.
srotas, *n. id.*
sva[3], *adj.* own: *in comp.* self; own.
svaka, *adj.* one's own.
svayam, *indec.* self.
svâmın, *m.* a lord.
svaıra, *adj.* free: *n.* free will.

svañj, 1. *m.* svajate, sasvaje, *and* sasvañje; svaṅ·ktâ; svaṅ·kṣyate; asvaṅ·kta; svakta: embrace.
svan[4], 1. *and* 10. *a.* svanatı; sasvâna, (*pl.* sasvanus, *and* svenus;) svanıtâ; svânıṣyatı; asvanit, *and* asvânit: sound.
nısvana, *m.* a noise.
svana, *m.* a sound, noise.
svap[5], 2. *a.* svapıtı, asvapit *and* asvapat; suṣvâpa; svaptâ; svapsyatı; asvâpsit; *pot.* svapyât, *prec.* supyât; suptvâ: *p. impers.* supyate; supta. sleep.
svapna[6], *m.* sleep: a dream.
svara, *m.* a sound; a vowel.
su-svara, *adj.* having a pleasant sound.
svasṛı[7], *f.* a sister.
svıt, *an interrogative particle.*
svıd[8], 4. *a.* svıdyatı; sıṣveda; svettâ; svetsyatı; asvıdat; svınna, *and* svedıta: *caus.* svedayatı; asısvıdat: sweat.
asveda, *adj.* without sweat.
sveda[9], *m.* sweat.
ha, *conj. an expletive.*
haṃsa[10], *m.* a swan; a goose.
han[11], 2. *a.* *The old form is* ghan. hantı, (hatas, ghnantı;) *imp.* 2. jahı, (*pl.* hata,) hanyât, 1 *pret.* ahan, (ahatâm, aghnan;) jaghâna, (*pl.* jaghnus;) hantâ; hanıṣyatı; *part. pres.* ghnat, *perf.* jaghnıvas, *and* jaghanvas; hatvâ: *p.* hanyate; jaghne, hantâ, *and* ghânıtâ; hanıṣyate, *and* ghânıṣyate, ghânıṣiṣṭa; aghânı, (*pl.* aghâ-

---

1 *Rus.* smyex".
2 memor.
3 sui, suus.
4 sonus.
5 *Pal.* sapatı; *Pers.* xuftan; *Rus.* spat'.
6 *Pers.* xvâb; ὕπνος; somnus; *Go.* slepan.
7 *Pers.* xvâhar; soror; *Wel.* chwaer; *Go.* svıstar.
8 *Pal.* sudatı.
9 *Pal.* seda; sûdor.
10 χήν; anser; *Rus.* gûs.
11 *Pers.* zadan.

nışata, *and* ahasata); hata:
strike, kill.
ahımsà, *f.* harmlessness.
-gha, *adj.* -striking, -killing.
-ghna, *adj. id.*
parıgha, *m.* a club.
vıghna, *n.* a hindrance.
-han, *m.* -striking, -killing;
slayer.
hanu¹, *m. f.* the jaw.
hıms, 7. 1, *and* 10. *a. m.* strike,
kill.
hımsà, *f.* harm, injury.
haya, *m.* a horse.
haya-kovıda, *adj.* skilled in
horses.
haya-jnatà, *f. and* haya-jnàna,
n. a knowledge of horses.
has, 1. *a.* hasatı; jahàsa; hasıtà;
hasısyatı; ahasit: *caus.* hàsa-
yatı: *des.* jıhasısyatı: *intens.*
jàhasyate: laugh. pra-, burst
into laughter.
parıhàsa, *m.* a joke.
-hàsın, *adj.* -laughing.
hasta², *m.* a hand; the trunk *of
an elephant.*
hastın, *m.* an elephant.
hà, *int.* alas! ah!
hàhà, *int. from pain, or fear.*
hà, 3. *a.* jahàtı, jahitas, *and* jahı-
tas; jahàtu (2 *pers.* jahihı,
jahıhı *and* jahàhı); jahyàt;
jahau; hàtà; hàsyatı; heyàt;
ahàsit; hıtvà: *p.* hiyate;
hina. leave, forsake.
jıhma, *adj.* crooked; wicked.
jıhma-ga, *adj.* going crookedly.
hina, *p. p. p.* forsaken; void of.
hı, *conj.* for.
hı, 5. *a.* hınotı; jıghàya; hetà;
hesyatı; ahaısit: go; send;
increase.
hetu, *m.* the cause *of a thing.*
hu, 3. *a.* juhotı; *imper.* 2. juhu-

dhı; juhàva; hotà; hosyatı;
ahausit: *p.* hùyate: sacrifice.
huta, *p. p. p.* sacrificed: *n.* an
offering.
hut'-àśa, *and* hut'-àśana, *m.* the
sacrifice-eater, fire, Agnı.
hotrı, *m.* a sacrificer.
hotra, *n.* a sacrifice.
hrı, 1. *a. m.* haratı, -te; jahàra,
jahre; hartà; harısyatı, -te;
ahàrṣit, ahrıta: *p.* hrıyate;
ahàrı: *des.* jıhirṣatı, -te: *caus.*
hàrayatı, -te: seize; take;
carry; steal. à-, bring. vyà-,
explain; speak, tell. vı-, a-
muse one's self; walk about;
spend time, live. sam-, bring
together, seize.
apaharaṇa, *n.* the act of taking
away.
àhartrı, *m.* one who brings an
offering.
àhàra, *adj.* -bringing: *m.* food.
uddhrıta = ut-hrıta, torn up.
jıhirṣ, *desid.* wish to take.
parıhàrya, *adj.* that may be
taken away, *or* avoided.
harı, *adj.* green; yellow: *m.*
Vıṣṇu.
harıṇa, *adj.* pale yellow.
harıṇi, *f.* a doe.
harıt, *adj.* green.
haritaki, *f. the name of a plant,*
termınàlıa chebula.
hıranya³, *n.* gold; wealth.
hrıd, *n.* the heart.
akṣa-hrıdaya, *n.* knowledge of
dice.
akṣa-hrıdaya-jna, *adj.* skilled
in dice.
asuhrıd, *adj.* unfriendly, hostile.
suhrıd, *adj.* friendly.
sauhrıda, *n.* friendship.
sauhàrda, *n. id.*

---

¹ γενυς; *Go.* kınnus.
² *Pal.* hattha; *Pers.* dast.

³ *Pal.* hıraṇṇa.

hṛic-chaya, (= hṛidi śaya, that dwells in the heart,) *m.* love.
hṛidaya[1], *n.* heart; knowledge.
hṛidya, *adj.* pleasant.
hṛiṣ, 4. *a.* hṛiṣyati; jaharṣa; harṣità; harṣiṣyati; ahṛiṣat; hṛiṣita, *and* hṛiṣṭa: *caus.* harṣayati; ajaharṣat, *and* ajihṛiṣat: *des.* jiharṣiṣati: rejoice: stand on end, *of the hair, whether from fright or joy.*
harṣa, *m.* joy.
hṛiṣṭa, *p. p. p.* delighted.
hrada, *m.* a lake.
hradini, *f.* a river.
hrasva, *adj.* short; narrow.
hrasva-bâhu, *adj.* short-armed.
hri[2], 3. *a.* jihreti, *pl.* jihriyati; jihrâya *and* jihrayâñcakâra; hretâ; hreṣyati; ahraiṣit; hriṇa *and* hrita: be ashamed.
hlâd[3], 1. *m.* hlâdate; jahlâde; hlâdità; hlanna. *caus.* hlâdayati, ajihladat: be glad.
hval, 1. *a.* hvalati; jahvâla; ahvâlit: tremble, stagger.
vihvala, *adj.* agitated, troubled.
hve, 1. *a. m.* hvayati, -te; juhâva, juhuve; hvâtâ; hvâsyati, -te; hûyât, hvâsiṣṭa; ahvat, ahvata, ahvâsta; hûya: *p.* hûyate; ahvâyi, ahvâyiṣṭa, ahvata, ahvâsta; hûta: call; call to. â-, call towards, challenge. samâ-, call towards *one* at the same time *or* place.
âhava, *m.* battle, war.
samâhrâna, *n.* challenge.

---

[1] *Pal.* hadaya; καρδια; cor; *Go.* hairto.

[2] *Rus.* sram"; *Pers.* ṣarm.

[3] lætus. *Go.* hlas.

A SKETCH

OF

SANSKRIT GRAMMAR.

A SKETCH OF SANSKRIT GRAMMAR[1].

1. The Sanskrit alphabet consists of forty-seven letters, of which thirty-three are consonants: these last are arranged according to the vocal organs on which they depend.

Vowels:

a, à, ı, i, u, ù, ṛı, ṛi, e, aı, o, au.

Consonants:

	hard.					hard.
	unaspirated	aspirated.	unaspirated.	aspirated.	nasals.	sibilants.
Gutturals,	k	kh	g	gh	n·	
Palatals,	c	ch	j	jh	ṅ	ś
Cerebrals,	ṭ	ṭh	ḍ	ḍh	ṇ	ṣ
Dentals,	t	th	d	dh	n	s
Labials,	p	ph	b	bh	m	

Semivowels, y, r, l, v.

The simple aspirate, h.

To these must be added ṃ, which is a slight nasal, called anusvàra, and ḥ, a soft aspirate, called visarga.

Each consonant is named by adding a short a; as ka, ca, ṭa, ta, pa.

The letter h here added to ten of the consonants shows that these letters are to be followed by an aspiration which does not change the sound of the letter itself.

2. The letters are divided into *hard* and *soft*. The *hard* consonants are k, c, ṭ, t, p, with their aspirates, as well as the *sibilants*; the remaining consonants and all the vowels are *soft*.

[1] The substance of this sketch is from Wilson's Grammar.

3. The vowels have the following relations with each other:

a + a = ȧ	ȧ + a = ȧ
a + ı = e	ȧ + ı = aı
a + u = o	ȧ + u = au
a + ȧ = ȧ	ȧ + ȧ = ȧ
a + i = e	ȧ + i = aı
a + u̇ = o	ȧ + u̇ = au
a + ṛı = ar	ȧ + rı = ȧr
a + e = aı	ȧ + e = aı
a + aı = aı	ȧ + aı = aı
a + o = au	ȧ + o = au
a + au = au	ȧ + au = au

The *change* in a vowel caused by prefixing a is called guṇa; and that caused by prefixing ȧ, is called vṛıddhı.

ı	becomes	y, before any vowel except ı, or i.
u		v " " u, or u̇.
o		av " " "
au		ȧv " " "
ṛı		r, before any vowel.
e		ay "
aı		ȧy "

4. *Mutation of consonants.* (*a*) When two consonants come together, without any intervening vowel, they must be either *both hard* or *both soft*, the former of the two being made to agree with the latter; thus tg, becomes dg, and dt becomes tt. (*b*) If the former of two consonants is an aspirate, it must be changed to its corresponding unaspirated letter; thus dhdh becomes ddh, and bhdh becomes bdh. (*c*) A *final* hard consonant becomes soft, and a final aspirated consonant becomes unaspirated; but a final hard consonant may be retained before a pause. (*d*) A final *palatal* may be changed to a *guttural.* (*e*) A *dental* preceding either a palatal, or a cerebral, (except ṣ), is changed to the corresponding letter of that class. (*f*) If a grammatical inflection begins with a *dental,* that letter is changed to a *cerebral,* when added to a word ending in a *cerebral.* (*g*) A *dental* letter before l is changed to l. (*h*) A final consonant may be changed into its *own nasal* before any word beginning with a *nasal.* (*i*) ṇ must be written for n, whenever the latter follows ṛı, r, or ṣ, either *immediately*, or with the intervention of a *guttural*, a

labial, a vowel, y, v, h, visarga, or an anusvâra derived from n or m. But if the n is final it must not be changed. (*k*) [*a*] ch is substituted for ś, whenever the latter follows any consonant except a *semivowel, nasal, or sibilant;* thus tat śrutvâ = tac śrutvâ, by (*e*).
= tac chrutvâ, by (*k*).

[*β*] When n ends a word and ś follows, the n must be written ṅ, and ś may be changed to ch. (*l*) s not final becomes ṣ after any vowel except a or â (even with the intervention of anusvâra or visarga), and also after the semivowel r or l, or after k. (*m*) ṣ before s becomes k; and a final ṣ is usually changed to ṭ, but sometimes it becomes k. (*n*) s becomes ś before a *palatal,* and s becomes ṣ before a cerebral. (*o*) s is dropped from sthâ, and stambh, when the preposition ut is prefixed. (*p*) When h follows any consonant that has an aspirate, that letter must be made soft, and then its aspirate may be substituted for h; thus vâk harati becomes vâg harati, for which we may write vâg gharati. (*q*) A final y or v, preceded by a or â, may be dropped before any vowel. (*r*) t may be inserted before a word beginning with ch, if the preceding word ends in a short vowel; it may also be inserted if the preceding word ends in a long vowel or has a long vowel immediately before its last syllable; and it may likewise be inserted after the particles â and mâ prefixed to verbal inflexions or derivatives beginning with ch.

5. *Visarga.* ḥ, s, *and* r are mutually interchangeable. (*a*) A final s becomes ḥ at the end of a verse or sentence; and it may be so changed before a sibilant, or before a hard letter followed by a *sibilant,* or a *hard guttural* or *labial.* (*b*) A final s becomes r after any vowel except a or â, the s being before any *soft* letter. (*c*) A final syllable as becomes o, when followed by a word beginning with a or a soft consonant, this a being rejected, and its place being marked by an apostrophe. (*d*) s final in the nom. mas. of the pronouns tat, etat is usually omitted. (*e*) s final, preceded by a, is dropped before any vowel except a; and, when preceded by â, is dropped before any soft letter.

6. *Number* and *Gender.* There are three numbers and three genders; the dual number being found in nouns, pronouns, and verbs; but there is no variation for gender in the verbs.

7. *Nouns.* Nouns have eight cases, which are arranged in the following order:

1. Nominative. 2 Accusative. 3. Instrumental. 4. Dative. 5. Ablative. 6. Genitive. 7. Locative. 8. Vocative. The instru-

mental has the sense of *by* or *with;* the ablative, that of *from;* and the locative, of *in*, or *on*.

The changes made for number and case will be seen in Table I. in which each noun is arranged according to its final letter.

8. *Adjectives.* Adjectives are declined like nouns, their terminations varying according to the gender. (*a*) The *comparative* is formed by adding tara, *m.* as, *n.* am, *f.* à, and the *superlative* by adding tama to the crude form; as puṇyas, -am, -à, *holy*, puṇyataras, -am, -à, *more holy*, puṇyatamas, -am, -à, *most holy*. A final n is rejected before these terminations, and the affix vas in participles becomes t; as yuvan, *young;* yuvatara, *younger;* yuvatama, *youngest;* vıdvas, *wise;* vıdvattara, *wiser;* vıdvattama, *wisest.* (*b*) Some adjectives add iyas for the comparative, and ıṣṭha for the superlative; thus bala, *strong*, baliyas, *stronger;* *m.* -iyàn, *n.* -iyas, *f.* -iyasi; balıṣṭha, *strongest*, *m.* ıṣṭhas, *n.* -ıṣṭham, *f.* ıṣṭhà.

9. *Numerals.* These are either *cardinals* or *ordinals;* the latter are all declinable, and some of the former, according to Table II.

10. *Pronouns.* The *personal* pronouns of the first and second persons are, asmat, the crude form of aham, *I*, and yuṣmat, the crude form of tvam, *thou.* *Adjective* pronouns are declined like sarva, *all.*

The declensions will be found in Table III.

11. *Verbs.* (*a*) The moods and tenses of Sanskrit verbs are as follows:

1. Indicative mood, present tense.
2. 1st preterite, denoting an action recently past or not completed.
3. 2nd preterite, denoting an action absolutely past.
4. 3rd preterite, denoting an action past of any period, especially very remote.
5. 1st future, properly an agent with the present tense of the verb to be[1].
6. 2nd future, denoting an action indefinitely future.
7. Imperative mood.
8. Potential mood.
9. Precative mood.
10. Conditional mood.

[1] In Russian the past tense is an agent or participle, not varying for the person, but for gender and number.

(*b*) There are three *Voices*, viz. *Active*, *Middle*, and *Passive*. The terminations marking the various tenses and moods will be found in Table IV; and it must be remembered that the *Passive* in most cases takes the terminations belonging to the *Middle* voice. Before these terminations are attached, the *root* usually undergoes some modification. In connection with these changes, the verbs are arranged in ten classes or conjugations; but, with the exception of the tenth conjugation, the roots limit these changes to the Present, and 1st Preterite, Tenses, with the Imperative, and Potential Moods. These four are therefore called the *conjugational* Tenses. (*c*) *Second Preterite.* [α] If a root ends in à, the a which ends certain persons becomes au. [β] There is usually a reduplication of a letter at the beginning of the root. Thus, if the root begins with the vowel a, that vowel becomes à, as, ad, *eat*, àda, *I did eat*. But if the a is followed by a double consonant, àn is prefixed; as, arc, *worship*, ànarca, *I worshipped.* [γ] If a verb begins with ı or u, the substitutes are either ıy and uv or i and ù; thus, ı, *go*, becomes ıyàya, *I went*, ıyetha, *thou wentest;* ukha, *wither*, uvokha, *it withered;* iyatus, *they two went*, ùkhatus, *they two withered.* [δ] An initial ṛı becomes àr; as ṛı, *go*, àra, *I went:* but when followed by a consonant it inserts n; as, ṛıȷ, *be firm*, ànṛıȷe, *m. it was firm.* [ε] A root beginning with a single consonant, which is neither a guttural nor an aspirate, doubles that consonant; as pac, *cook*, papàca, *I cooked.* [ζ] An initial *guttural* is changed to its corresponding unaspirated *palatal*, and *h* is changed to ȷ: thus kṛı, *make*, cakàra; khan, *dig*, cakhàna; grah, *take*, ȷagràha; ghas, *eat*, ȷaghàsa; hṛı, *take*, ȷahàra. [η] Sometimes the reduplication of a *semivowel* is the corresponding vowel; as, yaȷ, *sacrifice*, ıyàȷa; vac, *say*, uvàca. [θ] An aspirated consonant substitutes its corresponding unaspirated letter; as, bhram, *whirl*, babhràma. [ι] When the initial is a *double* consonant, the former only is repeated; as, śrı, *serve*, śıśràya. But if the double letter is a *sibilant* followed by a *hard* consonant, the latter is doubled; as, ṣṭù, *praise*, ṭuṣṭàva; sthà, *stand*, tasthau; while if the second letter is *soft*, the sibilant is doubled; as, smṛı, *remember*, sasmàra. If a sibilant is followed by a hard consonant and y, the middle letter is repeated; as ścyut, *ooze*, cuścyota. [κ] The vowel of the reduplication is a for a root whose medial vowel is a, à, ṛı, ṛi, or whose final is e, aı, or o; as, kṛı, *make*, cakàra; bhà, *shine*, babhau; gaı, *sing*, ȷagau. a is also the vowel in the reduplication of bhù, *be*, babhùva. [λ] Any other short vowel, whether medial or final, is repeated; as, mud, *be pleased*, mumude. A *long* vowel is made *short;* as, śik, *sprinkle*, śıśike. For a medial diphthong the corresponding short vowel is used: as, pel, *go*, pıpela; lok, *see*, luloka. [μ] Verbs which have a as their middle vowel, and which begin and end in a simple consonant, of which the former would be unchangeable in reduplication, do not allow reduplication before those terminations which begin with a vowel, or before an ı inserted before any termination, but such verbs change the a into e; as from pac, 2 *pret.* 3 *pers.* papàca, pecatus, pecus; 1st *pers.* papàca, pecıva, pecıma. [ν] There is another form of the 2nd preterite made up of the *root*, followed by the syllable àm, and the second preterite of either as, *be*, bhù, *be*, or kṛı, *make*, *do;* as, edh, *increase.*

S. 1.	edhàmàsa	edhàmbabhùva	edhàñcakre
2.	edhàmàsıtha	edhàmbabhùvıtha	edhàñcakṛıṣe
3.	edhàmàsa	edhàmbabhùva	edhàñcakre
D. 1.	edhàmàsıva	edhàmbabhùvıva	edhàñcakṛıvahe
2.	edhàmàsathus	edhàmbabhùvathus	edhàñcakràthe
3.	edhàmàsatus	edhàmbabhùvatus	edhàñcakràte
P. 1.	edhàmàsıma	edhàmbabhùvıma	edhàñcakṛımahe
2.	edhàmàsa	edhàmbabhùva	edhàñcakṛıḍhve
3.	edhàmàsus	edhàmbabhùvus	edhàñcakrıre

This form of the second preterite is taken by all verbs of more than one syllable, as well as all *derivative* verbs. In this form as and bhù take the *active* voice, and kṛı follows the voice proper to the root. (*d*) The remaining tenses call for no especial remarks, their forms being given in the tables of verbs. (*e*) [α] In the *first* conjugation, the vowel a is inserted *in the root* before a vowel either medial or final, and also a before the *terminations beginning with a consonant*, which last is changed to à before v and m; thus bhù becomes bho, before a vowel bhav, while ȷı becomes ȷe, and before a vowel ȷay. [β] In the *second* conjugation the terminations are added to the root without the intervention of a vowel. An a is sometimes inserted before the middle or final vowel of the root; but a *long* vowel is unaltered. [γ] In the *third* conjugation the radical syllable undergoes reduplication. [δ] In the *fourth* conjugation ya is inserted between the root and the terminations of the conjugational tenses. [ε] In the *fifth* conjugation nu is added to the root. [ζ] In the *sixth* conjugation, the vowel of the root is unchanged, but a is inserted before the terminations. [η] In the *seventh* conjugation na or n is inserted before the final consonant of the root. [θ] In the *eighth* conjugation u or o is inserted before the terminations. [ι] In the *ninth* conjugation nâ, ni, and n are inserted before the terminations. [κ] In the *tenth* conjugation a is inserted before a medial vowel and ay is affixed to the root. (*f*) Any verb may be made causal by adding to the root the vowel ı, which becomes ay before a vowel; the vowel â being prefixed to the radical vowel, thus bhû becomes bhau, which is changed to bhâvı, and before a vowel to bhâvay. (*g*) A verb becomes a *desiderative* by reduplication and the addition of s. The vowel of reduplication is ı, for a medial or final a, â, ı, i, ṛı, ṛi, e, or aı; and the vowel is u, for u, û, o, or au. When a root begins with a vowel, the reduplication is the radical syllable itself followed by the final consonant with ı prefixed. (*h*) In *frequentatives* the root is doubled. A verb beginning with a vowel repeats the whole, lengthening the syllable of the root. There are various modifications of the vowels. (*i*) *Participles* are either declinable or indeclinable. [α] The *Present Participle Active* is formed by changing into at, the termination of the 3rd *pl.* of the present tense. It is declined like tudat. [β] The *Present Participle Middle* is formed by adding âna to the same termination; but when, as in the *first*, *fourth*, *sixth*, and *tenth* conjugations, the inflective base ends in a, then mâna is added for the participle. These middle participles are declined like nouns in a, as pacamânas, pacamânâ, pacamânam. [γ] *Participles of the second preterite.* The *active* is formed by adding vas to the inflective base, as it occurs before the terminations of the dual and plural numbers of the second preterite. The augment ı is inserted after certain verbs. These participles are declined in the three genders as, from ı, *go;* iyıvas; *nom.* iyıvân, *m.* iyuṣi, *f.* iyıvat, *n.*: kṛı, *do*, cakṛıvas; *nom.* cakṛıvân, *m.* cakruṣi, *f.* cakṛıvat, *n.* The *middle* participle of the second preterite is formed by adding âna to the inflective base as it occurs before the termination of the third person plural; thus pac, *cook*, makes pecâna; vac, *speak*, ûcâna. [δ] The *indefinite past* participle *active* is formed by adding to the root tavat; as kṛıtavat, *having made.* It is used commonly with the verb as, *be.* The *passive* participle of the indefinitely past is formed by adding ta to the root, as kṛıta. This ta is sometimes changed to na. [ε] The *future active* participle is formed from the second future tense by changing the termination atı of the 3rd pers. sing. to at, for the *active* voice, and mâna for the *middle.* [ζ] *Future* participles of *fitness*, *likelihood*, or *necessity*, are formed by adding to the root the affixes tavya, aniya, or ya. These are declined in three genders; the feminine frequently being used as a noun. [η] *Indeclinable parti-*

ciples. There are two participles of the past tense which admit of neither gender, number, nor case. They are generally formed from the past passive participle by changing ta into två, or da into dvå; but when the verb has a preposition before it, the affix is tya, after a short vowel, and ya after a long one. (*k*) *Infinitive Mood.* This is an indeclinable noun and may be formed from the first future by changing tà into tum[1].

[1] In the Vocabulary are inserted the chief tenses of all the verbs occurring in Nala. These forms are from Westergaard, Rådicês linguæ Sanscritæ.